ALSO BY KEN JENNINGS

Ken Jennings's Trivia Almanac

Brainiac: Adventures in the Curious, Competitive, Compulsive World of Trivia Buffs

MAPHEAD

Charting the Wide, Weird World of Geography Wonks

Ken Jennings

Scribner

NEW YORK · LONDON · TORONTO ·
SYDNEY · NEW DELHI

Scribner
A Division of Simon & Schuster, Inc.
1230 Avenue of the Americas
New York, NY 10020

First Scribner hardcover edition September 2011

SCRIBNER and design are registered trademarks of The Gale Group, Inc.,
used under license by Simon & Schuster, Inc., the publisher of this work.

For information about special discounts for bulk purchases, please contact
Simon & Schuster Special Sales at 1-866-506-1949
or business@simonandschuster.com.

The Simon & Schuster Speakers Bureau can bring authors to your
live event. For more information or to book an event contact
the Simon & Schuster Speakers Bureau at 1-866-248-3049
or visit our website at www.simonspeakers.com.

Designed by Paul Dippolito

Manufactured in the United States of America

7   9   10   8   6

Library of Congress Control Number: 2010052219

ISBN 978-1-4391-6717-5
ISBN 978-1-4391-6719-9 (ebook)

Additional credit for illustration on page 53:
McArthur's Universal Corrective Map of the World. © 1979 Stuart McArthur.
Available worldwide from ODT, Inc. (1-800-736-1293; www.ODTmaps.com;
fax: 413-549-3503; e-mail: odtstore@odt.org). Also available in Australia from
McArthur Maps, 208 Queens Parade, North Fitzroy, 3068, Australia;
phone: 0011 614 3155 5908; e-mail: stuartmcarthur@hotmail.com.

Further credits:
Images on page 66 courtesy of NASA; map on page 81 courtesy of Altea Gallery
(www.alteagallery.com); map on page 118 © Dragonsteel Entertainment, LLC;
photograph on page 118 © Mayang Murni Adnin; photograph on page 171 by
Jim Payne; images on page 230 © OpenStreetMap and contributors, CC-BY-SA

For my parents.
And for the kid with the map.

CONTENTS

MAPHEAD

Chapter 1

ECCENTRICITY

[ek-ˌsen-ˈtri-sə-tē] *n*.: the deformation
of an elliptical map projection

My wound is geography.
—PAT CONROY

They say you're not really grown up until you've moved the last box of your stuff out of storage at your parents'. If that's true, I believe I will stay young forever, ageless and carefree as Dorian Gray, while the cardboard at my parents' house molders and fades. I know, *everybody's* parents' attic or basement has its share of junk, but the eight-foot-tall mountain of boxes filling one bay of my parents' garage isn't typical pack-rat clutter. It looks more like the warehouse in the last shot of *Raiders of the Lost Ark*.

The last time I was home, I waded into the chaos in hopes of liberating a plastic bucket of my childhood Legos. I didn't find the Legos, much to my six-year-old son's chagrin, but I was surprised to come across a box with my name on the side, written in the neater handwriting of my teenaged self. The box was like an archaeological dig of my adolescence and childhood, starting with R.E.M. mix tapes and *Spy* magazines on top, moving downward through strata of *Star Trek* novelizations and *Thor* comics, and ending on the most primal bedrock of my youthful nerdiness: a copy of Hammond's *Medallion World Atlas* from 1979.

I wasn't expecting the Proustian thrill I experienced as I pulled the

1

huge green book from the bottom of the box. Sunbeam-lit dust motes froze in their dance; an ethereal choir sang. At seven years old, I had saved up my allowance for months to buy this atlas, and it became my most prized possession. I remember it sometimes lived at the head of my bed at night next to my pillow, where most kids would keep a beloved security blanket or teddy bear. Flipping through its pages, I could see that my atlas had been as well loved as any favorite plush toy: the gold type on the padded cover was worn, the corners were dented, and the binding was so shot that most of South America had fallen out and been shoved back in upside down.

Today, I will still cheerfully cop to being a bit of a geography wonk. I know my state capitals—hey, I even know my *Australian* state capitals. The first thing I do in any hotel room is break out the tourist magazine with the crappy city map in it. My "bucket list" of secret travel ambitions isn't made up of boring places like Athens or Tahiti— I want to visit off-the-beaten-path oddities like Weirton, West Virginia (the only town in the United States that borders two different states on opposite sides) or Victoria Island in the Canadian territory of Nunavut (home to the world's largest "triple island"—that is, the world's largest island in a lake on an island in a lake on an island).* But my childhood love of maps, I started to remember as I paged through the atlas, was something much more than this casual weirdness. I was consumed.

Back then, I could literally look at maps for hours. I was a fast and voracious reader, and keenly aware that a page of hot Roald Dahl or Encyclopedia Brown action would last me only thirty seconds or so. But each page of an atlas was an almost inexhaustible trove of names and shapes and places, and I relished that sense of depth, of comprehensiveness. Travelers will return to a favorite place many times and order the same dish at the same café and watch the sun set from the same vantage point. I could do the same thing

---

* This "honor" is sometimes claimed by Vulcan Point, on Lake Taal in the Philippines. But point your Internet map of choice at 69.793° N, 108.241° W—the unnamed Canadian island-in-a-lake-on-an-island-in-a-lake on Victoria Island is much bigger.

as a frequent armchair traveler, enjoying the familiarity of sights I had noticed before while always being surprised by new details. Look how Ardmore, Alabama, is only a hundred feet away from its neighbor Ardmore, Louisiana—but there are 4,303 miles between Saint George, Alaska, and Saint George, South Carolina. Look at the lacelike coastline of the Musandam Peninsula, the northernmost point of the Arabian nation of Oman, an intricate fractal snowflake stretching into the Strait of Hormuz. Children love searching for tiny new details in a sea of complexity. It's the same principle that sold a bajillion *Where's Waldo?* books.

Mapmakers must know this—that detail, to many map lovers, is not just a means but an end. The office globe next to my desk right now is pretty compact, but it makes room for all kinds of backwater hamlets in the western United States: Cole, Kansas; Alpine, Texas; Burns, Oregon; Mott, North Dakota (population: 808, about the same as a city block or two of Manhattan's Upper East Side). Even Ajo, Arizona, makes the cut, and it's not even incorporated as a town—it's officially a CDP, or "census-designated place." What do all these spots have in common, besides the fact that no one has ever visited them without first running out of gas? First, they all have nice short names. Second, they're each the only thing for miles around. So they neatly fill up an empty spot on the globe and therefore make the product look denser with information.

But I also remember a competing instinct in my young mind: a love for the way maps could suggest adventure by hinting at the unexplored. Joseph Conrad wrote about this urge at the beginning of *Heart of Darkness:*

Now when I was a little chap I had a passion for maps. I would look for hours at South America, or Africa, or Australia, and lose myself in all the glories of exploration. At that time there were many blank spaces on the earth, and when I saw one that looked particularly inviting on a map (but they all look that) I would put my finger on it and say, "When I grow up I will go there."

When *I* was a "little chap," there were (and are) still a few mostly blank spaces on the map: Siberia, Antarctica, the Australian outback.* But I knew these lacunae weren't just empty because they were rugged and remote; they were empty because nobody really wanted to live there. These were the places on the Earth that, well, sort of sucked. So I never put my finger on the glaciers of Greenland and said, "I will go there!" like Conrad's Marlow. But I liked that they existed. Even on a map that showed every little Ajo, Arizona, there was still some mystery left *somewhere*.

And then there were those amazing place-names. My hours with maps featured lots of under-my-breath whispering: the names of African rivers ("Lualaba . . . Jumba . . . Limpopo . . .") and Andean peaks ("Aconcagua . . . Yerupajá . . . Llullaillaco . . .") and Texas counties ("Glasscock . . . Comanche . . . Deaf Smith . . .") They were secret passwords to entry into other worlds—more magical, I'm sure, in many cases, than the places themselves. My first atlas listed, in tiny columns of type under each map, the populations for thousands of cities and towns, and I would pore over these lists looking for comically underpopulated places like Scotsguard, Saskatchewan (population: 3), or Hibberts Gore, Maine (population: 1).† I dreamed of one day living in one of these glamorous spots—sure, it would be lonely, but think of the level of celebrity! The lone resident of Hibberts Gore, Maine, *gets specifically mentioned in the world atlas!* Well, almost.

The shapes of places were just as transporting for me as their names. Their outlines were full of personality: Alaska was a chubby

---

* My personal favorite has always been Bir Tawil, a tiny trapezoid of desert on the border between Egypt and Sudan that, by international treaty, neither nation can claim. (For complicated reasons dating back to the Anglo-Egyptian Condominium Agreement of 1899, both Egypt and Sudan would lose their claim to a much more attractive slice of territory called the Hala'ib Triangle if they were to call dibs on Bir Tawil.) As a result, Bir Tawil is one of the last remaining bits of *terra nullius*—land belonging to no one—on Earth.

† There's a downside to this kind of fame, *The Boston Globe* learned in 2001 when it profiled Karen Keller, the lone resident of Hibberts Gore. The Census Bureau doesn't release demographic information for individuals, but it does release *average* totals for all towns and cities, which means that Keller's salary, for example, was published as the average household income for Hibberts Gore.

profile smiling benevolently toward Siberia. Maine was a boxing glove. Burma had a tail like a monkey. I admired roughly rectangular territories like Turkey and Portugal and Puerto Rico, which seemed sturdy and respectable to me, but not more precisely rectangular places like Colorado or Utah, whose geometric perfection made them false, uneasy additions to the national map. I immediately noticed when two areas had slightly similar outlines—Wisconsin and Tanzania, Lake Michigan and Sweden, the island of Lanai and South Carolina—and decided they must be geographic soul mates of some kind. To this day, I see British Columbia on a map and think of it as a more robust, muscular version of California, just as the Canadians there must be more robust, muscular versions of Californians.

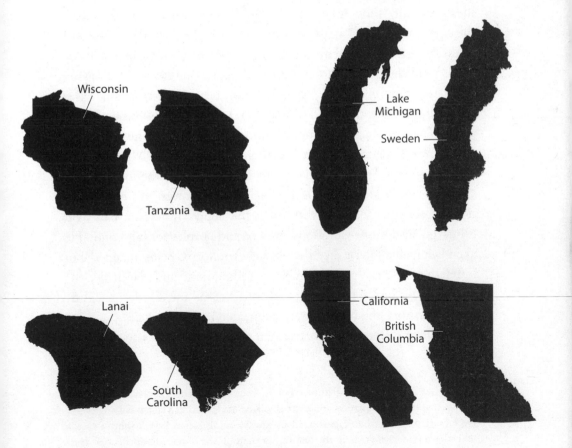

Separated at birth

These map shapes had a life of their own for me, divorced from their actual territories. Staring at a map for too long was like repeating a word over and over until all meaning is stripped away. Uruguay ceased to represent an actual nation for me; it was just *that shape,* that slightly lopsided teardrop. I saw these outlines even after the atlas was closed, afterimages floating in my mind's eye. The knotty pine paneling in my grandparents' upstairs bedroom was full of loops and whorls that reminded me of faraway fjords and lagoons. A puddle in a parking lot was Lake Okeechobee or the Black Sea. The first time I saw Mikhail Gorbachev on TV, I remember thinking immediately that his famous birthmark looked *just like* a map of Thailand.*

By the time I was ten, my beloved Hammond atlas was just one of a whole collection of atlases on my bedroom bookshelf. My parents called them my "atli," though even at the time I was pretty sure that wasn't the right plural. Road atlases, historical atlases, pocket atlases. I wish I could say that I surveyed my maps with the keen eye of a scientist, looking at watersheds and deforestation and population density and saying smart-sounding things like "Aha, that must be a subduction zone." But I don't think I was that kind of map fan. I wasn't aware of the ecology and geology and history manifest on maps at first; I was just drawn to their scope, their teensy type, and their orderly gestalt. My dad liked maps too, but he preferred the black British atlas in the living room, a Philip's one from the 1970s in which the maps were all "hypsometric." Hypsometric maps are those ones that represent terrain with vivid colors: greens for low elevations, browns and purples for high ones. He liked being able to visualize the physical landforms being mapped, but I preferred the clean political maps that Hammond and National Geographic published, where cities and towns stood out neatly on lightly shaded territory and borders were delineated in crisp pastels.

In fact, I dislike hypsometric maps to this day. They look stodgy

---

* Yassir Arafat once claimed that he spent an hour every day folding his *keffiyeh* headdress so that it would resemble a map of his longed-for Palestinian state, showing everyone he met that Palestine was—literally!—always on his mind. I don't think that the Thai people were always on Gorby's mind, but that was the impression he may inadvertently have been giving map nerds everywhere.

and old-fashioned to me, something you might see a matronly 1960s schoolteacher straining to pull down in front of a chalkboard.* But it's more than that. I have to admit that I still like maps for their order and detail as much as for what they can tell us about the real world. A good map isn't just a useful representation of a place; it's also a beautiful system in and of itself.

Maps are older than writing, so of course we have no written account of some Newton's-apple moment in cartography, some prehistoric hunter-gatherer saying, "Hey, honey, I drew the world's first map today." Every so often, the newly discovered "world's oldest map!" will be announced to great fanfare in scientific journals and even newspaper headlines. But whether the new old map is a cave painting in Spain or a carved mammoth tusk from Ukraine or petroglyphs on a rock by the Snake River in Idaho, these "discoveries" always have one thing in common: a whole bunch of annoyed scholars arguing that no, that's not a map; it's a pictogram or a landscape painting or a religious artifact, but it's not *really* a map. When a cryptic painting was unearthed from the Neolithic Anatolian settlement of Çatalhöyük in 1963, its discoverer, James Mellaart, proclaimed the eight-thousand-year-old artifact to be a map of the area. The domino-like boxes drawn at the bottom of the wall represented the village, he claimed, and the pointy, spotted orange shape above them must be the nearby twin-coned volcano of Hasan Dag. Cartographers went nuts, and historians and geologists even combed the painting for clues as to the history of prehistoric eruptions at the site. There's just one hitch: subsequent researchers have decided that the spotted thingy probably *isn't* meant to be a volcano: it's a stretched leopard skin. That's not lava spewing forth, just a set of claws. Ergo, the mural was never a map at all. Archaeologists' embarrassing inability to tell a leopard and a volcano

---

* Hypsometric maps are also out of fashion with many cartographers, who find them misleading. Readers often assume that the hypsometric tints represent vegetation, not elevation. But the most barren desert might be verdant green on one of these maps, if it's sufficiently low-lying. Conversely, lush highlands might be a lifeless beige.

The Çatalhöyük mural. Volcanoes or leopard? You make the call.

apart turns out to be the same syndrome that had me seeing coastlines in my grandparents' wood paneling. It's called "cartacacoethes": the uncontrollable compulsion to see maps everywhere.

Many early protomaps do share some similarities with modern cartography, but it's a blurry line: their primary significance was probably artistic or spiritual. The essential traits we associate with maps today evolved gradually over millennia. We first see cardinal directions on Babylonian clay tablet maps from five thousand years ago, for instance, but distances don't appear on maps for three thousand more years—our oldest such example is a bronze plate from China's Zhou Dynasty. Centuries more pass before we get to our oldest surviving paper map, a Greek papyrus depicting the Iberian Peninsula around the time of Christ. The first compass rose appears in the Catalan Atlas of 1375. "Chloropleth" maps—those in which areas are colored differently to represent different values on some scale, like the red-and-blue maps on election night—date back only to 1826.*

---

* Part of the reason for the long gaps here is that many early maps, though widely used, haven't survived to our day. The timeline is spotty and tattered for the same reason that, say, a Honus Wagner baseball card or a copy of *Action Comics* no. 1 is so valuable: because everybody's mom threw stuff away. Just as mapmaking is a science of omissions—the cartographer can't include *everything* on the map, no matter how tempting that sounds—so the history of maps is a series of gaps and omissions as well.

But if the historical "discovery" of maps was a slow and gradual process, the way modern mapheads discover maps as children is more like the way cavemen must have discovered fire: as a flash of lightning. You see that first map, and your mind is rewired, probably forever. In my case, the Ur-map was a wooden puzzle of the fifty states I got as a Christmas present when I was three—you know the kind, Florida decorated with palm trees, Washington with apples. On my puzzle, Nebraska, confusingly, wore a picture of a family of pigs. The two peninsulas of Michigan were welded together into a single puzzle piece, so that I believed for years afterward that Michigan was a single landmass in the lumpy shape of a lady's handbag.

For other kids, it was the globe in Dad's study, or the atlas stretched out on the shag carpeting of the living room, or a free gas station map during a family vacation to Yosemite. (Many cases of twentieth-century American map geekdom, it seems, began the same way that many twentieth-century *Americans* began: conceived in the backseats of Buicks.) But whatever the map, all it takes is one. Cartophilia, the love of maps, is a love at first sight. It must be predestined, written somewhere in the chromosomes.

It's been this way for centuries. That wooden map puzzle that took my map virginity when I was three? Those date back to the 1760s, when they were called "dissected maps" and were wildly popular toys, the ancestors of all modern jigsaw puzzles. For Victorian children, the most common first map was a page in a family or school Bible, since a map of the Holy Land was often the only color plate in a vast sea of "begat"s and "behold"s. Nothing like a dry two-hour sermon on the Book of Lamentations to make a simple relief map look suddenly fascinating by comparison! That single page probably drew more youthful study than the rest of the Good Book put together—Samuel Beckett makes a joke in *Waiting for Godot* about how his two characters, Vladimir and Estragon, have never read the Gospels but remember very clearly that the Dead Sea in their Bible maps was a "very pretty . . . pale blue." Joseph Hooker, the great British botanist, once wrote to his close friend Charles Darwin that his first exposure to maps had been a Sunday school "map of the world before the flood" that he said he spent hours of his "tenderest years" studying. That one map led to his lifelong interest in exploration and science, during which he helped Darwin develop the theory of evolution.

In the twentieth century, when kids were spending less time in front of Bibles, the inevitable map on their schoolroom wall served the same purpose: something to stare at when a dull monologue on fractions or *Johnny Tremain* started to turn into the wordless "wah-wah" drone of the teacher from a *Peanuts* TV special. I just now realized *why* I know all the Australian state capitals, in fact: my desk in second grade was right next to the bulletin board that had the world map on it. My head was just inches from Darwin and Adelaide and, um, Hobart. (See? I still got it.) If I'd been a little taller then, I might be an expert on Indonesia or Japan today instead.

Recently I was driving my friend Todd to the airport, and, while talking about his vacation plans, he outed himself as a bit of a geography nerd. (I'd known Todd for years, incidentally, but was only now finding out we had this in common. Map people sometimes live for years in the closet, cartophilia apparently being one of the last remaining loves that dare not speak their names.) He boasted that, thanks to the hours of his childhood he'd spent poring over atlases, he could still rattle off the names of every world capital, so that's how we spent the rest of the drive. We both discovered that the capitals we stumbled over weren't the obscure ones (Bujumbura, Burundi! Port-of-Spain, Trinidad and Tobago!) but rather major European cities like Bratislava, Slovakia, and Kiev, Ukraine. Why? Because these cities had committed the crime of becoming national capitals *after* the end of the Cold War, when Todd and I weren't map-memorizing nine-year-olds anymore! Apparently our knowledge of geography is like your grandparents' knowledge of personal computers: it ends in 1987.

I suspect that Todd and I are far from alone in this—that many people's hunger for maps (mappetite?) peaks in childhood. In part, this is due to the fact that nobody is ever as obsessed about *anything* as a crazed seven-year-old is; this week I'm sure my son, Dylan, thinks about dinosaurs more than any adult paleontologist ever. Next week it'll probably be spaceships or Venus flytraps or sports cars.

But there does seem to be something about maps that makes them specifically irresistible to children. Consider: most square, old-timey hobbies are taken up in middle age as a way to mortify one's teenage children. That's when Dad suddenly gets obsessed with Dixieland jazz or bird-watching or brewing lager in the basement. Not so with map love, which you catch either during your Kool-Aid years or not at all. In fact, I remember my map ardor abruptly cooling around puberty—you discover pretty quickly that it's not a hit with girls to know the names of all the Netherlands Antilles. In college, I briefly had a pleasant-but-bookish Canadian roommate named Sheldon. (Note: Nerdy first name not fictionalized for this story!) Sheldon moved into the apartment first that September and had the whole place—living room, kitchen, bedrooms—papered with dozens of *National Geographic* maps by the time the rest of us arrived. I rolled my eyes and resigned myself to the fact that we were never going to see a single girl inside the apartment. But in third grade, I'm sure I would have been over the moon at this development, making Sheldon pinky-swear to be my BFF and drawing detailed maps of Costa Rica on the back of his Trapper Keeper.

See, in elementary school, I was convinced that I was the only one in the world who felt like this. None of my friends, I was sure, ran home to their atlases after school. In the years since then, I've become vaguely aware that this, whatever it is, is a thing that exists: that some fraction of humanity loves geography with a strange intensity. I'll see a three-year-old on *Oprah* who can point out every country on a world map and think, hey, that was me. I'll read about a member of the Extra Miler Club who has visited all 3,141 counties in the United States or about an antique map of the Battle of Yorktown selling at auction for a million dollars. And I'll wonder: where does this come from? It's easy to see from my own life story, my *Portrait of the Autist as a Young Man*, that these mapheads are my tribe, but I'm mystified by our shared tribal culture and religion. Why did maps mean—why *do* they still mean, I guess—so much to me? Maps are just a way of organizing information, after all—not normally the kind of thing that spawns obsessive fandom. I've never heard anyone profess any particular love for the Dewey Decimal System. I've never met a pie-chart geek. I suppose indexes are good at what they do, but do they inspire devotion?

There must be something innate about maps, about this one specific way of picturing our world and our relation to it, that charms us, calls to us, won't let us look anywhere else in the room if there's a map on the wall. I want to get to the bottom of what that is. I see it as a chance to explore one of the last remaining "blank spaces" available to us amateur geographers and cartographers: the mystery of what makes our consuming map obsession tick. I will go there.

Chapter 2

BEARING

['ber-iŋ] *n.*: the situation or horizontal direction of one
point with respect to the compass

An individual is not distinct from his place. He is his place.
—GABRIEL MARCEL

James Joyce's alter ego, Stephen Dedalus, is bored in his geography classes—all those place-names in America seem so far away to him. But when the places are *his,* his native surroundings, he has no trouble with their names. This is what he writes on the flyleaf of his geography textbook:

Stephen Dedalus
Class of Elements
Clongowes Wood College
Sallins
County Kildare
Ireland
Europe
The World
The Universe

As a child, I liked to write my address using a similar hierarchy—though I was apparently more of a space geek than wee Stephen, so my address featured a few steps ("The Solar System, Orion Arm,

Milky Way Galaxy, Virgo Supercluster") that he skipped. I'm sure my elaborate envelope-addressing system annoyed the mailman, but it delighted me. One of the fundamental questions of childhood is "Where am I?" and children want to know the answer on every level, from the microlocal to the galactic.

"What was it that identified us as closet geographers, perhaps as children, long before we knew enough to put a name on our private passions?" Peirce Lewis, then the president of the Association of American Geographers, asked in a 1985 address. The "visceral love of maps" is only part of the equation, he said. "The second, common to us all, is topophilia, an equally visceral passion for the earth—more particularly, some magic or beloved place on the surface of the earth."

The word "topophilia," from the Greek for "love of place," was popularized by the geographer Yi-Fu Tuan in a 1974 book.* When I first read about the concept, I experienced a jolt of recognition and validation, like a patient finally getting the right diagnosis for an obscure malady. I had felt this weirdly intense connection to landscape my whole life, but it was a relief to finally have a fancy Greek name to hang on it. Lewis said he had been forged into a geographer by the white sand dunes on the shores of Lake Michigan where he used to spend his summers as a child. My own primeval landscape was the Pacific Northwest, where I was raised: the lush pastures of my grandparents' farm in Oregon's Willamette River Valley, and especially the drizzly cedar-and-fir forests of western Washington State, so thick with moss and ferns that even in winter the forest floor is a vivid shade of green you normally see only in children's books about dinosaurs. If you hooked me up to one of those hospital monitors, I imagine the graph of my heartbeat would look exactly like the pale contour of the Olympic Mountains seen across Puget Sound on a sunny day. Well, no, not really. That would be charming but probably fatal.

Young topophiles are most deeply shaped by the environments

---

* The term, however, seems to have been coined almost thirty years before, by no less than W. H. Auden, who used it to describe the strong sense of place in the work of his fellow poet John Betjeman.

where they first became aware they *had* an environment: they imprint, like barnyard fowl. Baby ducks will follow the first moving object they see in the first few hours after they hatch. If it's their mother, great; if it's not, they become the ducklings you see following pigs or tractors around the farm on hilarious Sunday-morning news pieces. When I was seven years old, my family moved from Seattle to Seoul, Korea; I've since lived all over the globe, from Singapore to Spain to Salt Lake City. (The alliteration has been a coincidence, not an itinerary.) These are all places with distinctive, beautiful landscapes, ranging from tropical jungles to Mars-like salt flats, and I happily explored them all, but it was too late for me. I had already imprinted on a different part of the world. Falling in love with places is just like falling in love with people: it can happen more than once, but never quite like your first time.

These early landscapes are the maps over which my mind wanders even while I'm asleep. I rarely dream about the office cubicle where I worked for years or the house I live in now. My dreams are far more likely to be set in more primal settings: my grandparents' sunlit kitchen, the hallways of my elementary school. And geography is an unusually vivid element in my dreams. Upon waking, I rarely remember the dream people I met or the jumble of events that took place, but I always have a very strong sense for where I stood, which direction I was traveling. Years later, I can still remember dreams that took place in nonexistent neighborhoods of major cities—Seattle, San Francisco, New York. Within those dreams, I always navigated with a very specific idea of where I was on a city map, and always, of course, with the dreamer's absolute certainty that I had been there many times before.

Not everyone thinks this way, of course. We all have our own filing systems. A history buff might mentally index things chronologically. ("Let's see, that must have been the summer of '84, because the Colts were already in Indianapolis but *The Cosby Show* hadn't premiered yet . . .") The quiz buffs I met when I was playing *Jeopardy!* excel at trivia because of strong associative memories; they are naturally gifted at storing new facts, and retrieving them, by topic. Some new factoid about, say, peanuts will stick in their mental mesh because it gets linked to clusters of thematically similar data, facts about circuses and Jimmy Carter and peanut butter, which in turn links to Annette Funicello and George Washington Carver, and so on.

But some of us organize the world by location.

"I wish I had a dollar for every time a student has walked into my office and said, 'I've always loved geography, and I've always loved maps, ever since I was young,'" says Keith Clarke, the University of California, Santa Barbara, geography professor who writes the "Ask Dr. Map" column for the American Congress on Surveying and Mapping's *Bulletin* magazine. "My theory is that these are people who reason spatially."

Good spatial skills are easy enough to measure; every intelligence test you've ever taken probably had a series of headache-inducing rotation and cross-section problems designed to test your spatial cognition. People with these abilities are far more likely than their peers to wind up in math- or science-heavy careers, even when general intelligence is controlled for. They might be engineers, geologists, architects—even dentists, since dental exams ask lots of spatial questions. You don't want your dentist asking you, in the middle of a root canal, "Wait, which molar was that again? I can't quite . . . can you turn your head the same direction as mine?"

Machines and molars may come easier to people with keen spatial sense, but maps *really* come alive for them. They engage with the map in a way that others don't. They can project their viewpoint right into its dots and lines and vividly imagine what the territory will look like ahead. Christopher Columbus's biographer Bartolomé de Las Casas wrote that the explorer's first Atlantic voyage was inspired by a nautical chart that the Italian mathematician Paolo Toscanelli had sent him. "That map set Columbus's mind ablaze," wrote Las Casas. "He did not doubt he should find those lands that were marked upon it." Columbus was clearly one of those people who could see a map once and enter its world immediately, and it changed the course of history.

Not everyone has the knack, of course. If you've ever stood in front of a shopping-mall map for ten minutes, craning your head at various angles in a vain attempt to visualize whether Sbarro's is to your left or your right, you know it's a frustrating experience.* People, especially kids, who have that experience over and over aren't going to want to read maps for fun. They're going to avoid them at all costs. When cartophiles trace the Zambezi River with one finger on a map of Africa, they can imagine rafting the river's serpentine jungle curves, the roar of Victoria Falls growing to deafening proportions in the spray ahead . . . but it's just not the same if the river stubbornly remains just a squiggly blue line on the map for you.

But you needn't despair every time you get lost in the mall. "There's tremendous evidence that we can learn these skills," says David Uttal, a professor of psychology and education at Northwestern University. "People's potential is grossly underutilized."

In study after study, lousy mappers and lousy spatial thinkers have "responded well and quickly to relatively simple interventions," Uttal tells me. This is academicspeak for "practice makes perfect." Test the baseline spatial cognition of a group of college freshmen and then repeat the test after they've taken a short introductory course in engineering graphics. Their scores will improve markedly. A famous 2000 study showed that the brains of London cabbies who had passed "The Knowledge," a licensing exam requiring encyclopedic expertise of the city's streets, had a markedly larger hippocampus than those of normal Londoners. (The hippocampus, a sea horse–shaped structure in the brain's temporal lobe, is the center of navigational function.) In fact, the cabbies' hippocampi continued to grow the longer they spent on the job. Apparently size matters.

"When people say they can't read maps, I just think they have a preference not to," says Uttal. "There are a lot of things I can't do right now, but I could if you gave me two weeks to study them."

I decide to test Uttal's two-week dictum on my wife, Mindy. Mindy,

---

* The costs of losing one's way in unfamiliar territory were much higher a few centuries ago, when you might be robbed or shipwrecked or eaten by hungry wolves every time you strayed off course. G. Malcolm Lewis has argued that maps were humanity's way of inoculating itself against that fear of the unknown: by staring at a map of new territory, you were forcing yourself to confront your fear of it via the behavioral therapy that today we would call desensitization.

I hasten to add, is a wonderful woman in every respect. Songbirds fly in through our bedroom window every morning to help her dress, and her woodland friends whistle cheerfully along with her as she makes breakfast. But—how do I put this?—a good sense of direction is not foremost among her many outstanding qualities. On a recent trip to Paris, she took us the wrong direction on the Métro so many times that I eventually had to take over the pathfinding, even though it was my first time in Paris but she used to live there. Her uncanny inaccuracy does have one useful application, though: if I'm lost while driving, I can always ask her which way she thinks we should go at an intersection and then turn in *the exact opposite direction*.

But we have a family trip planned to visit some friends in Washington, D.C., and I'm determined to give Mindy a second chance. So I haul out a road atlas one Friday night (weekends can get pretty wild in the Jennings house!) and we study the lay of the land. Greater D.C. is a bit of a navigational nightmare, with those diagonal state-named avenues colliding with the other streets at weird angles. (Scientists know that humans aren't terribly good at grokking diagonals—we have neurons in our brains that are biased toward horizontal and vertical arrangements, and they vastly outnumber the diagonal ones.*) But we plan on spending plenty of our trip down by the National Mall, which is a perfect test case: small, dense, orderly, with notable landmarks in every cardinal direction.† On the map, we take careful

---

* Quick—is Los Angeles east or west of Reno? What's the first U.S. state you'll hit if you travel due north from Ecuador, on the west coast of South America? The answers (east and Florida, respectively) may seem counterintuitive if you've never seen this particular type of geographic brainteaser before. The underlying misconceptions here are a result of our brain's inability to remember and manage diagonal relationships. We simplify them in our mental models so that California is due west of Nevada and South America due south of North America, when the actual relationships are much less rectilinear.

† The Dutch-born geographer Harm de Blij has claimed that, contrary to what you might expect, Americans actually have a much better innate sense of direction than Europeans do, because Americans have more experience navigating orderly, gridlike cities. Twisty cobblestoned streets apparently don't sharpen a person's skills—they just cause people to throw their hands up in the air, shout *"Zut alors!"* or *"Ach du lieber!"* or something, and give up.

note of where the monuments are, where the Metro stops are, how the lettered and numbered streets are ordered.

We drill relentlessly. "Mindy, you're standing at the Air and Space Museum facing the National Gallery! Point to Capitol Hill! Correct. Which way is the Lincoln Memorial? Correct!"

Rocky music plays. We jump rope, shadowbox with sides of beef.

This little exercise doesn't take us two weeks; we spend maybe an hour on it. But David Uttal turns out to be right. In D.C., a well-prepared Mindy successfully navigates me and the kids to the White House, the Washington Monument, and many, many Smithsonian food courts. Once, after coming out of the Metro at Federal Triangle, I am disoriented and, after a moment's hesitation, march us in the wrong direction. Mindy stops and closes her eyes tightly like a Jedi using the Force. "Aren't the National Archives this way?" she asks, pointing behind us. I don't believe her, but when we get to the corner I see my mistake.

"Aha, I was right!" she gloats, newly empowered. "It makes me think my sense of direction isn't actually all that bad. If I cared enough to actually work on it a little." I imagine that, like the Grinch's heart, her hippocampus has grown three sizes this day.

Show a map to a three-year-old, and what will the child say? Even without any specific training, there will probably be a basic under-standing that the map represents a place. Generally he or she will have no idea what place—one researcher noted that a map of Chicago was often mistaken for Africa, while a map of her young subjects' home state of Pennsylvania was charmingly identified by one as depicting "California, Canada, and the 'North Coast.'" They will have trouble understanding angle (an aerial view of a rectangular parking lot might be mistaken for a door) or representation (the states being different colors won't make much sense to them) or scale ("That line can't be a road! My car wouldn't fit on that!"). But they'll understand that it's a kind of picture of a place, and that you can use it to get around. Any younger than three, and children can't even grasp the idea that a piece of paper can stand for an area. If you show toddlers a two-dimensional object like a shadow or a photo, they'll reach for it as if it were real and rounded. This makes sense, I guess—2-D representations like maps and photos are fairly recent innovations. Evolutionarily, our instincts haven't caught up yet.

The fact that very young children can understand maps with no training led scientists, for many years, to conclude that there was something innate about the process of mapping—essentially, that all people, regardless of culture, were born mappers. But new research suggests that this isn't really true—not everyone maps. Anthropologists are now beginning to understand that a wide variety of artifacts from all over the world—the *quipu* knots of the Incas, the *toa* marker pegs of South Australian Aborigines, the *lukasa* memory boards of the African Luba tribe—did have some geographical import, but they're far from anything we'd call maps. One favorite curiosity of map lovers is the *rebbelib*, or stick chart, of the Marshall Islanders. These lattices of coconut fronds and seashells look like something the Professor might use to map Gilligan's Island, but they're actually detailed charts of ocean swells that were used by Marshallese canoe navigators for centuries. It's remarkable that these people could pilot from atoll to atoll on the open sea based solely on wave patterns, but it's also interesting that we haven't found a single map of the Pacific made by any of the hundreds of other island cultures. Some people, apparently, get by just fine without written maps.

"Mapmaking might be innate in the same way that reading is innate," Uttal suggests. "And that's a very complex thing: reading text is obviously *not* innate, but the language upon which it is based is."

So which parts of cartography might actually be as instinctive as language and not (fairly recent) cultural innovations? Well, we all make mental maps, models of our surroundings that we store in our heads. Calling such a construct a "map" might be misleading, though, since our mental maps don't have much in common with paper ones. They're not static; they're not one-to-one replicas of actual topography; they don't rely on symbols and in some cases may not even involve landmarks. (You also can't refold them badly and shove them back into your glove compartment.) When I ask my friend Nephi Thompson, who has the best sense of direction of anyone I know, to

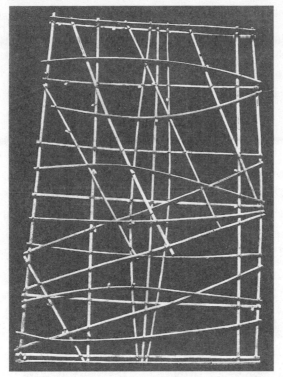

A Micronesian road map: the tiny seashells are islands and the bamboo strands currents

describe how he sees his mental map in his mind's eye, he says, "It's like a first-person shooter game, an over-the-shoulder perspective. It's not a bird's-eye view."

Humans have been making mental maps millions of years longer than they've been making written ones, of course. The very first time some hairy hominid ever decided to alter his hunting route to avoid an obstacle or a predator, he was drawing a mental map. In fact, when the term "cognitive map" was first coined in 1940, it wasn't used to refer to humans at all but to the surprising maze-solving abilities of lab rats.

It's well known that animals can perform navigational feats that make even the canniest human trackers look, in comparison, like blindfolded four-year-olds swinging cluelessly at a birthday party piñata. Baby loggerhead sea turtles, immediately after hatching in

Florida, embark straightaway on an eight-thousand-mile circuit of the North Atlantic, getting as far as the African coast before returning home a decade later. They do it alone, they start when they're less than two inches long, and they don't get lost. Scientists have translocated black bears hundreds of miles from their home in the forests of Minnesota and seen the majority quickly return. In 1953, a British ornithologist named R. M. Lockley heard that a friend, the noted American clarinetist Rosario Mazzeo, was flying home to Boston the following day. Lockley seized the opportunity to give Mazzeo two Manx shearwaters, seabirds whose homing abilities he had been studying. "In the evening, I enplaned for America with the birds under my seat," Mazzeo later wrote his friend. "Only one survived the flight." (Note to self: Don't let a woodwind player watch my pets next time I'm out of town.) He released the surviving bird from the east end of Boston's Logan International Airport and watched as it flew straight out to sea. Less than two weeks later, the bird reappeared in its British burrow. The shocked scientist, who hadn't heard from Mazzeo since his departure, assumed that he'd been forced to release the bird somewhere in Britain, but that very day his letter arrived from the United States, describing the shearwater's brief Boston visit. The bird had made it back home ahead of the mail, traversing 3,200 miles in just twelve and a half days.

Not all feats of spatial memory are long-distance migrations straight out of Walt Disney movies. The frillfin goby is a small tropical fish that's usually found in rocky pools along the Atlantic shore. When threatened in a tide pool, either by a predator or by falling water levels, it has a remarkable defense mechanism: it escapes by shooting itself up into the air, like James Bond from an Aston Martin ejector seat. If you ever had a suicidal goldfish as a child, you know that accurate jumping isn't always a fish specialty, but the goby always jumps straight into another (safer) pool. Sometimes it makes up to six consecutive pool hops until it arrives in open water. Obviously the fish can't see out of its own pool, so how does it make these leaps of faith? It plans ahead. It takes advantage of every high tide to explore its surroundings so it knows—and remembers—where the safest spots are likely to be once the tide goes out.

But just because an animal can perform an impressive bit of way-finding doesn't mean it's relying on a sophisticated cognitive map. The clarinetist's shearwater, for example, was crossing territory it had never seen before, the North Atlantic. It was obviously flying on instinct, not a mental map from past experience. We now know that many migrating birds rely on the position of the sun as a compass, as well as the sights and even smells of habitats along the way. Baby turtles are sensitive to tiny variations in the earth's magnetic field; you can get a loggerhead turtle to change directions in a swimming pool by placing powerful magnets nearby.*

We humans use many of the same tools to orient ourselves that animals do; we're just not as good at them. We don't have magnetite in our beaks like homing pigeons do, but otherwise the principles are the same. Take my family's recent trip to Washington, D.C.

- On our first day there, we walked from the Metro to the Air and Space Museum and then to the Natural History Museum. To get back to the Metro, we didn't retrace our steps through both museums. We mentally gauged the distances and directions we'd traveled and set out to walk directly toward the Metro. Animal species from fiddler crabs to ground squirrels can do something analogous, only with much greater accuracy. An ant, for example, can wander around aimlessly for two hundred meters (at human scale, the equivalent of run-

---

* For many years, the uncanny homing abilities of Tunisian desert ants were one of the great navigational mysteries of the animal kingdom. Most ant species find their way home by following the scent trails left by other ants, but that doesn't work well in the windy, sandy Sahara. A Swiss zoologist named Rüdiger Wehner spent decades trying to crack the secret of the ants' internal odometers with a series of ingenious experiments. To find out whether ants judge distances based on "optic flow," the speed with which they observe the landscape passing them by, he blocked their vision with tiny paint "blindfolds." To find out if they judge distances based on metabolic effort, he fitted each ant with a tiny weighted backpack. Finally, his team decided to alter the ants' pace length by putting them on tiny stilts made of individual pig bristles. Bingo! The stilt-walking ants drastically overshot their destination, proving to the researchers that ants reckon the distance they've traveled by counting their steps in some instinctive fashion. Best of all, the researchers now have an adorable set of ant-sized fashion accessories ready for all occasions.

ning a marathon) and then, from any point, return in a straight line to exactly where it started. This is called "path integration," and it's a crucial ability for foraging animals, which wander over a vast territory looking for food but need to be able to return directly to the nest as soon as they find enough to eat.

- Every time we double-checked our location by looking to see where we were relative to the Tidal Basin or the Washington Monument, we were mimicking another common animal trick: the use of landmarks. Many species of jays and nutcrackers, for example, are "scatter hoarders," meaning that they store little food caches in as many as eighty thousand locations over a single winter. These birds rely heavily on landmarks to recover their hidden goodies; if nearby visual cues are tampered with, the food will be lost forever.

- We even used some rudimentary celestial navigation on our trip, as the Manx shearwater does. In which direction is the late-afternoon sun? All right, then, the White House is that way.

By the end of the day, we had the lay of the land down pretty well; even Mindy could find her way between any two monuments we'd visited without resorting to landmarks or a sun compass. It's hard to be sure which animals can do the same. We can't exactly ask them. The current consensus is that mammals, and possibly even some insects, like honeybees, can think in terms of maplike models. In one experiment that's been repeated with both dogs and chimpanzees, an animal accompanies the researcher as food is hidden at various points within an enclosure. The animal is taken to a food cache, then back to a starting point, then on to another food cache, then back to the start, and so on. When the animal is released, it's vastly more successful at locating the food than are other subjects that didn't get the walking tour, of course. But, more suggestively, the dog or chimp won't just retrace the researcher's steps between the food and "home." It will actually invent efficient new routes to circle through nearby food caches without ever having to revisit the starting point.

"Every species is good in its own niche" when it comes to navigation, says David Uttal. "We're not at the top of some evolutionary ladder." This probably goes without saying, given that a Chinook salmon can swim a thousand miles upstream to the place it was born just by following its nose, whereas a human often struggles to find a car in a parking lot after ten minutes in a grocery store. "But what we have that no other species has is culture. We can share information, and that gives us an amazing flexibility."

That's where mapmaking comes in. When humans take information from mental maps and put it down on paper (or a cave wall or clay tablet), the game is fundamentally changed. Sure, a honeybee can share geographic information with his hive by doing a little dance, but according to Karl von Frisch, who won a Nobel Prize for translating the bee dance, it has only three components: the direction of the food source relative to the sun, its distance, and its quality. The maps we make for other humans are much more versatile. The same map of southern Africa that I used as a kid to imagine Tarzan-style adventures could be used by an environmentalist to study land use, a tourist to plan a safari, or a military strategist to plan a coup or invasion. It has thousands of potential routes on it, not just one.

There are plenty of possible ways you could express to others the geographical information in your mental map: a written description, gestures, song lyrics, puppet theater. But maps turn out to be an enormously intuitive, compact, and compelling way to communicate that information. To emphasize that they're not "innate" seems to stop just short of saying that maps are an accident, the product of dozens of arbitrary cultural decisions. I think that misses the point. Just because maps aren't innate doesn't mean that they're not optimal, or even inevitable.

Cast your mind back, for a moment, to the middle of the last century. Today, orbital imagery is everywhere and we take it for granted, but before the space race began, no Earthling had ever seen our home planet from high above—that is, from the viewpoint of a large-area map. If you look at science-fiction movies and comics from that era, you'll see that the Earth is almost always depicted like the Universal logo or a schoolroom globe: *without any cloud cover at all.* We had no idea what we looked like from outside ourselves! As a species, we were the equivalent of Dave Chappelle's famous comedy sketch character: the blind Klansman who doesn't know he's black.

But when John Glenn became the first man to orbit the earth

in 1962, he looked down in surprise and told the Bermuda tracking station, "I can see the whole state of Florida just laid out like a
map."* Think about what that says about the fidelity of maps: seeing
the real thing for the first time, the first thing that occurred to Glenn
was to compare it to its map representation. In that one sentence, he
validated that maps had been getting something fundamentally *right*
about Florida for centuries. That makes me think that we shortchange
maps by calling them mere cultural conventions. Sure, some of the
specifics that we take for granted might be arbitrary—the angle of
view, dotted lines for roads, blue ink for water, and so on—but not
the fact that we as a species rely heavily on pictorial representations of
the surface of our world. They're critical to the way we think. If maps
didn't exist, it would be necessary to invent them.

That's also demonstrated in our compulsion to turn *everything*—
not just spatial data—into map form. For centuries illustrators have
been drawing allegorical maps, which schizophrenically join the
beauty and detail of classic illustration with all the bag-of-hammers
subtlety of a 1980s after-school special. In the 1700s, it was popular
to draw romance as a nautical chart: watch out for the Rocks of Jeal-
ousy and the Shoals of Perplexity on your way to the Land of Mat-
rimony! Unlucky sailors would wind up marooned at Bachelor's Fort
on the unfortunately named Gulf of Self Love. The Prohibition era
gave us railroad maps of temperance, in which the Great Destruction
Route might seem like fun as you're chugging through Cigaretteville
or Rum Jug Lake but then quickly diverts you through the States of
Bondage, Depravity, and Darkness. One of the most popular illustrations of the 1910s was "The Road to Success," depicting a snare-laden
road through Bad Habits, Vices, and the carousel of Conceit, in which
only the tunnel of True Knowledge leads successfully through Lack
of Preparation mountain and inside the Gate of Ideals. A recent Matt

---

* You may have read that the Great Wall of China is the only man-made object visible
from orbit, but that's bunk. The Mercury astronauts reported seeing all kinds of stuff,
from trains to oil refineries to Tibetan monasteries. When Gordon Cooper told Houston that he was watching a white big-rig truck travel down a Texas highway, NASA
assumed that he must be hallucinating—until workers there later investigated and were
actually able to identify the truck in question.

The most popular allegorical map ever drawn.
Watch out for the slide of Weak Morals!

Groening cartoon updates this map for the twenty-first century. Now the road takes aspirants past the meadow of Parental Discouragement and the River of Unsold Screenplays, inside the House of Wrinkles, and up into the Tower of Fleeting Fame . . . which unfortunately leads straight to a long slide marked "Disappointing Sales of Second Album, Novel, Play or Film Followed by the Long, Long Slide Back to the Bottom* (*Drug Addiction Optional)."

Why this urge to turn every facet of life into a mappable journey? Hell, why see life itself as a journey to Heaven, the way medieval Christian maps always did? That whole metaphor isn't in the Bible anywhere. (Well, that's not strictly true. I'm sure there are lots of verses about walking in righteous paths and so on. But nowhere, as far as I know, does God tell the children of Israel, "Verily I say unto you that life is a highway. Yea, thou shalt ride it, even all the night long.")

For a long time I blamed writers like John Bunyan and Dante for this allegorical form of cartacacoethes. Desperate to extract a storyline from a possibly dreary and didactic subject—the struggle to live a life worthy of Heaven—they seized on a quest narrative, a "pilgrim's progress," and mapmakers were quick to follow suit.* I wonder: how would history be different if Bunyan or Dante had chosen to represent life not as a linear journey through a geographic territory but as something a little more holistic—a library, say? Or a buffet? (*Pilgrim's Potluck!*) What would Western civilization be like in that alternate universe? Would we value different things, set different goals for ourselves, if the governing geographic metaphor of our culture were replaced by something else—recipes instead of maps, cookbooks instead of atlases? Would shallow celebrities still tell interviewers they were "in a good place right now"? Or would they say things like "I'm at the waffle bar right now, Oprah"? ("You eat, girl!" Respectful audience applause.)

Maybe, but I think there would still be people like me who would

---

* Dante's dreamlike *terza rima* poetry doesn't really lend itself to cartography, but devising "accurate" maps of his Inferno, Purgatory, and Paradise nevertheless became a popular pastime during the Renaissance, attracting luminaries from Botticelli to Galileo. It was a faux-academic pursuit, like the "Sherlockians" today who write deadpan scholarly treatises about Holmes and Watson as if they were real historical figures.

see everything through the filter of geography, because of the spatial way our brains are wired. The sense of place is just too important to us. When people talk about their experiences with the defining news stories of their generation (the Kennedy assassination, the moon landing, the Berlin Wall, 9/11), they always frame them as where-we-were-when-we-heard. I was in the kitchen, I was in gym class, I was driving to work. It's not relevant to the *Challenger* explosion in any way that I was in my elementary school cafeteria when I heard about it, but that's still how I remember the event and tell it to others. Naming the place makes us feel connected, situated in the story.

And maps are just too convenient and too tempting a way to understand place. There's a tension in them. Almost every map, whether of a shopping mall, a city, or a continent, will show us two kinds of places: places where we've been and places we've never been. The nearby and the faraway exist together in the same frame, our world undeniably connected to the new and unexpected. We can understand, at a glance, our place in the universe, our potential to go and see new things, and the way to get back home afterward.

When my family moved overseas in 1982 so my dad could work at a Korean law firm, I missed my imprinted habitat of western Washington State. In many ways, South Korea was the polar opposite of Seattle: hot in the summer, dry in the winter, crunchy cicadas underfoot instead of slimy slugs. The Seoul air was so polluted that I developed a convincing smoker's hack at the tender age of eight. Before the end of World War II, Korea had been a Japanese colony, and the peninsula had been stripped of forests to help fuel Japan's massive industrial and military expansion. The neat rows of spindly pine trees assiduously replanted by the Korean government seemed like soulless counterfeits when compared to the dense, majestic forests of the Pacific Northwest.

I loved it anyway, but I felt very keenly that I had been transplanted; it's hard not to feel like a stranger in a strange land when you're the only American kid in a vast Korean apartment complex. Expatriates thrive on this sense of bold outsiderness, and it bonds them into tightly knit communities. But it isolates them from their homeland as well. My family would spend a month or so every summer on home leave in the States, just long enough to be reminded of what we were missing, before we had to hop wistfully on a plane back . . . where? Home? For the next decade, when people asked me where I was from, I would automatically say, "Seattle," even though I never spent more than two or three weeks a year there. This was pre-grunge, and nobody thought Seattle was a particularly hip place to be from, so I wasn't being a poseur—I just didn't want to deal with the follow-up of having to explain why, despite all appearances, a white kid was claiming to be Korean. The sociologist Ruth Hill Useem coined the term "Third Culture Kids" to refer to nationality-confused global nomads like me, because, she said, we fuse our birth culture and our adopted culture into some entirely new, blended culture. But I didn't necessarily feel like a man without a country. I knew where home was; I just wasn't living there.

I've never thought about it until now, but my obsession with maps coincided almost exactly with the move overseas. I wasn't traumatized by the news that we were going; just insatiably curious. Driving home from a movie with my parents that summer (I'm oddly certain it was Disney's *The Fox and the Hound*), my brother and I peppered them with questions about the upcoming move: What country would we be living in? Which city? There were *two* Koreas? Were we going to the north one or the south one? Crossing an ocean made me feel like an explorer; I wanted maps to explain this suddenly larger world. I bought my very first atlas from the only English-language bookstore in Seoul during our first months there.

But I also know that I spent just as much time looking at maps of the United States, looking backward. Maps became a way to reconnect with the country I'd left behind. And not just the Pacific Northwest but all of it, even places I'd never seen. I was annoyed by a kiddie atlas I'd been given that showed only three cities in the entire state of Delaware. (I can still name them: Wilmington, Dover, Newark.) When I finally got my hands on a Rand McNally U.S. road atlas, I relished the detail, planning imaginary road trips along open highways that seemed so unlike the cramped, noisy urban quarters where we now found ourselves. I recited the tiny towns of Delaware as if they were the most exotic names imaginable: Milford, Laurel, Harrington, Lewes.* To me, half a world away, they *were* exotic.

Fast-forward two decades. Mindy and I were living in Salt Lake City and happily settled, but I suddenly found myself working from home, and we realized that, as a result, we could really be living anywhere we liked. New York? Europe? Where would you go if you could go anyplace? We'd visited Seattle a couple times over the years, and I'd always cleverly arranged these visits for the summertime, when Seattle likes to fool out-of-towners by not drizzling three weeks out of every month. Mindy fell for it; she wasn't "imprinted" on the Pacific Northwest like me, but it was growing on her. I proposed a trip up to Washington and Oregon to see how we felt about moving there. It was May, and everything—even the parking lot of the extended-stay hotel where we were encamped—smelled like rain and cedar. Nine days later we put down an offer on a house outside Seattle, where we still live happily today.

"To be rooted," wrote Simone Weil, "is perhaps the most important and the least recognized need of the human soul." It took twenty-five years—longer than the Manx shearwater, longer even than the loggerhead sea turtle—but I finally found my way back home.

---

* There are also a Riverside, Delaware; a Centerville, Delaware; and a Fairview, Delaware. But you'd expect that—according to the U.S. Geographic Names Information System, Riverside, Centerville, and Fairview are the three most common place-names in America.

Chapter 3

FAULT

['fôlt] *n.*: a fracture in the earth's crust, along
which parallel displacement occurs

To the people of Bolivia!
—RONALD REAGAN, OFFERING
A 1982 TOAST—IN BRASILIA

O n the very first day of the University of Miami's spring semester in 1983, assistant professor David Helgren sprang a pop quiz in his introductory geography classes. He gave each of his 128 students, mostly business and liberal arts majors, a blank world map. They were to pinpoint the locations of thirty different places, ranging from the obvious (Miami, London, the South Pacific) to the then-newsworthy (the USSR, the Falkland Islands) to the slightly more exotic (New Guinea, Cairo). They didn't need to write their names on their papers but were instructed to try their best.

Dr. Helgren, a five-year veteran of freshman geography instruction, wasn't expecting the students to blow him out of the water with their astute global knowledge. As a rule, geography professors are pretty cynical about the public's command of geography. (In your school days, did you assume your teachers were all gossiping about your personal ineptness in smoke-filled break rooms? Well, you were probably right.) But if the scores were lousy, at least the department could use them to seek increased university funding for geography instruction. Helgren could give his students a similar quiz at the end of the semester as a way to benchmark their improvement. He was coming up for tenure soon, after all.

But when the results came back, even Helgren was a little shocked. He had graded the maps, he thought, pretty leniently, but more than half his students still couldn't find Chicago. Or Iceland or Quebec or the Amazon rain forest. Fewer than one in three knew where Moscow and Sydney were. Eleven of his Miami students had even misplaced Miami! It's hard to imagine an easier item on a test like this than the city where all the students live, unless you add two more items— "Your Ass" and "A Hole in the Ground"—and give credit to anyone who doesn't mark them in exactly the same spot. Helgren circulated the depressing scores to his dean and a few other campus contacts but heard nothing back. He assumed that was the end of the story.

A month later, the student newspaper wrote a small article on the quiz, a first tiny domino in the unlikely chain that would completely change Helgren's life. Both local Miami papers picked up on the story in *The Miami Hurricane* and sent reporters to interview Helgren. Viewing this as an opportunity to put in a good word for his field, Helgren waxed expansive to both reporters about America's widespread problems in geography education. The next day was February 14, Valentine's Day. All hell broke loose.

"This was a really dull news day," David Helgren remembers. "It was a Tuesday. Did you ever notice there's no news on Tuesdays?"

Decades after his brush with fame, I've tracked Helgren down at his Salinas, California, home on a bluff overlooking miles of strawberry and lettuce fields. You can guess at his academic specialty— African deserts and archaeology—just by walking through his home, which is full of antelope horns and tribal masks. ("My wife is Afrikaner," he says, and I wonder briefly if, in his shoes, I'd be able to resist the temptation to always tell people, "My wife is a Boer" instead.) A zebra skin hangs above the dining room table where we're talking. Now sixty-two years old, Helgren is a big man with piercing blue eyes and a snowy beard, and he strokes his pet cat pensively as he talks, like a Bond villain.

"So I wake up that morning, and I'm getting phone calls. I have the London papers calling me at home before seven A.M. because they're in a different time zone. I didn't know what the hell was going on! I'd never been interviewed by a newspaper in my life. I was a reclusive academic."

The Miami Herald, it seemed, had titled its story, "Where in the World Is London? 42% Tested at UM Didn't Know." When that headline came across the wire, the British papers jumped at the story, which was also spreading across the United States as the sun moved westward. Soon every national network wanted an interview. The overrun media relations people at the university called Helgren in a panic. "They said, 'Come into your office and try to look respectable!' So they put a globe in front of me and a map on the wall. I was wearing a tie, which was very not like me." He spent the entire day soberly lecturing TV news crews on the importance of geography. The camera crew from NBC's Miami affiliate happened to be an international news team, on an R&R break from covering the contras in Nicaragua. They were savvy. After getting their sound bites from Helgren, they hurried over to the giant swimming-pool complex at the heart of the Miami campus and started asking good-looking kids in swimsuits where Chicago was. As the camera rolled, one unconcerned but well-muscled young man told them, "Well, I don't know where it is, but I can look it up." Journalistic gold!

Helgren was hustled onto a plane to New York—*Good Morning America* had decided to do a story about map illiteracy. While he was in the air, all three Miami networks were airing their news pieces, and just about every newspaper in the English-speaking world was preparing a story or a scolding editorial on the "crisis." Johnny Carson was making map jokes in his monologue. The next morning, Helgren was the biggest news *Good Morning America* had, so he got the prime morning-show spot: ten minutes after eight o'clock. At the exact same time, over at the *Today* show, they were running clips from the previous night's NBC interview. No matter which channel Americans were tuned to,* they were seeing David Helgren.

---

* Well, pretty much. Even back in 1983, nobody watched CBS's morning show.

After showing the clip in which the tanned himbo confessed to not knowing where Chicago was, the *Today* show's Bryant Gumbel remarked to the camera, "Well, you know, some folks down there call that place 'Suntan U.'"

Ouch. By the time Helgren returned home to Miami, the residents had the torches and pitchforks ready. His wife fielded anonymous threatening phone calls to their home number. "My daughter is not a dummy!" one Hurricane mom blustered. "I'm going to have you fired!" The university president called the incident "very unfortunate," and a group of law students threatened to sue Helgren, the university, and even Bryant Gumbel for all the loss of future income they'd undoubtedly suffer. ("Why didn't you make partner last year, Bob?" "Oh, you know, the usual. Bryant Gumbel.") The campus public relations staff had been working that year to rebrand Miami, long sensitive to its reputation as a party school, as "a global university in a global city," so the media circus came at the worst possible time. One miffed publicist even compared *l'affaire Helgren* to the famous case a decade earlier in which a Miami researcher had kidnapped a young woman at gunpoint, then buried her in a fiberglass box in rural Georgia.

"I was in the worst shit ever, from the institution and the city," Helgren tells me. It's been twenty-five years, but he still looks completely bewildered as he describes his unwitting career suicide, the result of a few geographically inept undergrads and one slow news day. "At any other campus, this wouldn't have been an issue. That's the weirdness of Miami. It's essentially a freak show in American culture."

Though Helgren had been awarded a quarter of a million dollars in grants for his research—"more than anyone had ever got in the whole place," he says—and was up for promotion, he learned the following year that he'd be out of a job in May. A colleague who had stood up for him in the media, Jim Curtis, was dismissed a month later. The university denied that the map-illiteracy kerfuffle had anything to do with the firings. As a consolation prize, at least the Helgren story got the *National Enquirer* to run a nice, serious piece on geographic illiteracy. It appeared right between an article on a Turkish woman whose left hand weighed forty pounds and an interview with an expert who claimed that 20 percent of America's dogs and cats are space aliens.

David Helgren wasn't the first to discover, of course, that lots of people are pretty lousy at geography. In fact, geographical ignorance is such an engrained part of our culture that it's become an easy bit of comedy shorthand for ditziness, the same way you might show a character wearing a barrel with suspenders to represent poverty. Marilyn Monroe, in *Gentlemen Prefer Blondes,* insisted that she wanted to visit "Europe, France"; fifty years later, Sacha Baron Cohen deployed the exact same joke on *Da Ali G Show,* annoying his United Nations tour guide by complaining about the fact that Africa isn't a U.N. member. Joey on *Friends* thought that the Netherlands was where Peter Pan lived, and Bart Simpson was once surprised to discover the large Southern Hemisphere country of "Rand McNally" on his sister Lisa's globe.

Snickering at the cartographically cloddish dates back centuries. You'd think that, in the more provincial 1600s, *everyone* would have been a little hazy on geography, but that didn't prevent the French educator Denis Martineau du Plessis from filling the preface of his 1700 book *Nouvelle Géographie* with Joey Tribbiani–worthy stories of map woe. He recounts a (probably apocryphal) tale of the English ambassador to Rome in 1343, who caught wind of the fact that the pope had given away the "fortunate islands" (the Canary Islands were then called the "Islas Fortunatas") to the Count de Clermont. Assuming that the world's only *truly* fortunate islands were the British Isles, the outraged ambassador rushed back to London to tell the king that some French count was taking over England! Making fun of the English was a popular French pastime, then as now, but du Plessis takes some shots at his own countrymen as well, citing French authorities who wondered which river the Pont Euxine crossed ("Pont Euxine" was an ancient name for the Black Sea, not a bridge) and assumed that Moors came from Morea (another name for Peloponnesia, in Greece).*

---

* Even for three-hundred-year-old jokes, I'll grant you that these aren't really very funny. But, hey, *Friends* hasn't aged all that well either.

Jokes like these never would have been comic tropes if there weren't some truth behind them, of course. Real government officials, and not just apocryphal Renaissance-era ambassadors, make geographical gaffes all the time. In his autobiography, Henry Kissinger told the story of the prime minister of Mauritius's goodwill visit to Washington in 1970. Somehow the confused State Department had briefed the president to meet not with the leader of Mauritius, a tiny tropical island in the Indian Ocean, but of Mauritania, a vast Saharan nation that had recently cut off diplomatic relations with the United States. This improbable *I Love Lucy* setup led to the comic hijinks you might expect: President Richard Nixon led off the discussion by suggesting that the prime minister *of a valued American ally* restore diplomatic relations with the United States! That way, he said, he could offer American expertise with dry farming. The flummoxed Mauritian, hailing as he did from a lush jungle nation, had little interest in desert farming, so he tried to change the subject, asking Nixon about a space tracking station the United States operated in his country. The bewildered Nixon scrawled something down on a yellow legal pad and handed it to Kissinger. The note read, "Why the hell do we have a space tracking station in a country with which we don't have diplomatic relations?"

During the 2008 presidential race, both campaigns dealt with elementary school–level geography blunders that could have come from the pen of any sitcom hack. At a rally in Beaverton, Oregon, Barack Obama told the crowd, "Over the last fifteen months, we've traveled to every corner of the United States. I've now been in fifty-seven states. Just one left to go." (He was apparently channeling the *Friends* episode in which Joey crowns himself the winner of Chandler's name-all-the-states game, with a high score of fifty-six.) Then John McCain, when asked by a Spanish radio interviewer if he would invite Spain's President José Zapatero to the White House, seemed amenable, stressing "the importance of our relationship with Latin America." (Hey, just like that *Arrested Development* episode where Gob thinks his brother has fled to "Portugal, down South America way!") And that's not even counting Fox News's report that Sarah Palin believed that Africa was a country, not a continent. See, she's a real-life Ali G, only with—respek!—more stylish eyewear. On those rare occasions when a politician does display a knack for geography, he's treated as a sideshow freak. Al Franken's favorite party stunt has long been his ability to draw a near-perfect map of the United States freehand, a skill he's used to great effect doing electoral coverage for *Saturday Night Live*'s "Weekend Update" and on Comedy Central. In 1987, he amazed a Letterman audience by whipping off one of his Sharpie maps in less than two minutes. When the former comedian somehow got elected to the Senate in 2008, his onetime Stupid Human Trick got rebranded as a wonkishly patriotic bit of Americana and became a staple at campaign events and fund-raisers. But the audience result is still the same: shocked gasps that a U.S. senator *might actually know what the United States looks like!**

You know that geographic ignorance is a serious societal problem when even Miss Teen USA candidates are grilled about it! In 2007, South Carolina's Caite Upton was asked, "Recent polls have shown a fifth of Americans can't locate the U.S. on a world map. Why do you think this is?" Upton finished only fourth in the pageant, but her answer to that question made her an international celebrity overnight.

"I personally believe," she answered with absolute confidence, "that U.S. Americans are unable to do so because, uh, some people out there in our nation don't have maps and, uh, I believe that our, uh, education like such as in South Africa and, uh, the Iraq, everywhere like such as, and, I believe that they should, our education over here in the U.S. should help the U.S., uh, or, uh, should help South Africa and should help the Iraq and the Asian countries, so we will be able to build up our future, for our children."

In the much-watched YouTube video, even host Mario Lopez can't quite swallow his grin at the gratuitous "for our children" tacked onto the end, as he mercifully pulls away the mike.

But educators are worried too, and have been for a while. In

---

* My sense of celebrity geography knowledge was shaped as a child by watching the daytime game show *Win, Lose, or Draw,* a *Pictionary* clone produced by Burt Reynolds, of all people. Whenever the clue was an American place, the celebrity guest—whether it was Tony Danza or Loretta Swit or Dom DeLuise—would always start by drawing on their easel the exact same "map" of America: a vaguely rectangular blob almost tipping over on the right side due to the presence of a ginormous, phallic Florida.

1857, Andrew Dickson White, who would go on to cofound Cornell University, was put in charge of assessing the geography acumen of the University of Michigan's sophomore class. Michigan took great pride in the geography curriculum in its public high schools, but White wrote that "in the great majority of my students there was not a trace of real knowledge of physical geography, and very little of political." White told his students to throw away their rote lists of memorized place-names and browse atlases instead, with great success. During World War II, a Harvard professor named Howard Wilson was featured in *The New York Times,* insisting that German geographical expertise gave the Nazis a leg up on the United States. "Geographic illiterates cannot be counted on to create a public mind alert to the geographic factors of either war or peace," he scolded. If you don't study maps enough, in other words, you're studying for Hitler! Paging through back issues of *The Journal of Geography,* an education journal, I discover a regular stream of articles bemoaning the sad state of geographic knowledge. David Helgren wouldn't have been surprised by his findings if he'd read a 1950 study by an Oregon professor named Kenneth Williams, who'd sprung a blank-map test on his freshman class, with similar results: less than half his students could label Wisconsin on a U.S. map, and only a third could find New Hampshire. At one school, 15 percent misplaced their own state.

What's remarkable about these stories is the surprise that journalists and educators always express about the kids' ineptitude. This tired dog-bites-man story is still capable of grabbing the front page, even after a century of wear. Why? At some point, isn't this news only if the kids suddenly start doing *well* on map quizzes?

Part of the blame can be chalked up to the tendency, in both academia and the media, to attract readers to unsurprising developments by breathlessly overhyping them. Besides, reporters tend to be just as much "in the tank" on map knowledge as academic geographers are, since journalism is one of the few careers in which detailed global knowledge is still expected and rewarded.* And because journalism

---

* When the media is disproportionately interested in a story, you're going to hear about

and academia are somewhat insular private worlds, these stories get written by people who *are* genuinely surprised that college students couldn't find Kenya or Chile on a map; in their odd bubble worlds of geographic expertise, *everyone* would ace that test! Some people with odd obsessions become acutely aware of how their expertise makes them different (cf. my childhood love of maps). But others blithely assume that everyone shares their fanaticism, as you probably know if you ever had a college roommate whose favorite band was Rush.

It's easy to see why these stories are popular with readers as well—they make us feel better about ourselves. Reporters always cherry-pick the studies for items that make the subjects look as dumb as possible. Three-quarters of David Helgren's students knew where the Falklands were, but that's not shockingly bad. In fact, it seems pretty reasonable. So the half of the students who couldn't find London provided the headline instead. Such studies usually come with at least one easy-sounding task, like locating Canada or the Pacific Ocean, that a small minority will still fail. Even if only 10 percent answer incorrectly, it'll be a big part of the story, enabling us to marvel that these dumb kids could botch a question *we* certainly would have aced—no matter that the vast majority of respondents actually got it right. In a culture where geographic illiteracy is used as comic shorthand for stupidity, nobody's willing to own up to a little map vagueness of their own.

But there's another possible way to explain the viruslike persistence of the geographic illiteracy meme, and it's a little more sobering. What if this story has stuck around for centuries because every generation has been surprised by the rising generation's *even poorer* mastery of maps? In other words, what if we're continually getting worse?

---

it, whether it's newsworthy or not. An example that immediately springs to my mind: my six-month residence on the quiz show *Jeopardy!* in 2004 was, I was convinced, just a minor bit of quirky local news that only my close relatives would ever be aware of. I had reckoned without one fact: trivia and game-show geeks, otherwise unemployable, often become pop-culture pundits and radio personalities when they grow up. So my *Jeopardy!* streak became a staple of blogs and drive-time radio, whether anyone else cared or not.

It's not hard to find evidence to support that gloomy idea. In that 1942 *Times* interview, Howard Wilson bemoaned the fact that the average American didn't "comprehend the significance" of places such as Dakar and the Caucasus. Forget the "significance"—I doubt that many Americans today could even tell you what continent they're on. Indiana University's Rick Bein recently performed a fifteenth-anniversary follow-up to his massive 1987 study on the geographic literacy of Indiana college freshmen. Indiana had put major efforts into improving geography education in the interim, so Bein was anticipating a big bounce in his results. Instead, scores declined by 2 percent. For the most part, the students who knew their stuff were the ones who'd moved around a lot or traveled; those who had taken high school geography classes did no better than those who hadn't. In other words, the state's big initiatives hadn't done a lick of good. In recent National Geographic polls, one in ten American college students can't find California or Texas on a map, ten times worse than the same numbers in Dr. Williams's 1950 study.

There are obvious ways to explain an ongoing drop in geographic literacy. Geographers like to blame the curriculum revolution of the 1960s and 1970s, in which the clear-cut history and geography classes of grade schools past were replaced by a wishy-washy amalgam called "social studies." The adoption of social studies was the well-intentioned result of academics in a wide variety of social sciences hoping to expose kids to their pet fields: anthropology, economics, political science, and so on. But, as a side effect of the new curriculum, classes specifically devoted to geography virtually disappeared from the nation's schools. The United States is now the only country in the developed world where a student can go from preschool to grad school without ever cracking a geography text.

So kids are spending less school time with maps than ever before. And that generation gap becomes a huge part of the problem: in our cultural memory, geography becomes that thing that your parents or grandparents studied. We associate it with dusty old pull-down wall maps and Dick-and-Jane readers and "duck and cover" drills. On the TV series *Mad Men,* set in the early 1960s, the protagonist, Don Draper, has a large world globe prominently displayed not just in his den at home but at the office as well. It's a neat bit of production design, immediately signaling to viewers under thirty: See how old-timey this show is? *People actually still owned globes!* Convincing someone today that geography, of all things, is a serious and important field sounds a little like pushing a typewriter or phonograph repair class on them.

Geography seems to be a struggle for Americans, specifically. In 2002, National Geographic conducted a survey of college-aged people in nine different countries, testing place-name knowledge, current events geography, and map skills. No country aced the test, but the top scorers—Sweden, Germany, and Italy—answered around 70 percent of the questions correctly. U.S. students, with a dreary 41 percent, were next to last. (Thank you, Mexico!) These results are similar to what researchers see when they stack American students up against the rest of the world in other subjects, like math and science, so maybe they're just a symptom of our dumbed-down curricula in general. "Geography is just a subset of Americans not knowing *anything*," says David Helgren with a shrug. "I hate to say that."

But it isn't hard to imagine that there might be some peculiarly geographic reasons why Americans lag in global knowledge. One is our isolation—drive east from France for ten hours, and you might cross five different nations. Drive east from El Paso, Texas, and ten hours later you won't even be in Houston yet. Americans don't know much about other nations because we can so easily pretend that they don't even exist, the way Rosencrantz says he doesn't believe in England in Tom Stoppard's play *Rosencrantz and Guildenstern Are Dead*. ("Just a conspiracy of cartographers, then?" asks his friend Guildenstern acidly.) If Americans want to go to the mountains or the desert or the beach, we don't need to hop on an international flight: everything's right here. Our isolation isn't just a geographic accident; it was practically a mission statement when America was founded. The first people who settled here came to break connections with the rest of the world, so the American approach to geography has always been to expand our reach into new frontiers, not study up on old ones. The global interconnectedness of the modern world hasn't come easily to us.

There are international factors for the decline as well. For much of the twentieth century, the Communist threat of the Cold War era made geopolitics seem sexy and urgent: university geography department's couldn't keep up with the flood of applicants, and Kennedy's Peace Corps was staffed largely by geography students. Many U.S. embassies even had "geographic attachés" on staff, whose job was to monitor local maps.* The collapse of the Soviet Union killed that Risk-board view of the world with shocking suddenness, and the post-2001 rise in world tension, interestingly, hasn't led to a corresponding Cold War–style boom in geography interest. Arthur Jay Klinghoffer, a professor of political science at Rutgers University, has argued that geography seems less relevant than ever in a world where nonstate actors—malleable entities like ethnicities, for example—are as powerful and important as the ones with governments and borders. Where on a map can you point to al-Qaeda? Or Google, or Wal-Mart? Everywhere and nowhere.

Another reason for sagging geographic knowledge may strike closer to home. Today's kids live increasingly in a world without place—without personal exploration through real-life geographies of any kind. In one of the great ironies of the last century, many Americans moved from overcrowded cities out to the suburbs in order to "reconnect with nature," but those dreams of carefree country life didn't materialize; there's little that's carefree or natural about the soulless sprawl of modern suburbia. We've chosen insulated lifestyles—insulated by car, by TV, by iPod or Internet or cell phone—that distance us from our surroundings, that treat *any* kind of navigation through or interaction with our environment as a necessary evil.

And children have it worst of all. It's not just technology holding them back—it's us, their well-meaning parents. Seventy-one percent of us walked or rode a bike to school as children, but only 22 percent of our kids today do. The radius around home where kids are allowed to play has shrunk to a ninth of what it was in 1970. Not that we leave them time to explore in their overscheduled lives anyway;

---

* This may seem a little silly, but local maps have often provided crucial intelligence. In the late 1980s, for example, maps in Iraq started labeling Kuwait as the nineteenth Iraqi province, an early warning sign of trouble years before the tanks actually rolled in.

between 1981 and 2003, kids' free time dropped by nine hours per week. And why don't we let them wander? American parents often cite "stranger danger," without seeming aware that only 115 U.S. children are abducted by strangers every year—almost a one-in-a-million occurrence, not something to base a lifestyle on. Yet 82 percent of U.S. moms cite safety concerns as a reason to bar their kids from even leaving the house. Dear Abby recently urged parents to take a picture of their kids *every morning* before they head to school, so they'll always have an up-to-the-minute photo in case of abduction. That's not just helicopter parenting. That's, like, *Airwolf* parenting.

I'm part of the problem myself—this particular paragraph is getting written only because I plopped my young daughter down in front of the TV to watch *Yo Gabba Gabba!*, whereas thirty years ago my mom probably would have told me, "Go play outside." But I worry about what my two children are missing, living in this unbrave new world where kids can't spend a summer day out building forts and climbing trees. A mom in Columbus, Mississippi, made headlines in 2009 when cops threatened her with child endangerment charges just for letting her ten-year-old son walk a third of a mile to soccer practice. If letting your kids walk alone for fifteen minutes is a criminal act, I wonder how many concurrent life sentences my parents would be serving. My siblings and I ran around pretty freely even in Seoul, kings of the city at eight or nine years old. We knew the back-alley shortcuts, the bus and subway routes, the local shops that sold the weirdest hand-lotion-tasting chewing gums and squid-based snack foods, the best places to hail cabs in a downpour. I credit my Seoul upbringing with the proud, Batman-like sense of ownership and mastery I've felt in the many cities where I've lived since then.

Today, we're starting to see the effects on society as the first generation of acutely overparented children reaches adulthood. We know that their sedentary lifestyle has led to spikes in obesity and other health problems. We know they're technology addicts, spending every free waking hour—nine hours a day, on average!—staring at little glowing screens. We know that they're not exactly models of self-sufficiency—in fact, employers like Merrill Lynch and Ernst & Young now provide job information packets and seminars for their adult recruits' parents, who are increasingly involved in hiring negotiations.

But this generation's collective geo-awareness is in just as much jeopardy as its emotional independence or its body mass index. Today's stuck-inside kids feel little connection to nature and landscape. In 2002, one study found that eight-year-old kids could identify more varieties of Pokémon than real native species in their area. Meanwhile, most measures of outdoor activity—camping, fishing, hiking, visits to national parks and forests—are steadily declining by about 1 percent a year. The boomers are still going outside, say park rangers and pollsters, but not their kids and grandkids. Never having been given free rein to explore an area and then find their way home, these kids' responses to real-world navigation range somewhere between discomfort and abject terror. A *Harvard Magazine* article on the 2009 freshman class related the story of a new student who ventured into Boston by subway but panicked at a downtown intersection. Not sure whether to turn left or right, she called—who else?—her father in Chicago, who supplied the answer.

And they'll pass their geographical ineptness on to their children. A recent study at England's Hertfordshire University found that British moms now refuse to let their children explore the countryside because they themselves feel so clueless about geography. "None of the mothers I spoke to could read a map," said the study's author. "They did not know how to make up circular walks or work out where it might be safe to go cycling." If, as Peirce Lewis claimed, a love of place is what turns young people on to geography, then the discipline is in trouble. We're becoming a society not of topophiles but of topophobes.

But maybe the discipline of geography would be in trouble anyway. For centuries, it was considered one of the pillars of a good liberal education, as illustrated by the philosopher Edmund Burke's famous observation, "Geography is an earthly subject, but a heavenly science." No poetry or history "can be read with profit . . . without the helpe and knowledge of this most Noble Science," Wye Saltonstall enthused in the preface to his 1653 English translation of Mercator's atlas. But today, only one of *U.S. News & World Report*'s ten top-ranked U.S. colleges even has a geography department. (There's still an eight-person "committee" at the University of Chicago.) This trend dates back to 1948, when Harvard president James Conant proclaimed, "Geography is not a university subject!" and abolished his department. Most other campuses followed in short order.

The decline of geography in academia is easy to understand: we live in an age of ever-increasing specialization, and geography is a generalist's discipline. Imagine the poor geographer trying to explain to someone at a campus cocktail party (or even to an unsympathetic administrator) exactly what it is he or she studies.

"'Geography' is Greek for 'writing about the Earth.' We study the Earth."

"Right, like geologists."

"Well, yes, but we're interested in the whole world, not just the rocky bits. Geographers also study oceans, lakes, the water cycle . . ."

"So it's like oceanography or hydrology."

"And the atmosphere."

"Meteorology, climatology . . ."

"It's broader than just physical geography. We're also interested in how humans relate to their planet."

"How is that different from ecology or environmental science?"

"Well, it encompasses them. Aspects of them. But we also study the social and economic and cultural and geopolitical sides of—"

"Sociology, economics, cultural studies, poli sci."

"Some geographers specialize in different world regions."

"Ah, right, we have Asian and African and Latin American studies programs here. But I didn't know they were part of the geography department."

"They're not."

(Long pause.)

"So, uh, what is it you *do* study, then?"

And . . . scene.

It's misleading to think of geography as a single discipline at all. Instead it's the ultimate interdisciplinary study, because it's made up of *every other discipline* viewed spatially, through the lens of place. Language, history, biology, public health, paleontology, urban planning—there are geographers studying all these subjects and aspects of geography taught in all of them. In one sense, geography's ubiquity is an argument for its importance, but it's also the very thing that makes it so hard to define to administrators and so easy for universities to defund and divvy up into other departments.

In fact, the little one-act play above is probably too optimistic. The real cocktail party conversation would probably go something like this:

"Actually, I have a degree in geography."

"Geography? Wow, I'm terrible with maps. I bet *you* know all your state capitals, though!"

(Geographer's smile freezes, left eye starts to twitch uncontrollably.)

Maps, see, are a huge part of geography's ongoing identity crisis today. As late as the end of the eighteenth century, geography and cartography were synonymous—interchangeable words for the same science. The world was still being charted and explored, and geographers were the ones drawing the maps. But then geography began to grow into a holistic scholarly discipline, and a funny thing happened on the way to the symposium: it lost maps as its center.

This happened for many reasons. Most obviously, the world got pretty thoroughly mapped; making maps wasn't at the brave frontier of anything anymore. As a result, geographers began to see cartographers as mere technicians, not scientists or scholars. Second, once digital tools like geographic information systems, or GIS, began to be used to manage spatial data, focusing on maps felt old-fashioned. Finally, there's been an academic trend toward emphasizing the unreliability of maps: their cultural baggage, their selectivity, the agendas that drive them. "All maps distort reality" is the moral of Mark Monmonier's 1991 classic *How to Lie with Maps*. They're artifacts to be deconstructed, like literary texts. It's not fashionable to see them as the authoritative bedrock of a science anymore.

Without maps, we lose our way, and some people have argued that in its new, less cartographic incarnation, academic geography has done exactly that. "Here's the leading journal of American academic geography," says David Helgren, tossing me the latest issue of *Annals of the Association of American Geographers,* which is sitting on his dining room table, "and it is boring. It is terrible. You can look at those titles, and they just put you to sleep."

I flip through it. I consider myself a reasonably literate guy and a geography buff to boot. But I can't really muster up too much enthusiasm for "Cognitively Inspired and Perceptually Salient Graphic Displays for Efficient Spatial Inference Making" or "A Top-Down Approach to the State Factor Paradigm for Use in Macroscale Soil Analysis." Or even "Spaces of Priority: The Geography of Soviet Housing Construction in Daugavpils, Latvia." So many choices—where to begin?

"See? You can't even read it. They invent new words along the way. But that's the paragon of world academic geography. I'm proud to say I've published in it twice, which makes me somewhat of a star. But I was never a good member of the culture. Instead of the *Annals,* I refer to it as the 'anals.' I always had a bad attitude toward some of this stuff, because it wasn't making the world better. It wasn't even making the world more interesting."

Lay readers tend to be befuddled by academic writing in many subjects, of course, but geography has an additional image problem: people seek it out expecting to find out about maps. When parents tell you their child is into geography, what they mean is "she really likes looking at maps," not "she's oddly curious about housing construction in Soviet-era Latvia." When a news anchor reports that American children are failing geography, all that means is that they couldn't match place-names to locations on a map. David Helgren's account of his own media circus in the July 1983 *Journal of Geography* is careful never to call his quiz a geography quiz: it's a "place-name quiz." He never uses the phrase "geographical illiteracy," preferring "place-name ignorance."

This was of course intentional; geographers don't like to see their field of study reduced to a list of facts that children can master. "If I told you I was a professor of literature, you wouldn't ask me if I knew how to spell," says Doug Oetter, a geography professor at Georgia College & State University. "But people find out I teach geography, and they ask, 'What's the capital of Texas?'"

It's an understandable concern, and one motivated by, frankly, a century of pretty crappy geography instruction. For many years, when schoolkids were made to study geography, they were just memorizing long lists of names: all fifty states in alphabetical order, the world's tallest mountains. "You think you are teaching him what the world is like; he is only learning the map," wrote the French philosopher Jean-Jacques Rousseau in his novel *Émile*. "He is taught the names of towns, countries, rivers, which have no existence for him except on the paper before him. I remember seeing a geography somewhere which began with: 'What is the world?'—'A sphere of cardboard.' That is the child's geography." Who wouldn't want to rebel against that, to insist that geography should be something more? Even as recently as 2002, Rick Bein's Indiana study showed that students were actually better at identifying place-names than they were at basic map skills. In linguistic terms, we're still teaching them the words but not the grammar and then being surprised that they can't speak the language.

But I wonder if geographers haven't brought some of their marginalization on themselves by shunning maps—the only thing that laypeople know about their discipline—so thoroughly. You'd never be able to attract respect (or students or funding) to a college literature program if the prevailing attitude there to books was "Oh, those old things? We never look at *them* anymore." Peirce Lewis warned in 1985 that geographers were pooh-poohing the public's love for maps and landscapes at their own peril: "I know of no other science worth the name that denigrates its basic data by calling them 'mere description,'" he said. Many academic geographers entered the field because of a childhood love of maps; now they should embrace them again, as a gateway drug if nothing else. Once a student is looking at a map, you can dive into how geography *explains* the map: why this city is on this river, why this canyon is deeper than that one, why the language spoken here is related to the one spoken there—even, perhaps, why this nation is rich and that one is poor.

Media coverage of geographic illiteracy tends to take it as a self-evident article of faith that schoolchildren not being able to find Canada is a biblical sign of the Apocalypse. Amid all the hand-wringing, one question is never asked: could the Miami pool hunk be right? Does it really matter if someone who will probably never go to Siberia can't find it on a map? After all, if you really need to know, you can always just look it up, right?

Well, one problem with that is the obvious one: people *can* look it up, but that doesn't mean they will. We live in an increasingly inter-linked world where developments an ocean away affect our daily lives in countless ways. A collapsing Greek economy might affect my 401(k) and delay my retirement. A Taliban cell in Pakistan might affect my personal safety as I walk through Times Square. A volcano in Iceland might affect my plan to fly to Paris during spring break. These aren't hand-waving hypotheticals used in chaos theory classes, like that damn butterfly in China that's always flapping one wing and thereby causing a Gulf Coast hurricane. They are concrete and direct. On any given day, we might hear about a dozen of these events, each tied to a place-name. If I know where those places are, I can synthesize and remember the events that I hear about taking place there. But without an understanding of where those places are, they become just names that wash over me: Iraq is someplace Out There. Afghanistan is too. Are they close to each other? Far away? Who knows?

In the past, people would have known. During the brief Crimean War, the British public had an insatiable appetite for maps of that region, buying them up "until every hamlet and foot-road in that half-desert and very unimportant corner of the world became as well-known to us as if it had been an English county," remembered one writer in 1863. The American Civil War also sold countless maps in both north and south, and during FDR's "fireside chats," he often instructed his listeners to follow along with him at home on their world maps, as he described events in both theaters of World War II. Not so with today's far-off wars. Most of us *could* look at a map, but we probably won't. Instead, we'll just make decisions that are less and less informed—at the ballot box, sure, but in other ways too: investment decisions, consumer decisions, travel decisions. Some of us will take jobs in public policy or be elected to national office, and lives will start to hinge on the decisions we make. In his book *Why Geography Matters,* the geographer Harm de Blij argues that the West's three great challenges of our time—Islamist terrorism, global warming, and the rise of China—are all problems of geography. An informed citizenry has to understand place, not because place is more important than other kinds of knowledge but because it forms the foundation for so much other knowledge.

Second, Mr. Pool Hunk's analysis overlooks the fact that map savvy isn't just an abstract academic arena—it's also a critical survival skill in daily life. If schoolchildren can't find Europe on a map, it's probably because they're not looking at maps much at all, and that's going to make adulthood pretty hard on them. In 2008, a survey designed by Nokia to hype some new map offerings found that 93 percent of adults worldwide get lost regularly, losing an average of thirteen minutes of their day each time. More than one in ten have missed some crucial event—a job interview, a business meeting, a flight—because they got lost. Sometimes the results are even more dire: do a search in any news archive for a phrase like "misread a map," and you'll be introduced to hikers getting lost in snowy wilderness, military commanders calling down air strikes on the wrong coordinates, city work crews accidentally cutting down the town Christmas tree, and those poor kids from *The Blair Witch Project*. Private First Class Jessica Lynch, the American soldier rescued from Iraq to much fanfare in 2003, had been captured in the first place only because the exhausted officer commanding her truck convoy had made a map error and wound up on the wrong highway.

Finally, there's a growing body of research that shows that these map woes are just a symptom of a larger problem. In 1966, the British geographers William Balchin and Alice Coleman coined the word "graphicacy" to refer to the human capability to understand charts and diagrams and symbols—the visual equivalent of literacy and numeracy. Perhaps "graphicacy" doesn't exactly trip off the tongue (and its opposite, "ingraphicacy," is even uglier), but there's a convincing case to be made that we struggle with subway maps for the same reason that we have a hard time with PowerPoint graphs and Ikea assembly instructions: no one ever spent much time teaching us to read them. "High schools shortchange spatial thinking," says Lynn Liben, a Penn State psychology professor who advised *Sesame Street* on its geography curriculum, among many other accomplishments. "We focus on language and mathematics, and we ought to be equally focused on spatial thinking and representation." Teaching maps helps kids sharpen all these visual skills, which are increasingly important today: the rise of computers means that we use spatial interfaces and visualization tools for many complicated tasks that would have been text-based just a decade or two ago.

Maybe that's why old-school geography failed: it was just lists of names and places. It was better than nothing, we found when we lost it, but it wasn't what kids really needed. If I grew up a maphead just because of some innate knack for spatial thinking, maybe that's the magic bullet for our map-impaired society. Imagine the rallying cry: "Spatial ed now!" Or maybe "We are all spatial-needs children!" There are plenty of ways to teach maps without making them into a litany of "mere description," as Peirce Lewis put it. In 1959, the cognitive psychologist Jerome Bruner complained, as Rousseau had, that geography was too often taught passively, without any thought or exploration on the students' part. He hit upon the idea of dividing a group of children into two classes. One would learn an entirely descriptive geography: "that there were arbitrary cities at arbitrary places by arbitrary bodies of water and arbitrary sources of supply." The other class was, like David Helgren's, given a *blank* map. They were asked to predict where roads, railroads, and cities might be placed and were forbidden to consult books and maps. A surprisingly lively, heated discussion on transportation theory emerged, and an hour later, Bruner finally acceded to their pleas to check their guesses on a map of the Midwest. "I will never forget one young student," wrote Bruner, "as he pointed his finger at the foot of Lake Michigan, shouting, 'Yippee, *Chicago* is at the end of the pointing-down lake!'" Some students celebrated their correct prediction of St. Louis; others mourned that Michigan was missing the large city at the Straits of Mackinac that they themselves would have founded.

Bruner had succeeded in taking the thing we take most for granted—the map of our home—and making it new, making it into an adventure. You can do the same thing just by turning a map upside down, as the writer Robert Harbison observed when he inverted a map of Great Britain. "Its meanings have shifted and the whole as an integer easily graspable has disappeared," he wrote. "Now features have explanations, so the portentous interruptions in the coast of Britain are caused by rivers, self-justifying and uncaused no longer." In a map shop recently, I came across an Australian-made wall map that inverts the entire world, so that Australia sits proudly atop the other, lesser continents, while the Northern Hemisphere superpowers sink away into the abyss below it.* Southern Hemisphere residents will no doubt be happy to hear that I felt a moment of gripping existential nausea as I considered this Aussie-centric view of our planet, no doubt ruled by Yahoo Serious from his cavernous throne room within the

---

* And why not? There's no magical reason for our hemisphere to be at the top, beyond our insidious "north-ism." Medieval maps were usually aligned so that east was "up," which is why we use the same word, "orient," to mean both "the east" and "to spatially align." NASA's famous "Big Blue Marble" photo of the Earth from space had south on top when it was taken, so the agency flipped it for publication.

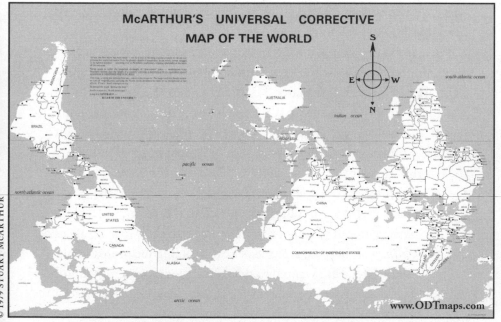

The first south-up world map, published by Stuart McArthur in 1979.
Hey, Australia: if south is so great, where's Antarctica?

Sydney Opera House. But it was thrilling as well to see familiar annotations like "Japan" and "Mediterranean Sea" printed over strange new contours, as if the whole planet had been redecorated overnight. At its best, this is what geography education can do: give maps back their sense of wonder and discovery.

In 1984, David Helgren found himself out of a job, but he was also surprised to find himself being consulted as an expert in geographic education, thanks to his brief splash of media fame. "It was an area where I never would have gone," he tells me as we polish off some tacos at a little family-run Mexican place near his home. He started doing in-service training for teachers and then founded a center for geographic education at San Jose State, where he taught for the next two decades. "I wrote some textbooks, and it turned out I was good at it. That's a world where academic geographers are not supposed to go, because it's financially successful. Academic geographers are supposed to be poor, and most of them are. But I wound up with a nice royalty check for thirty years." Three years ago, his textbook royalties allowed him to retire early from teaching.

Helgren's fame may not have lasted much more than the Warhol-allotted fifteen minutes, but "geographic illiteracy" is still in the spotlight almost three decades later. He didn't create the meme, but he was the one who moved it from the back pages of educational journals to the front pages of the nation's newspapers, and from there it became a movement. Other schools and pollsters began conducting their own regular place-name surveys. *Good Morning America* hired Helgren's former Miami colleague Harm de Blij as its on-air "geography editor." A 1985 computer game called *Where in the World Is Carmen Sandiego?*, full of geography facts and bundled with a copy of *The World Almanac*, became America's best-selling educational game. A couple years later, PBS wanted to develop a geography program for children but didn't have the budget for a full-fledged geoversion of *Sesame Street*. So the network adapted Carmen into a successful game show, which taught kids geography basics for the next five years.

Helgren also worked with the National Geographic Society, which at the time was facing a bit of an identity crisis: professional geographers tended to sneer at the magazine for being insufficiently academic, and the publication's core competency—delivering colorful photos of exotic locales to curious lay readers—didn't seem quite as fresh in 1984 as it had in 1924. (As a means of delivering pictures of topless women to curious young boys, it was still unparalleled, but that market was probably shrinking too, thank you very much, *Sports Illustrated* Swimsuit Issue.) The Helgren news cycle galvanized the society into taking on the new mission of geographic education—lobbying Washington, developing new curricula, and providing schools with millions of free maps. As of 2008, National Geographic's Education Foundation had spent more than $100 million to return geography to the nation's schools. At the time of its founding, only five states required the teaching of geography; today, all fifty states have geoliteracy standards. But still, more than half of the young adults in National Geographic's last poll say they've never taken a single geography course. We're not there yet, but—thanks in large part to David Helgren's accidental celebrity—some of the smartest people in the nation are working on the problem.

Being a geography buff, or even a one-eyed geography buff in a nation of the blind, isn't easy. I was mystified as a child to read about adults—college-educated adults!—who couldn't point out the United States on a world map. I was accustomed to the fact that not all of my odd little obsessions were shared by the general public, but geography was the only case where I had to read headline after headline about America's mass dismissal of what I held so dear. But we try not to take it personally, we mapheads. Maybe it makes some of us a little smug, to be so obviously superior to the unwashed masses who couldn't tell Equatorial Guinea from Papua New Guinea if their lives depended on it. But in my experience, most of us just want to be helpful: we like to give directions to confused tourists, and tell our Trivial Pursuit teammates that the Caspian Sea is the world's largest lake, and explain where Bangladesh is every time CNN says it's flooding again. We're not as important a public utility as we were in the days before Google and GPS, but we're not going to change now. Deep down, we naively believe that *everyone* could fall in love with maps the way we did. They just haven't given them a chance yet.

Chapter 4

BENCHMARKS

['bench-ˌmärks] *n.*: brass disks set in concrete to indicate elevation,
used as a reference for topographical surveying

*This information is what we need, you know. This shows history
and how people fit the places they occupy. It's about what gets erased
and what comes to replace it. These maps reveal the foundations
behind the ephemera.*

—BARRY LOPEZ

To enter the Geography and Map Division of the Library of Congress, you need to mess with Texas: set in the tile floor of the entryway is a circular detail from a geologic map of the Lone Star State. That's not an accident, according to map division chief John Hébert, a proud Louisiana native. "If anyone wants to, I encourage them to"—here his mild Cajun accent breaks off, and he makes a show of stamping his feet on the map, using the Texas Hill Country to dust off his shoes. Apart from the Texas-bashing twinkle in his eye, Hébert is a serious-looking sixtysomething man with round bifocals and a shock of wavy white hair above his oft-knitted brow. His eyebrows, though, still have a little pepper mixed in with the salt. We cross the patrons' reading room and pass through a secure set of doors at the other end. "You're in my world now," he says.

Hébert's world, located in the basement of the library's James Madison Building, is a row of metal map cases so long it momentarily takes my breath away. I always feel a certain sense of reverence in libraries, even small city ones that smell like homeless Internet users. Being so close to so much laboriously gathered information gives me a strange satisfaction with the scope of human ingenuity, the way other people might feel visiting Hoover Dam or the Great Wall of China. But this library is different from any I've ever seen, a seemingly endless expanse straight out of a Borges story. I can follow the fluorescent-lit lines of shelves almost to a single vanishing point in each direction. There are 8,500 of these cases, with five drawers per case, two entire football fields just for maps. And they're heavy, which is why we're two stories underground. "We have to be on this floor," explains Hébert, "because if we were on the sixth floor, we'd be down here pretty soon anyway." It's the largest map collection ever assembled in human history.

Maps have been Hébert's passkey to a larger world ever since he was a boy growing up in the bayou country. He and his older brother stretched a ham radio antenna out the bedroom window in their Houma, Louisiana, home and attached it to a tree in the vacant lot next door, and he spent hours tapping away at the transmitter in Morse code. "I'd always have an atlas on my lap," he remembers. "Because all of the sudden I'd be talking to Tamaqua, Pennsylvania, and where the hell is Tamaqua, Pennsylvania? Where is it?" As he tells the story, his finger traces a highway on an imaginary road atlas. But when he arrived at Georgetown to work on his master's degree in 1965, there was no geography department—those had been unfashionable for more than a decade. He studied Latin American history instead and was already working for the Library of Congress by the time he received his doctorate in 1972. He's been here ever since.

Most of Hébert's staff of forty-five librarians aren't professional geographers—they came to love maps by seeing the power of cartography in their own fields, whether that was art history or public affairs. Hébert was no different. "Maps drew out points of history that the text wouldn't tell me," he says.

Indeed, history seems to be all around us as we begin to trek through the geographically arranged stacks: first world maps, then (from north to south): Canada; the United States in the order of its appearance, from the Atlantic to the Pacific; Latin America; then across the Atlantic to Europe and Asia; and then Africa and Oceania at the far end of this cavernous space. It's the world in miniature, and Hébert displays a missionary zeal in showing off his beloved collection not as some dry scholarly archive but as a vast treasure trove of Americana, from the earliest days of Spanish exploration to the present. There are maps of the Brazilian rain forest drawn by Theodore Roosevelt himself, during his nearly fatal expedition down the "River of Doubt" in 1913. There's Welthauptstadt ("World Capital") Germania, Albert Speer's plan for a monumentally redesigned Berlin, recovered by American troops when Nazi Germany fell. There are the original maps that divided Europe at the end of World War I, brought back from Versailles by the American Geographical Society team that accompanied Woodrow Wilson there. "We have the original military maps from the Battle of Chapultepec and charts from the Barbary Coast War," boasts Hébert, "so I can honestly say we have the halls of Montezuma *and* the shores of Tripoli." If there's a History Channel special on it, it's in here.

Just about every luminary in history, it seems, makes a Mylar-covered cameo appearance in the Map Division's shelves. As he shows me around, Hébert is dropping so many famous names that he starts prefacing them with the faux-humble-sounding disclaimer "a man called"—"a man called Stonewall Jackson," "a man called Ferdinand Magellan." At one shelf, he points offhandedly to a high drawer. "I have Lewis and Clark in there," he says, alarmingly. Seemingly at random, he opens another drawer and shows me a colonial map of Alexandria, Virginia, before the town was even built. It's an unremarkable survey listing the names of local landowners, and I'm not quite sure why I'm looking at it. People sure did have nicer handwriting back then, I guess. Then I see on an indexing sticker the mapmaker's name: a young Virginia surveyor who later went on to other things. George Washington. I feel a little twinge of vertigo—not just that I'm holding *in my hands* a map personally drawn by The Father of His Country, Mr. First President, Ol' Ivory Teeth himself, but also that this priceless artifact is sitting seemingly unnoticed in a nondescript drawer ("Virginia 3884.A"), lost among dozens of similar maps.

The number of mind-blowing items like this one in the library's collection is powerful testimony to the omnipresent *Zelig*-like role that maps have played, always just behind the scenes, in the history of the world. I already described how Columbus's fateful voyage was inspired by his study of a map by Paolo Toscanelli. But there was also the 1854 cholera outbreak in London, which killed hundreds of people until a physician, John Snow, drew a map demonstrating that a single contaminated water pump was the source of the illness, thereby founding the science of epidemiology. There was the 1944 invasion at Normandy, which succeeded only because of the unheralded contribution of mapmakers who had stolen across the English Channel by night for months before D-Day and mapped the French beaches.* Even the moon landing was a product of mapping. In 1961, the United States Geological Survey founded a Branch of Astrogeology, which spent a decade painstakingly assembling moon maps to plan the Apollo missions. The *Apollo 11* crew pored over pouches of those maps as their capsule approached the lunar surface, much as Columbus did during his voyage. It seems that the greatest achievements in human history have all been made possible by the science of cartography.

The Library of Congress has had maps in its collection since its founding under President John Adams; in fact, the library's very first shipment of books, purchased in London in 1801, included three maps and an atlas. There were one hundred maps in the library, then located in the U.S. Capitol, when the original collection was burned during the War of 1812. Today the collection holds more than five and a half million maps and more than eighty thousand atlases, and Hébert, though choosy about acquisitions—"we don't buy crap," he assures me—is still adding between sixty and eighty thousand new maps every year.

They come from everywhere. The library has offices in Cairo, Islamabad, Jakarta, Nairobi, New Delhi, and Rio scouring the world for maps. "We don't know what's going to come through our door,"

---

* In 1942, the BBC asked its listeners to send in prewar postcards and holiday snaps from the beaches of Europe. Seven million poured in, showing coastlines from Norway to the Pyrenees, and they were used to select Normandy as the site of the initial landing.

says Hébert. "We have languages you've never seen before." Every map submitted for copyright in the United States automatically joins the collection. And by law, every time a U.S. government agency prints a map, it must deposit a copy with the Library of Congress—and these maps are generally free of copyright, since your taxes financed them, making them a remarkable publicly held resource. The best-known government maps are probably the United States Geological Survey's "quadrangle" topographic maps, whose pale green forests and bubbly brown contour lines are permanently etched into the subconscious minds of generations of hikers. The USGS began this series after World War II—in an echo of their military origins, the green woodland areas on the maps are still officially defined as "cover for small detachments of troops"—but it wasn't completed until 1992. Today these maps depict every creek, every ridge, and every grove of trees in the fifty states in remarkable 1:24,000 detail, each mile of territory measuring almost three full inches on the map. If you were to lay out the whole country in quadrangle map form—even the blank blue maps representing the middle of Utah's Great Salt Lake, which probably aren't ordered much—it would stretch 783 feet by 383 feet, the area of three city blocks.

But the USGS is far from the only federal agency that makes maps. In 2000, the Library of Congress was contacted by the National Geospatial-Intelligence Agency, which sounds like a made-up group from *24* or *Alias* but is actually the mapping arm of the Department of Defense. The NGA had 360,000 map sheets sitting in a vault in Arizona that it wanted to get rid of, so Hébert sent a staffer down to take a look. It turned out to be a gold mine: 40 percent of the maps were new, so they were brought back to the library for filing. Among the stuff the NGA had relegated to its yard sale: 1:50,000 coverage of Afghanistan (that's amazing detail, a little over an inch to a mile) that no one thought they'd need anymore. But after September 11, 2001, says Hébert, it didn't take long before the Defense Department was knocking at his door, wondering if maybe the Library of Congress didn't have any good tactical maps of Afghanistan, please . . . ? America's heroic map librarians saved the country's bacon yet again.

The Geography and Map Division serves a broad range of patrons.

Some requests are vitally important to national security, as in the case of the Afghanistan maps. Hébert says the State Department has lately been checking out lots of ethnological maps of Iraq over time—where have the Sunnis and Shiites historically lived? What about the Kurds? (Sigh. Better late than never, I guess.) Other governmental requests are a lot less urgent: the most common request from members of Congress is for a classy, sepia-toned historical map of their district that they can hang in their office. Or they might want area maps to help them understand some issue in their home state: natural resources on an Indian reservation, for example, or sex offenders living near elementary schools. If all politics is local, so is all geography—to someone, anyway.

You need to be a high-ranking official to be able to check stuff out from the Geography and Map Division or any other part of the nation's library. But even if you don't plan on running for Congress or getting appointed to the Supreme Court anytime soon, you can still get a library card there. Anybody can. It's called a Reader ID and it's free, and cardholders can look at maps in the reading room to their hearts' content. Most of the patrons here today, quietly turning atlas pages, are private researchers of one kind or another. When the division began scanning its maps and putting them on the Internet in 1995, they started with what the history buffs wanted: the Civil War, then the railroads, then the American Revolution, then World War II. More than twenty thousand maps and charts are now viewable online. My favorites are the panoramic maps, beautiful bird's-eye lithographs of American cities and towns that were fashionable at the turn of the last century. A print of Augustus Koch's 1891 panoramic view of Seattle, reproduced from the Library of Congress's copy, hangs above my piano at home.

But Hébert's most frequent request isn't so scholarly. "Most of the time we're getting people who think treasure maps exist," he says with a rueful smile.

Boy's-own-adventure pirate maps, with carefully counted paces from the gnarled tree to the big X on the sandy island shore, were a big part of my childhood love affair with maps. "*Are* treasure maps real?" I ask eagerly.

Hébert has evidently had some experience answering this question without popping the bubbles of wide-eyed kids and gullible get-rich-quickers. "I'd say it's very hard to say that they are," he hedges.

Translation: no, there's not a single documented case of a pirate drawing a map to buried treasure. This was a trope invented by the likes of Edgar Allan Poe and Robert Louis Stevenson, not Captain Kidd and Blackbeard. I make a mental note not to mention this at my son's upcoming birthday party, for which a buccaneer theme is planned. I'm still reeling from my geographic faux pas of a few months back—when I told my kids that there's no land at the North Pole the way there is in the Antarctic, just water and sea ice, it led to some uncomfortable Santa-related follow-up questions. Sometimes careful cartography is good for the imagination, but other times you'd rather have the mystery.

The Map Division's visitors come from all over the world. Recently, scholars flew in from Beijing to look at nineteenth-century plans of the Chinese capital, because Washington had better maps than anything they could find in China. In 2001, a Japanese research group stopped by the library to see what they could find on Ino Tadataka, the legendary shogun-era surveyor whose team produced the first modern map of Japan in 1821. That map was later lost in a fire, and modern scholars had been able to locate only 46 of his map's 214 tatami-mat-sized pages in Tokyo's Diet Museum. They were shocked to find that 207 pages—nearly a complete set—had been gathering dust in the Geography and Map Division for decades and soon secured a quarter of a million dollars from the Japanese government to scan and restore them. The final map was finally exhibited in a Nagoya baseball stadium, laid out neatly along the right-field line. Thirty-five thousand people filed by to look. "This collection is full of gems like that, just waiting to be discovered," says Hébert. In fact, there's no catalog at all for the vast majority of the pre-1970 material here; there's just too much of it. Millions of maps will sit unseen until someone looks for them.

Sometimes the foreign visitors are officials looking to settle—or start—a border dispute. It might be a South Korean delegation hoping to discredit Japanese claims to some tiny islets in the Sea of Japan or a group of Congolese and Ugandan bureaucrats wondering where exactly in Lake Victoria their nations meet. "They had gone to Brussels, they'd been to London, couldn't find the official maps. We had 'em," says Hébert proudly. In the late 1970s, Chile and Argentina were locked in a dispute over who controlled the eastern end of the Beagle Channel, a narrow strait running between the islands of Tierra del Fuego. This wasn't just an obscure issue of national pride for Chile, which would lose its only access to the Atlantic Ocean if Argentina's version of the border was drawn. The ruling junta in Argentina at the time seemed ready to go to war over the boundary, refusing to accept an International Court of Justice ruling for Chile and even preparing a military invasion of the contested islands for December 1978. At the eleventh hour came a diplomatic development straight out of the sixteenth century: the Vatican intervened, and both nations agreed to let the pope draw the boundary line. During the height of the conflict, Argentine and Chilean delegations spent months sitting at tables at opposite sides of the Geography and Map Division reading room like warring cliques in a high school cafeteria. They would request the same maps of Tierra del Fuego in turn and study them carefully, never acknowledging the enemy across the room. "We're neutral ground," claims John Hébert, but it might be more accurate to say that, for a few months, the border between Chile and Argentina ran north, right through the basement of 101 Independence Avenue in Washington, D.C.

Boundary lines can arouse stronger feelings than perhaps any other feature on a map. Marking property was the purpose of many of the earliest surviving maps, and boundary markers—piles of rocks, for example, the human equivalent of a dog peeing on a tree—probably go back millennia earlier. In medieval Europe, the surveyor was a hated figure, something like the "revenuer" in mountain moonshiner lore: a corrupt lackey always looking to stick it to poor farmers. His new map might take away part of your field, or it might raise your rent or your taxes. In Poland, surveyors were so dreaded that even death couldn't end their menace. The flickering lights of swamp gas—what we call will-o'-the-wisps—were said to be the ghosts of dead mapmakers wandering the marsh by night. Better finish your cabbage, kids, or the *surveyor* will come and get you!

A nice thick border and a carefully chosen color scheme can serve to unify a nation, as on those Victorian maps in which every far-flung corner of the British Empire was always the same uniform pink, to impress on generations of schoolchildren the constancy and reach of the Crown—the "pink bits," students called the empire.* Map boundaries also define, with a simple stroke of the pen, who *isn't* on our side: an enemy to guard against or even territory we might take back someday. These aren't just lofty scholarly concerns. Google fields so many complaints about the national borders on its maps that it's started delivering localized versions to different users: an Indian user might see a border in one place while a Pakistani user sees it somewhere else, and everyone stays contented in their own little cocoons of geographic superiority. In 2006, when the Israeli education minister, Yuli Tamir, announced that textbook maps of Israel would put a border around the West Bank, rather than depicting it as undemarcated Israeli territory, hard-line rabbis announced that God would strike her down for her blasphemy. You can't explain this all away as mere political posturing; it's genuine offense. The clarity and simplicity of the lines on a map make them powerful symbols.

Borders have fascinated me since childhood: I remember staying very alert on family vacations so I could register the *exact moment* our 1979 Mercury Zephyr crossed the line between, say, Washington and Oregon. To this day, I like to see borders when I travel; many give up secrets in person that you can't see on the map. You know that seemingly straight line of Manitoba's western border, the one that makes Saskatchewan such an eye-catching trapezoid on a globe? It's actually a pixelated zigzag, running maybe twenty miles north at a time before taking an abrupt one-mile "stair step" to the west. The Belgian town of Baarle-Hertog is even more intriguing: it's made up of no fewer than twenty-six separate pieces of Belgium sitting, thanks to a complicated series of medieval treaties between two warring dukes, in the middle

---

* British mapmakers used every trick in the book to make the empire look its biggest and best. A carefully chosen cylindrical projection would make Canada balloon to many times its actual size, for example, and some maps even spanned the globe through 420 degrees, so that Australia and New Zealand would appear twice, once on each edge of the map.

of the Netherlands. Some of these little bits of Belgium have little bits of the Netherlands inside *them*, leading to an impossibly intricate border that divides some village homes in half between the two nations. Your nationality depends on where your front door is, and residents have been known to "emigrate" by moving their door every time the tax laws change. When bars and restaurants in the Netherlands close, landlords just move their tables onto the Belgian side of their establishment and keep on serving.

In search of the most exotic border crossing of all, I insisted to my wife that our trip to Thailand last year should include a side trip to the Angkor temples of Cambodia—by bus. Why? Because I'd always wanted to find out what happens when you cross between a drives-on-the-left country (like Thailand) into a drives-on-the-right one (Cambodia). Would there be an overpass? A roundabout? An endless stream of hilarious traffic accidents? We were disappointed to learn that the border between Aranyaprathet, Thailand, and Poi Pet, Cambodia, is a traffic-free no-man's-land with only the occasional semi pulling through after it clears customs. Maybe most people wouldn't go to the length of a four-hour bus trip through the Thai jungle, but I know I'm not the only one who gets this liminal thrill from standing on borders. Four Corners Monument, where Utah, Colorado, Arizona, and New Mexico meet, is in the middle of nowhere. But two hundred thousand visitors make the trek each year to straddle a small round plaque and enjoy whatever the strange rush is that comes from being in four states at once.*

Borders may start out as arbitrary, but they don't stay that way for long. The British travel writer Mike Parker has noted that the Earth, seen from orbit, is no longer a borderless, utopian "big blue marble": where nations meet, so do their agendas and policies. From miles above the Earth, you can see the straight line where heavily forested western Russia meets the cow pastures of eastern Finland or where a stretch of

---

* Most of the tourists will never know that the location of Four Corners isn't just desolate—it's completely arbitrary. The current monument is a result of inexact nineteenth-century surveying, and sits 1,807 feet east of the actual quadripoint mandated by Congress in 1863. The "real" spot, in case you're curious, is identical bleak desert, but with fewer souvenir stands selling Navajo blankets.

Montana grassland meets irrigated strips of farm country in southwest Saskatchewan. The most dramatic example is the heavily militarized "demilitarized zone" between the two Koreas, just a half hour's drive north of Seoul, where I grew up. By day, the rift in the divided peninsula is almost invisible from space, but by night, the cities of South Korea are brightly lit, while isolated, agrarian North Korea is abruptly dark, as empty as the remotest stretches of Siberia or the Sahara. The distinct line between light and dark looks like a power outage moving across a cityscape grid by grid, except that this blackout has been going on for sixty years. By night, South Korea isn't a peninsula. It's an island.

Borders may divide us, but, paradoxically, they're also the places

South Korea's secret double life: peninsula by day, island by night

where we're nearest to one another. Borders on a map may start out as a useful way to separate Us from Them, but then they become symbols of our own complacency; by their very existence, they dare us to cross them. The breaching of a border doesn't have to be the result of an invading barbarian horde; when the Berlin Wall collapsed in 1989, it was gleefully sledge-hammered into the past by those on both sides of it. Even Chile and Argentina signed a Tratado de Paz y Amistad ("Treaty of Peace and Friendship") at the Vatican in 1984, ending the century-long Beagle Channel conflict for good. "We'll meet on edges soon," as Bob Dylan once sang.

John Hébert is also the chairman of the U.S. Board on Geographic Names, a federal body created in 1890 by President Benjamin Harrison to standardize American place-names. For more than a century, the board has worked to sort out tangles of inconsistency and confusion that can plague even some of the nation's most prominent spots. Take the Mount McKinley controversy: in 1975, the state of Alaska officially changed the name of North America's highest point to "Denali," the native Athabascan name for the peak. But the Board on Geographic Names has been repeatedly stymied in making this change official, thanks to the congressional delegation of Ohio, William McKinley's home state, which has been introducing anti-"Denali" clauses into appropriations bills for thirty years. Occasionally the board makes blanket changes, as in 1967, when 143 occurrences of America's direst racial slur were globally replaced on maps with the word "Negro." (In a similar move, "Jap" later became "Japanese.") This didn't solve every uncomfortable map issue, of course. The USGS quadrangle maps are still littered with Dago Springs and Chink Peaks and Polack Lakes, and it's not as if "Dead Negro Creek" is a huge improvement over the alternative anyway. But the board's goal is typically historical correctness, whether that aligns with political correctness or not. In 1983, for example, it returned the name "Whorehouse Meadow" to the map of Fish Lake, Oregon, after determining that the limp 1968 replacement, "Naughty Girl Meadow," was a bowdlerization concocted by embarrassed park officials. Today, says Hébert, the board's workload consists mostly of hundreds of requests to name things after Ronald Reagan. Between McKinley and Reagan, we're apparently spending a *lot* of time and paperwork on the iffy cartographic legacies of two-term Republicans.

As long as I've loved maps, I've been an enthusiastic toponymist: a student of place-names. Maps that aren't dotted with text look barren and lonely to me—what could be more soulless than one of those grade-school outline maps of a region with only a few sad oil derricks or ears of corn drawn on it to depict industry or agriculture? Those are the abominations that make kids hate geography. Names are the alchemical infusion that bring a map to life. There may be poetry in the curl of a coastline, but there's *personality* in a Humpty Doo, Australia, or Oaxaca, Mexico, or Chililabombwe, Zambia. The great Flemish cartographer Abraham Ortelius evidently agreed with me. In his 1570 atlas,* he labeled his imaginary southern continent of Terra Australis with tantalizing place-names like "Land of Parrots," "Cape of the Good Signal," and "Sweetest River." No one had ever actually *been* to these nonexistent places, but hey, it was either that or leave an entire landmass suspiciously naked.†

To this day, I feel a nostalgic warmth when I see obsolete map labels like "Tanganyika" and "Ceylon" and "British Honduras"—I've never been to these countries, of course, but their names are as direct a conduit to my childhood as the smell of a school cafeteria or the piano line from an Air Supply song. I plan my vacations around places like Llanfairpwllgwyngyllgogerychwyrndrobwllllantysiliogogogoch, Wales ("St. Mary's church in the hollow of the white hazel near to

---

* That book—*Theatrum Orbis Terrarium,* or "Theater of the World"—is now considered the first modern world atlas. If Ortelius had had his way, today's atlases would be called "theaters," but we've instead chosen to use the nomenclature of Ortelius's friend Gerardus Mercator. He dedicated his map book to Atlas—not the Titan who supported the heavens on his shoulders but another mythical character of the same name, a Phoenician philosopher-king said to have invented the first globe.

† Speaking of Ortelius and continents: the cartographer was also the first person to propose the theory of continental drift, based on the way the African and South American coasts seemed to fit together. But others have always gotten the credit, since Ortelius's 1596 note on the subject wasn't noticed until 1994!

the rapid whirlpool of Llantysilio of the red cave," as every trivia fan should know) and made sure to get my picture taken, during our trip to Thailand, next to the block-long sign at Bangkok's city hall that prints the city's full 163-letter name. Names don't have to be long to be memorable. You could spend months in Britain just visiting all the naughty little lanes and villages that seem to have been named by Benny Hill: Titty Ho, Scratchy Bottom, Wetwang, East Breast, Cockplay. In an American road atlas, the eccentric town toponyms all seem full of folksy roadside history: Cheesequake, New Jersey; Goose Pimple Junction, Virginia; Ding Dong, Texas.

Most of these places came by their names honestly. Goose Pimple Junction was once home to a warring couple whose noisy obscenities would make neighbors' skin crawl. Cheesequake is just a corruption of the Lenape Indian word "Cheseh-oh-ke," meaning "upland village." Ding Dong, Texas, was named for a local sign painting of ringing bells (it's located in Bell County). But sometimes such names seem a little too good to be true because they are. Take that fifty-eight-letter Welsh village. It was plain old "Llanfair Pwllgwyngyll" until the 1860s, when an enterprising local tailor concocted the longer name as a publicity stunt, hoping to bring in tourist revenue. (Perhaps the town needed to buy a vowel.) So Llanfairpwll is the spiritual ancestor of all those desperate American towns today that sell their souls by renaming themselves for dot-coms and celebrities. Sometimes the contest-winning names stick: the former Hot Springs, New Mexico, is still called "Truth or Consequences" more than thirty years after the game show for which it was named went off the air. The former Mauch Chunk, Pennsylvania, will probably be called "Jim Thorpe" as long as the renowned Olympian is still buried there.* But more often than not, the new name fades almost as soon as the headlines do. Half.com, Oregon, went back to being Halfway, Oregon, after only a year of sellout-hood. Joe, Montana, is just plain Ismay, Montana,

---

* Thorpe was a native of Oklahoma who had never set foot in Mauch Chunk, but in 1953, the Pennsylvania township shamelessly *bought* the athlete's remains from his widow and built a fancy memorial, hoping to stay on the map though its coal industry was dying.

again. Such gimmicky name swaps have always rubbed me the wrong way—maps are sacred! Would you sell ad space on the side of Mount Rushmore? So I applauded in 2005 when the tiny hamlet of Sharer, Kentucky, turned down the chance to earn $100,000 by changing its name to PokerShare.com. The town's Bible Belt residents, it seems, didn't cotton to none of that Internet gambling.

But name notoriety can be a two-edged sword. For every Half.com, Oregon, happily taking big checks and a new high school computer lab from a money-mad dot-com, there's a Butt Hole Road in Conisbrough, South Yorkshire. Cabbie Peter Sutton, who lives on the road, told the *Daily Mail* that the road's cheeky name was a big draw for him when he first moved there—he couldn't believe the previous owners were moving out because they didn't like the name. But the novelty soon wore off, thanks to the endless stream of prank calls, skeptical delivery drivers, and busloads of tourists posing for pictures while mooning the street sign. The street was named for a communal rain barrel (or "water butt") located on the spot long ago, but history didn't matter: in 2009, the neighbors collected the three-hundred-pound fee and the city changed the name to the much less distinctive Archers Way.*

The residents of Dildo, Newfoundland, have been more stalwart in the face of world attention. The town believes it was named for one of the Spanish ships or sailors that first explored the rocky coast. "I feel sure that we've been here longer than artificial penises have been around," says Dildo's assistant postmistress, Sheila White. Locals seem filled with Dildo pride, in fact; every summer, during Dildo Days, the traditional boat parade is led by Captain Dildo, a wooden statue of an old fishing-boat skipper. In the 1980s, a Dildo electrician named Robert Elford circulated a petition trying to change the town's name to something like "Pretty Cove" or "Seaview," but his neighbors poked fun at his crusade, and he soon gave up. But many other towns

---

* Similarly, the Filipino town of Sexmoan was a popular destination for American GIs after World War II, but they all made the same disappointing discovery: the name was just a Spanish-era corruption of the local name, "Sasmuan." In 1987, Sexmoan officially became Sasmuan again for good.

near Dildo *have* changed their names to avoid the sniggers of outsiders: Famish Gut is now Fair Haven, Cuckolds Cove is now Dunfield, Silly Cove is now Winterton, and Gayside is now Baytona. The new names in these stories are always tragedies; they sound like the made-up settings of comic strips or soap operas. Something important is lost when an authentic bit of history is replaced with a bland town-meeting consensus.

You'd think that the labels on maps would be the easiest bits to get right, but the struggles and compromises of the Board on Geographic Names belie that idea. Names aren't neutral; they come with agendas. In 1614, John Smith coined the name "New England" for the North

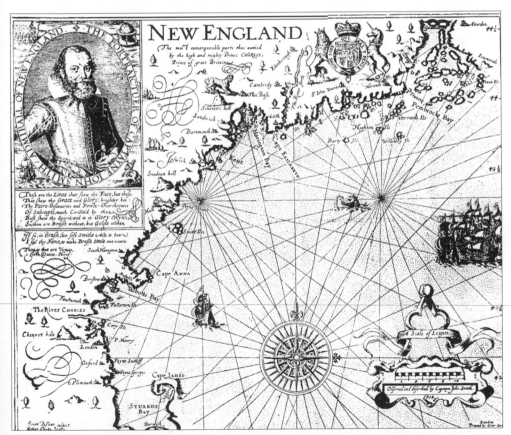

Somehow the unsettled Maine coast is full of charming little English villages. Also, as a special bonus: no Indians!

American coast he was exploring; his map of the area pointedly left off any Native American settlements or place-names. Instead, every place got a cozy—and completely arbitrary—British name: Ipswich, Southampton, Cape Elizabeth. Most of Smith's names never caught on, but one of his choices was adopted by the *Mayflower* pilgrims when they founded their colony there six years later: Plymouth, a spot that the Wampanoag Indians, then as now, actually called "Patuxet." As late as 1854, Commodore Matthew Perry steamed into Tokyo Bay and returned to Washington bearing a map of Edo, with all the parts of the harbor given suspiciously un-Japanese names like "Mississippi Bay" and "Susquehanna Bay." On the map, some islets in the Uraga Channel have even been labeled "Plymouth Rocks." "Look!" the maps say, all wide-eyed and innocent-like. "These places *must* be ours! Why else would they have our names on them?"

It's hard for Americans to understand the patriotism that can get bound up in place-names. We're a young country. We're also accustomed, in our cockeyed cowboy fashion, to everything else revolving around us, so we can afford to let slide the fact that, say, the Gulf of Mexico isn't called the Gulf of America. (Although, according to John Hébert, that is the pet issue of one frequent complainant to the Board on Geographic Names.) If America Ferrera announced tomorrow that she was changing her first name to "Canada," we'd be okay with it. We'd get on with our lives. But elsewhere in the world, toponymy *is* national identity. The imported Western atlases I saw on Korean shelves as a kid always had the words "Sea of Japan" blacked out on the Asian maps and the traditional Korean name, "East Sea," hand-lettered below. Greece got so angry about the name of the newly independent Republic of Macedonia (historically, Macedonia was a region of northern Greece) that it blackballed Macedonia's entrance into NATO in 2008. The hottest rhetoric has come out of (surprise!) Iran, after the 2004 edition of the *National Geographic Atlas of the World* added to the Persian Gulf a smaller parenthetical label reading "Arabian Gulf." Iranians sensed a conspiracy and went bonkers. "Under the influence of the U.S. Zionist lobby and the oil dollars of certain Arab governments, the society has distorted an undeniable historical reality," wrote the *Tehran Times*. All National Geographic publications and journalists were banned from Iran. Resourceful Internet users from the Persian global community sent National Geographic thousands of e-mails, left hundreds of angry Amazon reviews of the atlas, and even Google-bombed the phrase "Arabian Gulf," so that the top Web result for that phrase is now a mock error page reading, "The gulf you are looking for does not exist. Try Persian Gulf." National Geographic finally issued a correction, but tensions in the Gulf are still running high over the issue: Iran created a national "Persian Gulf Day" every April to celebrate the nomenclature, canceled the 2010 Islamic Solidarity Games when Arab nations objected to the phrase "Persian Gulf" on the medals, and has even threatened to ban any airline that doesn't use the "right" name on its display boards.

The closest American equivalent to this kind of toponymic pride is the way we use place-names to confer insider or outsider status in our communities. Woe unto the Manhattan tourist who asks where "Avenue of the Americas" is (the official renaming is such a mouthful that New Yorkers still say "Sixth Avenue") or pronounces "Houston Street" like the city in Texas. In my neck of the woods, the magic names are Puyallup, the Tacoma suburb that's home to Washington's largest state fair every fall, and Sequim, a retirement mecca on the Olympic Peninsula. To pronounce these towns "poo-YAL-lup" and "SEE-kwim," the way they're spelled, is to instantly brand oneself a clueless tourist or, worse, a California transplant. (I could tell you the real pronunciations, but then, under Washington State law, I'd have to kill you.)

In Marcel Proust's *Remembrance of Things Past*, the narrator remembers that the names on maps were often more magical for him than the places themselves. "Even on a stormy day the name Florence or Venice would awaken the desire for sunshine, for lilies, for the Palace of the Doges and for Santa Maria del Fiore," he says. The names fool him into thinking that each place he visits will be "an unknown thing, different in essence from all the rest," and he's disappointed when he actually visits them. "They magnified the idea that I had formed of certain places on the surface of the globe, making them more special, and in consequence more real." A friend of mine once fulfilled a lifelong ambition to visit Mongolia, and when he got home, I was excited to hear about the trip. "It's just a horrible venture," he said, to my surprise. "The real thrill is in your head: the name of the capital city, 'Ulan Bator.'" Nothing he'd actually seen could live up to the strange promise of those nine letters. He shook his head and said it again slowly: "Ulan Bator . . ."

"Getting people to know what we have here is a crucial challenge," says Hébert, pointing out a 1950s Soviet moon globe ("The only one in this hemisphere!") sitting atop a filing cabinet next to Marie Tharp's 3-D map of the Mid-Atlantic Ridge. Inside the cabinet is a fascinating collection of maps inscribed on powder horns, including one with a map of Havana harbor dating back to the French and Indian War. "My challenge is not to get those who love maps in here. It's how to get the *other* people in here, the ones who don't even know what a map is."

Pam van Ee, one of John Hébert's map history specialists, tells me that one of the library's biggest influxes of congressional staffers comes at four every Friday afternoon, as weekend hikers wander into the collection looking for a trail map. This shocks me even more than the idea of a congressman visiting the map division only to check on public school locations in his district. Here we have the most monumental map collection in the history of the world, one that makes the library at Alexandria look like a bookmobile, and we're using it to appease PTA moms and help Capitol Hill staffers see the Blue Ridge Mountains? It seems like a waste of an almost sacred resource, like gargling with Communion wine. But I reconsider after a moment. Maybe that's the power of this collection, the fact that so many people can find exactly what they need here, no matter what their interest. It shows, above all, the versatility of maps, and how we all rely on them in different ways.

The greatest cartographic treasure in the Library of Congress actually sits a block north of John Hébert's vault, in the grand exhibition gallery of the library's opulent Thomas Jefferson Building. In 2001, the library paid a German prince a whopping $10 million (half allocated by Congress and half from private donors) for the only surviving copy of a 1507 world map by a cartographer named Martin Waldseemüller.

Why did the so-called Waldseemüller map command a price of

almost ten times what any other map had ever fetched at auction? For one thing, the map was believed lost for centuries; of an original print run of one thousand, it seemed that not a single copy had survived. Some geographers even claimed that the much-ballyhooed map had never existed. "No lost maps have been sought for so diligently as these," proclaimed the Royal Geographical Society. "The honor of being their lucky discoverer has long been considered as the highest possible prize . . . in the field of ancient cartography."

That prize was finally claimed in 1901 by Joseph Fischer. Father Fischer was a Jesuit scholar researching early Viking navigation when he happened to come across a map folio in the south tower garret of Wolfegg Castle, near the German-Swiss border. As he paged through the pristine map sheets, Fischer realized he had unearthed a lost treasure. The map depicts a Western Hemisphere divided into two continents, north and south, separated by a narrow strait and the Caribbean Sea. Westward, there's a vast ocean separating this new continent from (a rather sketchily defined version of) eastern Asia. And in the northern part of modern-day Argentina was inscribed one fateful word: "America."

These are familiar sights on a world map today, but in 1507, they weren't just unexpected—they were revolutionary. Christopher Columbus had gone to his grave the year before still convinced he had visited the East Indies on his four voyages, but here was a vast new continent stretching almost from pole to pole between Europe and Asia. Europeans wouldn't glimpse the Pacific across the Isthmus of Panama for another five years, yet there it is on the map. The western coast of South America hadn't been explored at all yet, but Waldseemüller's simple rendering is extraordinarily accurate—within seventy miles at several key points, John Hébert tells me.

Scholars will no doubt be studying the map's remarkable verisimilitude for years to come, but its chief historical claim to fame—and the reason that Congress would pony up the cool five mill to rescue it from its German tower prison—is that single "America" at the lower left. This isn't just the earliest surviving use of the term; the text that accompanied the map makes it clear that, when we peer at the map, we are witnessing the word's coining in action. "A fourth part of the

world has been discovered by Amerigo Vespucci," wrote Waldseemüller.* "Since both Asia and Africa received their names from women, I
do not see why anyone should rightly prevent this from being called
Amerigen—the land of Amerigo, as it were—or America, after its
discoverer, Americus, a man of perceptive character."

Columbus's biographer Bartolomé de Las Casas huffily insisted
that the new continent "should have been called Columba instead,"
after its *real* discoverer. But Vespucci was a different kind of proto-

---

* Or possibly his collaborator, an Alsatian schoolmaster named Matthias Ringmann.
There's good evidence that Waldseemüller drew the maps but left the writing of the
preface to his friend.

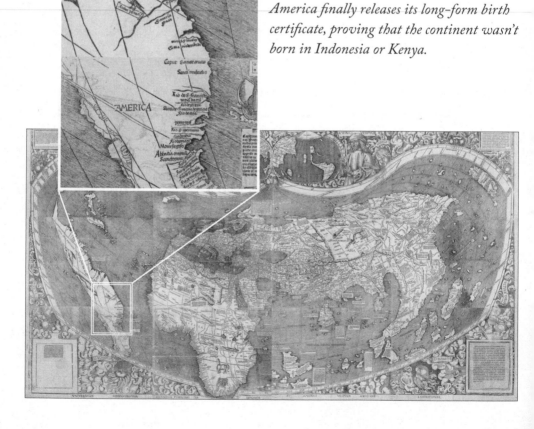

*The fateful word on the Waldseemüller map.
America finally releases its long-form birth
certificate, proving that the continent wasn't
born in Indonesia or Kenya.*

American: a showman and a shameless self-promoter. He was a Florentine merchant who probably deserved only a solid place on the exploration B-list for tagging along on a couple of Portuguese voyages to Brazil. But his (no doubt exaggerated) accounts of those travels took Europe by storm, testament to one eternal advertising dictum: that sex—even if you write about it in Latin—always sells.

Unlike Columbus's dull, G-rated journals, Vespucci's letters are obsessive and vivid on the subject of native sexuality. "They . . . are excessively libidinous," he leers, "and the women more than the men; for I refrain out of decency from telling of the art with which they gratify their immoderate lust." But—luckily for us—he doesn't refrain for long! "It was to us a matter of astonishment that none was to be seen among them who had a flabby breast, and those who had borne children were not to be distinguished from virgins by the shape and shrinking of the womb; and in the other parts of the body similar things were seen of which in the interest of modesty I make no mention. When they had the opportunity of copulating with Christians, urged by excessive lust, they defiled and prostituted themselves." Check it out, Europe: Caribbean women are all *hawt*! And, like, total sluts!

Vespucci's letters went on to be printed in no fewer than sixty editions; Columbus's journals, only twenty-two. So Waldseemüller could be forgiven for thinking that Amerigo was the one who deserved the naming honors. After all, Vespucci wrote that the land he'd visited (the "New World," he called it) "is found to be surrounded on all sides by the ocean." Readers like Waldseemüller got the distinct impression—which turned out to be right—that there was a new continent out there, over the horizon. The new map may never have reached Spain, where Vespucci lived until his 1512 death, so he probably died without knowing what his legacy would be. But what a legacy! This Renaissance rock star had managed to get 28 percent of the earth's land area named after him—*in his own lifetime*.

When he drew his map, Waldseemüller extended conic projection used in the first century by Ptolemy to the new ends of the Earth, so Europe, Africa, and the Near East look pretty good but eastern Asia and the Americas are distorted, as if seen through a fish-eye lens. The effect is oddly immersive as I walk toward the map; it rises out of its case to engulf me on all sides like a Hunter S. Thompson hallucination. The library has spared no expense in preservation—the case, modeled on the ones that house the Constitution and Declaration of Independence over in the National Archives, cost $320,000. The map sits in dim light behind an inch and a half of glass, the air inside having been replaced with inert argon gas. Gold letters on the case read, "America's Birth Certificate."

That tagline isn't just a politically canny way to raise $10 million for a single map—it's also a very perceptive statement about maps in general. The history of the world is just as much a history of places as it is of people—cities and nations that were born in obscurity if not bastardy but later grew into greatness. The English comic poet E. C. Bentley once observed that "The science of geography / Is different from biography: / Geography is about Maps, / But Biography is about Chaps." The Waldseemüller map—in fact, the whole of John Hébert's vault of wonders, its portolans and panoramas and powder horns— reminds us that history is about both. It makes us wonder: if one map can change the world, what can five and a half million do?

They have power only if we use them, of course. I wonder how many dusty drawers of the Geography and Map Division might hold unseen treasures like the one that Father Fischer found in a German castle garret. We'll never know if nobody looks. As we walk out of the Waldseemüller exhibit, our footsteps echo on the marble floor. Today, the vast, dim gallery that houses the world's most valuable map is, except for us, completely empty.

Chapter 5

ELEVATION

[ˌe-lə-ˈvā-shən] *n.*: the height of a landform above sea level; altitude

More delicate than the historians' are the map-makers' colors.
—ELIZABETH BISHOP

L owther Lodge, a bountifully gabled and chimneyed Queen Anne town house just south of London's Kensington Gardens, has been home for the last century to Britain's Royal Geographical Society. This is the crew that sent Speke and Burton up the Nile and Scott and Shackleton to the South Pole. During the age of empire, whenever a doughty, broadly mustached Briton returned to London from some manly adventure abroad, he would address his fellow explorers there and they would pass around his souvenirs, squinting appreciatively at them through their monocles. Henry Morton Stanley bequeathed them the pith helmet he was wearing when he found Livingstone. They have Charles Darwin's pocket sextant and Edmund Hillary's oxygen canisters.

Normally the society's headquarters is closed to nonmembers, but today the halls are packed. For the last three years, the Royal Geographical Society has played host to the London Map Fair, Europe's largest event for buying and selling antique maps. Thirty-five dealers are exhibiting their cartographic wares here, from both sides of the English Channel and both sides of the Atlantic: Athens, Berlin, New York, San Diego, Rome. The squeaky blond floorboards of the Victorian building are lined with card tables and makeshift booths, all

79

covered with thousands and thousands of Mylar-sheathed maps. The most colorful samples hang from walls in no particular order: Australia continental-drifting into West Africa, the Falklands spotted off the coast of France.

The once obscure pastime of map collecting has grown, over the last thirty years or so, into a big, big business. This weekend's sales are expected to top £750,000, a record for the fair. "Today, there are more map *societies* than there were map collectors when I started out," the Chicago map dealer Ken Nebenzahl has said. Certainly the shoppers here today are a diverse bunch. Many are examples of the stereotypical private collector: middle-aged, male, bespectacled, quiet, perhaps a bit of an "anorak," to use the Brit slang term for a niche obsessive. (It's a sunny June day, so the anoraks, not wearing their eponymous piece of outerwear, are slightly harder to spot.) But there's also the shaved-headed hipster with an Eels T-shirt and a huge brown poodle on a leash, not to mention the glamorous French woman with pearls, a Louis Vuitton handbag, and a baby in a stroller, flipping through a New York dealer's map stacks. I mentally tag the first as a curiosity seeker (this year's fair has been widely advertised to the general public) and the second as a representative of that recent addition to the map scene: the wealthy, noncognoscenti buyer. Some are poseurs who have hopped aboard the bandwagon now that maps are trendy antiques or possible investments; others are decorating a new condo and just think maps look pretty. ("Is that a 1584 Ortelius map of Burgundy? I'll take three. Do you have it in blue?") Map dealers often set up shop near tourist meccas, and they live or die by these impulse shoppers, who will pay exorbitant prices for even historically unremarkable maps as long as they're handsomely matted and framed and match the sofa. Collectors, on the other hand, sniff at the nonaficionados: they don't *really* care about maps, they just drive up prices.

But Ian Harvey, manning the International Map Collectors' Society booth here, doesn't blame them. "If you're decorating, by and large, maps are cheaper than pictures," he says. Unlike in the art world, map collectors can still find beautiful seventeenth- or eighteenth-century pieces for just hundreds of dollars—a steep rise from decades past but still entry level. In fact, the most attractive maps are sometimes the most affordable. They were popular, so they were widely printed and saved. "The rare ones are the scruffy little things," says Harvey. "There are only four in the world, but they are ugly." The fair's leaflets boast that the maps on sale today range in price from £10 all the way to £100,000, and that's not just hype. Many dealers have brought cardboard boxes of small £5 and £10 maps for souvenir hunters to rummage through, as if they were LPs at a garage sale. Massimo De Martini of the Altea Gallery, one of the fair's organizers, has brought the only six-figure item I see for sale: a pristine 1670 world map by Willem Blaeu, uncolored and unremarkable to the lay eye. I'm a little surprised at how the high-end merchandise here is treated: this map costs as much as a Bentley, but it hangs casually in one corner of the Altea booth among dozens of other maps, as if in a Covent Garden stall.

I walk up to the Blaeu and study its hemispheres intently, as if somewhere in their crowded text hides the secret of why anyone would

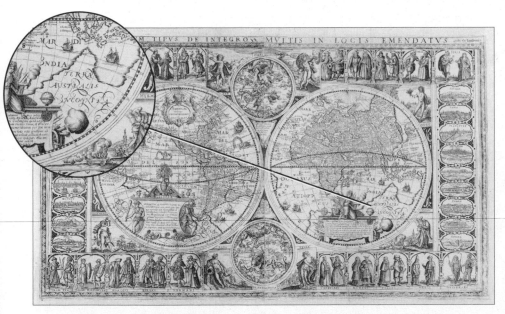

A one-of-a-kind Italian copy of Willem Blaeu's famous world map, making it a $150,000 item. Check out "Terra Australis" in the lower right, nonexistent but nevertheless drawn large enough to dwarf Eurasia and Africa combined.

pay $150,000 for an old map. I know the obvious answer—because it's rare, and they're not making new seventeenth-century maps anymore—but I still can't get my head around this particular variety of map love. I grew up loving maps for their completeness, their accuracy, their confident sense of order—all qualities that are conspicuously missing in these antiques.

"Why old maps?" I ask Jonathan Potter, the veteran London map dealer who is running the fair's largest setup. Potter recently announced that he was retiring from the map game and has put his prodigious collection, which has been valued at more than $6 million, up for sale. He laughs, as if he's been ambushed by a question too big to answer. "Well, they combine all sorts of facets of art, history, scarcity, antiquity, intrinsic interest—it's all in one. There aren't many things that have all of that."

The antiquity and historical importance of these maps are certainly behind much of their popularity. Map collectors tend to specialize in a particular niche: they collect only maps of Australia, say, or Scandinavia or Texas. And they don't just *accumulate* like a man with a giant ball of string in his attic; they become scholarly authorities on their niche, intently studying the period and the region the maps come from. The definitive book on niggly cartographic subjects is most often written not by a curator or an academic but by some enthusiastic amateur. Map collectors are history buffs, in other words, and often ones with deep pockets. The world's most valuable maps aren't necessarily the beautiful ones but rather the ones that, like the Library of Congress's $10 million Waldseemüller map, changed history in some way. In February 2010, a Maine auction house sold a map of the siege of Yorktown for $1.15 million, a record price for a map at auction. The map is creased, somewhat roughly sketched, and not particularly colorful—but that doesn't matter much when you find out it was George Washington's personal copy of his most crucial victory.

But it's not just cold matters of historical fact that give old maps their allure. Most maps on the market are, when you think about it, of comparatively recent vintage. Almost none are more than five hundred years old—a mere blip in the march of time. Yet old maps come to us with an aura of ancient mystery and romance wildly out of proportion to their actual age. Their mottled parchment is the tawny color of sandstone and mummy linen. Their novel and faintly untrustworthy coastlines seem to have arrived from another world altogether: Atlantis, maybe, or ancient Mu. They're not just artifacts; they are relics. National Geographic recently unveiled an "earth-toned" version of its standard world map, based on the faded palette of old sea charts Envisioned as a bit of a novelty, it now outsells the familiar schoolroom-blue version. The message is clear: we count on our maps to be up to the minute, but we like them to seem venerable as well.

Studying the six-figure Blaeu world map in the Altea booth, my eye is immediately drawn to the parts that aren't quite right, the way you might find yourself awkwardly unable, in conversation, to stop staring at a wart or a scar. Australia is connected to New Guinea and then extends southward to the pole, forming a landmass larger than Asia that the mapmaker called "Terra Australis Incognita." A broad, imaginary swath through Canada, the so-called Strait of Anian, provides a northerly route from the Atlantic to Asia, the mythical "Northwest Passage" that many Europeans died trying to find.

But to the collector, these aren't warts. Time has freed antique maps from the shackles of serving as reference objects, so their mistakes are lovingly prized by collectors, the way a printing error can add a zero or two to a stamp's value. Dealers' catalogs carefully enumerate these little quirks as major selling points. "California appears an island," reads Altea's description of a neighboring New World map.* Or "Australia is connected to Tasmania," or "the Great Lakes are open-ended to the west." I'm a little alarmed to find that, if you go by most eighteenth-century French maps, my Seattle home is underwater, part of a vast "Bay of the West" that the Pacific Ocean has apparently carved out of Washington, Oregon, Idaho, British Columbia, and Alberta.

Why pay more for a map that's wrong? Some of it is sheer novelty value: a map where California is floating in the middle of the Pacific

---

* There are plenty of American collectors who will buy *only* maps in which California is an island. Maybe they're hoping to make a killing when Lex Luthor carves off the Golden State, the way he tried to do in the first *Superman* movie.

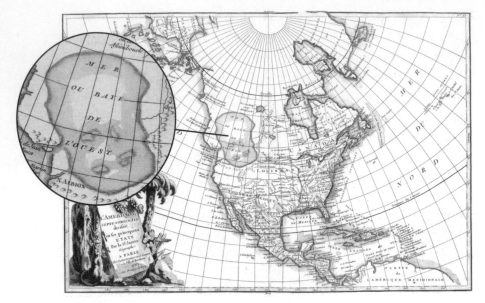

Jean Janvier included the "Baye de l'Ouest" on his 1782 map of North America. The Pacific Northwest may be wet, but it's not that wet.

makes a great conversation piece in an L.A. living room. But it's also a charming memento of human ignorance and imperfection. It reminds us that maps are never completely reliable, should never be mistaken for the actual territory. Once drawn on one map, a fanciful invention like the "Bay of the West" would propagate through decades of later maps like a virus, sometimes appearing long after actual exploration had corrected the original goof. The tiny sickle-shaped island of Mayda first appeared on sixteenth-century maps just southwest of Ireland; as the oceans were more carefully charted, it gradually moved westward, toward Bermuda. Remarkably, it stuck around for four hundred years, making its final appearance on a Rand McNally map of 1906.* The

---

* In the future, however, when islands disappear from maps, it will probably be because they've disappeared from the ocean as well. In March 2010, New Moore Island, a tiny dot in the Bay of Bengal, vanished under the waves due to rising sea levels. India and Bangladesh had hotly disputed claims to the island for years; that problem is now solved, but the region faces more serious problems. Almost a fifth of Bangladesh will be underwater if sea levels rise just one meter over the next forty years, as some climate models predict.

Mountains of Kong, an imaginary range in western Africa, appeared in *Goode's World Atlas* as late as 1995!

Mayda's odd westward drift isn't unusual in the annals of map errata. The crazily awesome stuff on old maps always gets pushed to the edge of the paper as time goes on. The Garden of Eden started out in Asia Minor and kept drifting over the horizon until finally it landed outside the map altogether. The fabled Seven Cities of Gold were originally believed to sit on an island in the North Atlantic,* before being relocated to the American plains and finally winding up in the Southwest. You have to admire the dogged confidence of the mapmaker, never daunted by actual real-world evidence. "Okay, so nobody who goes to Turkey has managed to find Eden where we drew it on the last map. Well, it's got to be over there somewhere . . . hey, how about Armenia? Are you guys cool with Armenia? All righty, then." It's easy to see this process as a metaphor for almighty reason sweeping superstition away from the center of human thought into the dustbin of history—or, if you're a little more sentimental, for the tragedy of lost dreams and invention. According to that school of thought, Mayda's final winking out of the North Atlantic in 1906 would be the equivalent of a child's disillusionment at recognizing Daddy under Santa's beard or Tinkerbell's light fading because the audience refuses to applaud. In the case of the Seven Cities of Gold—an ideal ever receding just past the frontier of civilization until it comes to rest in the bleakest, least hospitable bit of the desert—you could even draw a parallel with the endless relocations of native people as Europeans advanced across the globe.

Perhaps these old maps seem to have more personality because they're credited to actual personalities. Modern maps have, essentially, no origin at all: they simply emerge—fully formed, as if from the mind of Zeus—onto computer screens and chain bookstore remainder tables. They are maps *of* something—Tuscany or Antarctica or Philadelphia—but not maps *by* anyone. At best, a connoisseur can

---

* The existence of this island was taken as an article of faith by sailors of the time, though none of them had ever seen it. Columbus even planned on stopping there on his 1492 voyage and was confused when it was nowhere to be found.

glance at an atlas and derive its corporate parentage—Goode's, Hammond, Oxford University Press—from the fonts and color scheme, but we still know nothing, imagine nothing about the hands that prepared it. Today, we might suppose (correctly, to a degree) that *no* hands really prepared it—that, instead of careful men with green eyeshades airbrushing artboard and scratching acetate overlays with crow-quill pens, the map was immaculately conceived of a GIS database.

By contrast, the maps at this fair are *by* someone. The name of the mapmaker appears in the largest type on every placard and first in every catalog listing: Pieter Goos, Nicolas de Fer, Thomas Kitchin. I've never heard of any of these people; they all sound to me like the fake names on Jason Bourne's passports. But the right name on a map—Speed or Ortelius or Mercator—allows a seller to bump up its price substantially. This is the auteur theory of cartography. It draws on the memory of a time when mapmakers left fingerprints all over their maps, and it requires the expertise to tell the craftsmen from the true artists. No matter how important they were in their field, none of these mapmakers ever became a household name (except perhaps for Gerardus "Hey, ladies, how'd you like to come up and take a look at my projection?" Mercator), but in this room they are the Old Masters: the map collectors' da Vinci and Rembrandt and van Gogh.

The early mapmakers deserve every bit of this attention. Today we're so surrounded by high-quality maps that we have the tendency to take them for granted. Well, of course this is what my hometown looks like! See, here it is on Google Earth. Maybe we can remember or imagine a time when there was no aerial imagery or airborne radar or GPS, but 250 years ago, before John Harrison invented the marine chronometer, there wasn't even a reliable way for sailors to measure their own longitude. Think about that for a moment: the best technology on Earth couldn't tell you how far east or west you were at any given moment. That's a wee bit of an obstacle when it comes to drawing reliable maps. When Ptolemy mapped the known world in the second century, he had to rely on oral histories and a series of rough mathematical guesses to gauge east-west distances. As a result, he drastically elongated the Mediterranean, making it half again as wide as it is in reality. A millennium passed without any improvement on his method, and so Columbus relied on Ptolemy's fuzzy math to calculate the length of his proposed voyage to India. He was about ten thousand miles off, and was very lucky there was a huge unknown continent in his way, or he would never have been heard from again.

Without modern mapmaking tools, scale can be tricky. Francis Billington was a teenager when his family landed at Plymouth Rock in 1620, and records of the time make him out to be the colony's Bart Simpson, an incorrigible juvenile delinquent. He nearly blew up the *Mayflower* in harbor by firing his father's musket inside a cabin where flints and gunpowder were stored.* On January 8 of the following year, Francis climbed a tree on a nearby hilltop and was surprised to see "a great sea" three miles away. This discovery led to a good deal of pilgrim excitement—could this be the famous Northwest Passage?—but when the vast "Billington Sea" (as it is still known) was explored, it turned out to be a pond only seven feet deep. Oops.

When soldiers like Zebulon Pike and Stephen Long first explored the high plains of Kansas and Nebraska, they thought the region "wholly unfit for cultivation and, of course, uninhabitable." Pike wrote that the plains "may become in time equally celebrated as the sandy deserts of Africa," and Long's map even labeled the area "The Great American Desert." As a result, the plains were held to be valueless and settlers avoided them for decades. As it turned out, the explorers had visited during a dry period in the region's drought cycle, and of course they had no idea of the vast aquifers under their feet that made the area ideal for irrigation farming. Today, the same region is called "America's breadbasket."

I mention these misconceptions not to discredit the early mapmakers but to show what they were up against: they were writing the first records of every single thing they saw. Their horizon was only three miles away, and they had no way to transcend the limits

---

* Raise a toast this Thanksgiving to Francis "Bad Boy" Billington! I love the idea of a rebel pilgrim, presumably with his big black hat worn at a jaunty angle and the silver buckle on it shamefully unpolished. "What art thou rebelling against, Francis?" the town elders would ask him, and "What hast thou got?" would come the surly reply.

of their own viewpoint. Consider the laborious process of making the first survey of a region using eighteenth- or nineteenth-century technology. First you need to establish a baseline—a precisely known distance between two points. Today you'd do that with a laser; measure the time it takes light to reflect off a prism, and within seconds you'd have the distance. But back then it meant inching across the countryside with a sixty-six-foot chain, moving the chain like a football referee every time it got fully extended and always taking great care to keep it straight and at a constant elevation (on wooden trestles, if necessary). Marking off a single seven-mile baseline could take weeks.

And *then* the fun would really start. From both ends of your baseline, you use a bulky instrument called a theodolite to measure the angle to a single landmark—a hilltop, maybe, or a distant church steeple. With a little tenth-grade trigonometry, you use the baseline length and the two angles to compute the distances from each endpoint to the third landmark. Well done! You have just surveyed a single triangle! Now take one of your endpoints and the new landmark, and make that distance the baseline of a second triangle, and one of that triangle's sides the baseline of a third triangle, and so on. Now please try to resist blowing your brains out when I tell you that the Great Trigonometrical Survey that mapped British India two centuries ago required more than *forty thousand triangles* to complete and stretched from a five-year project into an eighty-year one.*

It was a Herculean task, the Indian survey. This kind of triangulation is difficult enough if you're mapping, say, Devonshire. It's almost inconceivable on a subcontinent of dense jungles and the world's

---

* The first survey of this kind was begun in France in the 1670s by Giovanni Cassini, and it proved so daunting that his *grandson* wound up finishing it more than a century later. This was the first topographic map of an entire nation ever made, but it revealed France to be much smaller in area than it had always been drawn. "Your work has cost me a large part of my state!" King Louis XIV reportedly huffed. Large-scale triangulation surveys like Cassini's proved too laborious for other nations to emulate, and so the science died out before roaring back in the 1840s, driven by, well, shit. The new sanitation systems being installed in Europe's large cities were the first construction projects big enough to require the precision of trigonometry.

highest mountains,* where torrential rains might halt mapping for months at a time and you have to constantly replace the surveyors killed by malaria. Where there were no easily visible landmarks to sight to or from, rickety bamboo scaffolds would be built, and many of the flagmen stationed atop them fell to their deaths. James Rennell, the "father of Indian geography," was almost killed on the Bhutanese border in 1776 when his small party of sepoys was attacked by hundreds of Sannyassa fakirs, who had been terrorizing local villages. Armed only with a cutlass, Rennell fought off two lines of the bandits and crawled back to the British camp, bleeding copiously from at least five sword wounds, one more than a foot long. The nearest doctor was three hundred miles away, but Rennell somehow clung to life, though he was never the same after surviving the attack. Even more remarkable is the story of Nain Singh, the Bhotian schoolteacher who spent the better part of ten years exploring the Himalayan "roof of the world" for the British. Tibet was closed to Westerners under penalty of death, but Singh was able to smuggle himself across the border and complete the five-hundred-mile trek to Lhasa, where he met the Dalai Lama himself. Singh's Buddhist prayer wheel concealed a hidden compartment for notes and a compass; his rosary had been doctored so he could use the beads to count his paces. At every place he stopped, he would secretly use his sextant to determine latitude and boil a pot of water to measure altitude. Though he received only twenty rupees a month for his pains, his measurements formed the basis for the only maps of Tibet available for the next fifty years. In 1877, the Royal Geographical Society awarded him its prestigious Victoria Medal "for having added a greater amount to our positive knowledge of the map of Asia than any individual of our time."†

---

* Before the Great Trigonometrical Survey, in fact, no one had any clue what the world's highest mountain even *was*. When Surveyor General Andrew Waugh first published Everest's height in 1856, he announced it as 29,002 feet above sea level. In fact, the surveyors had calculated the figure at 29,000 feet exactly, but Waugh was afraid no one would believe that suspiciously round number.

† The British borrowed a Hindi word meaning "learned one" to describe these native scouts, and from this we derived a modern word for any self-proclaimed expert. They were called "pundits."

Today, collectors might be the only people who can look at a map and still see the heroism, the sacrifice—sometimes the lifeblood—that went into the drawing of its contours. There's no better place than the Royal Geographical Society to consider the human face of mapmaking. As I stand in the society's main hall, John Singer Sargent's portrait of Lord Curzon, Asian explorer and viceroy of India, considers me coolly from its post above the great marble fireplace. Behind me is an intricate scale model of the *Discovery,* one of the last three-masted wooden ships ever built in Britain, which in 1901 took Scott and Shackleton to Antarctica, a continent from which, in the end, neither would return alive. To my right is an odd oil painting of Richard Francis Burton, spotlit in the dark, huddled under a blanket on a dirt floor. The setting might be a Mecca alley or a prison cell, but either way, as Burton stares warily out at the viewer, he gives the impression that he'd rather be somewhere else entirely.

There's a funny disconnect between the rugged adventurers painted in oils here and the meek little men walking through the halls and poking through their maps. But then I reconsider: is the divide really all that wide? All the sweaty tropical valor of the Indian surveys was performed in the service of trigonometry, of all things—it's hard to get nerdier than that. Eratosthenes, the mapmaker who was the first man to accurately measure the size of the Earth, was a *librarian.* The great mariners of the Age of Exploration, for all their naval derring-do, never would have left home if they hadn't been map geeks as well: Columbus etched maps in his brother's Lisbon print shop ("God had endowed me with ingenuity and manual skill in designing spheres, and inscribing upon them in the proper places cities, rivers, and mountains, isles, and ports," he once wrote the king of Spain), and Vespucci was a map collector from his youth. We think of trailblazing as a tough, brawny pursuit, but there's something solitary and nerdish at the heart of it. What is exploration if not the urge to go somewhere where there's no one else around—where no one, in fact, has *ever* been?

On the wall next to Lord Curzon, Mindy points out a photograph of the *current* president of the Royal Geographical Society. "Is that a joke?" she asks incredulously. It's none other than Monty Python's

Michael Palin—who, I explain to Mindy, has become a respected globetrotter and travel documentarian in recent years. He's so influential that the travel industry speaks of a "Palin effect," a sudden influx of tourists pouring into any destination he features on his TV programs. I guess that seals the deal regarding the nerd/explorer overlap: if a geek icon like Monty Python can take over the Royal Geographical Society, then exploration isn't just for jocks and probably never was. But Mindy can't stop laughing at the idea of "K-K-K-Ken" from *A Fish Called Wanda* having been placed in charge of British geography. I guess I can see her point; it would be like an Englishman coming to the United States only to find that William Shatner runs NASA now.

The now-valuable maps of the Age of Discovery made the world a much bigger place, but the world of map collecting itself is small. "It is a tiny subculture," says the New York dealer Henry Taliaferro. "I'm an expert in rare maps, but saying you're the greatest expert in rare maps is like saying you're the best ballet dancer in Galveston, Texas." It's an insular, incestuous world where everyone knows everyone else. Dealers sell maps to collectors but might buy them back later when a collector moves on or decides to refine his or her collection, and then sell them again to someone else. (Many of the best maps on display here today are on consignment from private collectors looking to sell.) Dealers sell to museums and libraries as well—Nikolaus Struck, a map dealer here from Berlin, tells me he makes most of his living selling to museum curators. This is why the year's big map fairs—London, Miami, Paris—are such important events in the trade: they're symposia as well as marketplaces, chances for colleagues to meet up and swap stories. "In the evening we go out together, eat and drink," says Massimo De Martini.

But that cozy world is changing. "The one thing that's transformed everything is the Internet," says Taliaferro's partner, Paul Cohen. "Before, the dealers had special knowledge." In fact, many dealers could make a living as trusted tastemakers, shepherding a small but elite clientele through the confusing world of copperplates and cartouches. Today the balance of power has swung to the collector: I can go online and comparison-shop the catalogs of dozens of antiquarians. There are now price guides and standardized condition guides. It's hard to see this wider spread of information as a problem, but for the dealers, accustomed to their position as gatekeepers of all map lore, it's been a bitter pill to swallow. "Collectors used to be loyal," sighs Cohen.

That exclusivity made the rare-map world one of cliquish secrecy, and old habits die hard, as I learn every time I tell someone in the trade that I'm working on a book about maps. Stories become as vague as the South American coastline on a Sebastian Münster map; lips tighten into a single etched line of latitude. Dealers working with wealthy collectors don't want rival sellers finding out about their golden-egg-laying clients and vice versa. Collectors don't want their personal list of Holy Grails to be widely known, for fear they'll be quoted higher prices when one comes up for sale. They don't even want you to know what they already own, and maybe I wouldn't either, if I had pieces of vellum that each cost more than my first house hanging in my den. Especially if they weren't all insured. "It's almost like the confidential relationship between a psychiatrist and a patient," Cohen explains in all seriousness. "I'm limited in what I can say, like someone who's been indicted of a crime."

This reticence surprises me at first; in my experience, the main conversational problem with hobbyists is getting them to *shut up* about their odd pastime. But map knowledge has always been guarded with great secrecy. In 1504, King Manuel I of Portugal declared that anyone leaving his kingdom with a single Portuguese map would receive the death penalty. He did so for the same reason that map dealers keep mum about their clients today: to protect a trade monopoly. The geopolitical equivalent of the space race at that time was a "spice race" for Asian cinnamon, pepper, and nutmeg, and Vasco da Gama had just given Portugal a crucial edge by charting a sea route to India. Keeping Spain in the dark about his discoveries was a crucial matter of national security. Likewise, until the dawn of glasnost in 1988, the KGB was charged with making sure that essentially every detail of every publicly available map of the Soviet Union was wrong. "Almost everything was changed," said chief mapmaker Viktor Yashchenko. "On the tourist map of Moscow, only the contours of the capital are accurate." Visitors to the city would invariably rely upon the CIA's Moscow map, the only one that actually got the streets right.

You might assume that falsified maps are a Cold War relic that could never survive in the age of satellite photography, but you'd be wrong. For most of the decade my family lived in Seoul, we lived less than a mile from Yongsan Garrison, the largest U.S. military installation on the Korean Peninsula. Yongsan is a bustling miniature city, home to more than seven thousand troops stationed in Seoul. My family wasn't military, but lots of my friends' parents were, and my mom worked at the high school there, so I spent more time on that post than many GIs did. Today, when I look at maps of Yongsan on Google Earth, little has changed—I can see the barracks, the bowling alley, the chapel where I played in my sixth-grade piano recital, the tennis court where my Boy Scout troop sold Christmas trees. But if I bring up the same coordinates on Naver, by far the most popular South Korean search engine, my childhood has been erased. The contours of the military garrison have been carefully filled with imagery of forested mountainside, no doubt for government-imposed security reasons. There's now a trackless 620-acre wilderness sitting incongruously in the middle of one of the world's most densely populated cities,* a lie as whoppingly transparent as any Soviet-era skewing of railroad lines.

But competitive advantage isn't the only reason why antique map dealers are wary of outsiders these days. There's been a flurry of recent media interest in their quiet little community, but nobody's covering the standard map-world controversies: whether it's good form for collectors to add new outline color to uncolored maps, for example, or whether the "Dieppe maps" of 1547 provide evidence that the Portuguese were the first to land in Australia. Instead, the articles have been written by crime beat reporters, because of a recent rash of high-profile map thefts that have rocked the trade to its foundations. Maps have gone missing in libraries from Madrid to Mumbai, but by far the most notorious case is that of E. Forbes Smiley III.

---

* Seoul boasts a remarkable 17,219 people per square kilometer. That's twice as dense as Mexico City and eight times as dense as New York City.

Smiley was one of the world's most knowledgeable map dealers, but if his name makes him sound instead like a sitcom millionaire, that's not a coincidence. By all accounts, this scion of a middle-class New Hampshire family carefully cultivated an über-preppy image—"right down to the deck shoes with no socks," said one dealer—in order to project reliability and taste to his high-roller clients. He had helped build some of the most magnificent collections of colonial American maps ever assembled and sat on the steering committee of the New York Public Library's Mercator Society. On the morning of June 8, 2005, Smiley was sitting with four valuable map books in the reading room of Yale's Beinecke Library for rare books and manuscripts when a library employee found an X-Acto knife near him on the floor. A small blade in a university library is a red flag; a best-selling book had recently told the story of Gilbert Bland, the Florida map dealer who'd used a hobby knife to slash valuable maps and prints out of old books in libraries coast to coast. After learning that Smiley had been looking at rare maps and that some maps he'd recently handled at Yale's Sterling Library had been reported missing, the librarians began videotaping Smiley and had him followed by campus police when he left the building. When detectives stopped him, they discovered that his metal briefcase was full of old maps and that an inside pocket of his tweed blazer contained a John Smith map of New England that, it turned out, had gone missing from the very book he'd been reading.* He was charged with first-degree larceny and led away in handcuffs.

"The Forbes Smiley case did a lot of damage, because he was one of us," says Paul Cohen. His own gallery had recently bought a large number of high-quality maps from Smiley and faced huge losses if they too turned out to be stolen property. Other libraries began to report missing maps from books that Smiley had handled over a period of years. The Boston Public Library was missing thirty-four; the New York Public Library, his old stomping ground, was missing thirty-two. The total value of the heisted maps was close to $3 million. In the end, the FBI could link Smiley to only eighteen thefts; as part

---

* This was a copy of the same John Smith map discussed in the previous chapter, the first one to feature the name "New England."

of his plea bargain, he copped to eighty others and helped authorities recover the maps from dealers like Cohen & Taliaferro, which found itself out $880,000. Smiley explained to prosecutors that he had stolen because of mounting debts and had chosen institutions that he blamed for some past slight. Outraged map librarians testified that Smiley was "a thief who had assaulted history" and argued for an eight-year sentence, but in light of Smiley's cooperation, the judge sentenced him to only three and a half years in a minimum-security Massachusetts prison. That seemed plenty harsh to her. "When he leaves prison," she pointed out, "he will have no assets, no career in the field he loves. He will be a pariah, he will lose years of liberty, and years with his young son." Indeed, in his courtroom appearances, the once oversized and ebullient Smiley appeared to be a broken man, haggard and hesitant.

Stealing antique maps sounds like such an esoteric niche of felony that it's hard to believe it's becoming commonplace all over the world. In fiction, a sudden rash of old map thefts would mean only one thing: a cunning new criminal genius in town. ("Holy hachured contour, Batman! It's the Cartographer!") But when real-life map thieves are apprehended, they're disappointingly ordinary: desperate, underpaid misfits from the world of rare books or academia. In fact, their obvious nonmastermind status explains the recent popularity of this kind of crime: maps are pilfered because they're so easy to pilfer.

It's the nature of the beast: the whole purpose of a library is to make rare materials available to the public. These materials are valueless if *nobody* can see them. It's hard to spirit a big bulky book out of a reading room—they get checked in and out carefully—but removing pages is, as Gilbert Bland and Forbes Smiley have demonstrated, heartbreakingly easy. (Smiley might never have been caught if not for a fluke: he accidentally dropped his knife.) They're light and small, and their absence might not be noticed for years. But which pages to remove? "If you take a page out of a rare book, you've got a worthless piece of paper," says Tony Campbell, a former map librarian at the British Library. "But if you take a map, you haven't destroyed its worth. It's likely to have a fair value, and it's virtually untraceable." Maps, unlike books or paintings, are almost never sold with a provenance; their history, a cartographer might say, is Terra Incognita. Most often, they bear no identifying marks at all. (Yale was able to prove ownership of Smiley's maps only by matching up wormholes with those on adjacent pages.) During the Smiley trial, the defense made much of the fact that many of the institutions he targeted reported maps missing that he had never handled or that later turned up elsewhere in their archives. Libraries, frankly, don't always know what they have, especially if little larcenies like this have been going on under the radar for decades, as seems likely.

Despite the gloomy predictions of some dealers, the map trade didn't collapse with Forbes Smiley's downfall. Even in a major recession, sales have been strong and prices have stayed high. The antiquarian world, having lost its innocence, has begun to take precautions: libraries are keeping a closer eye on patrons, and dealers and auction houses are becoming more inquisitive about the provenance of the items they buy. For many years, "tome raiders" like Smiley were tacitly abetted by their victims—institutions were reluctant to report missing items, since the security lapses were embarrassing and might discourage future donors while encouraging future thieves. That's now starting to change. Map librarians share more information on losses as they happen, so that dealers and auction houses know to be on the lookout for specific missing items, as the art world has done for decades. But there's still no central online index of thefts and no map dealer who requires proof of title every time a map is offered for sale.

As much as I love maps, I've never felt the need to possess them. I understand the completist instinct of the collector, but I've always regarded maps as a kind of public utility. Like a nice sunset, I can look at one without wanting to take it home. But the recent crime wave in cartography demonstrates that maps do exert that kind of pull over many, many people. Not every map thief is a Forbes Smiley, stealing big-ticket items and quickly reselling for fear of losing a cabin on Martha's Vineyard. Many just see a beautiful map and *have to have it*. My favorite case is that of Farhad Hakimzadeh, a wealthy London publisher sent to prison in 2009 for scalpeling hundreds of thousands of dollars' worth of maps and illustrations out of rare books in London and Oxford libraries. He had no plans to resell, he told the court—he was just deeply attached to his collection and couldn't help wanting to improve it. He testified that, on his wedding night, he even kept his new bride waiting in bed while he polished the covers of his beloved rare books. Perhaps she misunderstood when he warned her he was into "leather binding."

The world's most distinguished collectors of maps may keep their treasures very private, but luckily for me there's a second tier filling out map societies around the world: the garrulous amateur enthusiasts. Leonard Rothman, a longtime Annapolis gynecologist who retired to California a decade ago, is one of them. "I love to expound," he says as he welcomes me into his thirty-first-floor condo in San Francisco's posh Russian Hill neighborhood. "I'm not allowed to mention maps when we have people over. I get in trouble." In fact, he can't help talking about every map we pass as we walk across the Persian rugs in his entryway. The vignette on this John Tallis map is supposed to be a giraffe, but clearly the engraver was working from vague secondhand descriptions—it looks more like a kangaroo with a bad case of acne. The outline color on that map—rust and teal, like two-strip Technicolor—is a dead giveaway as to its German origins, and you can even tell how old it is by how the pigments have oxidized. A cabinet holds part of a collection of almost one hundred thirteen inch globes. Most are antiques, but one is from the 1998 World Cup and plays the anthem of each competing nation when you press its corresponding flag.

"I've never seen that before," says Phil Simon, pointing at a strangely elliptical globe on a lower shelf. Phil, a retired United pilot, is the president of the California Map Society and has come with me to take a look at his friend's collection. In his sixties, he's a grandfatherly man with bushy black eyebrows and a penchant for sweater-vests.

Leonard is delighted to have the oddity noticed. "You know what that is? It's an ostrich egg!"

"That's a beauty! Who made it?"

"Who made it? The ostrich made it."

We sit on Leonard's terrace, which gives us a breathtaking three-hundred-degree view of San Francisco on a cloudless day, from the Golden Gate Bridge in the northwest all the way around to the Bay

Bridge eastward. We're on top of the tallest building on one of the city's highest hills, which might make us the uppermost people in the city right now. (I can't tell if we're quite higher than the tip of the Transamerica Pyramid or not.) When I mention this to Leonard, he points out that there's actually a penthouse above us; his upstairs neighbor is no less than George Shultz, longtime secretary of state under Reagan. "And his deck keeps leaking onto our ceiling!" he complains.

Yes, this is what even the middle tier of serious map collecting looks like: an elite world where the most serious annoyances are the leaky hot tubs of former Cabinet officials. There may still be entry-level maps around, but, by and large, soaring prices have made this a hobby for the affluent. But Phil and Leonard still get moony when they talk about the *real* elite West Coast collectors, the David Rumseys* and the Henry Wendts. "Leonard and I will *never* amass a collection like Wendt's," sighs Phil. "This man is *extremely* wealthy. One of his maps, there's only five of them in the world."

Maps have been luxury items ever since the Renaissance, when there are the first records of people collecting them. It was fashionable at the time for wealthy Dutch burghers, German nobles, and Italian merchants alike to keep "cabinets of curiosities"—little home museums full of rarities.† Back then, the idea of owning things and looking at them as a pastime was so novel that you weren't necessarily a collector *of* anything specific, like coins or seashells or porcelain. You were just *a collector*, full stop. You wanted it all, and the world was still limited enough for that to be a reasonable goal. Surviving inventories of such chambers reveal an amazing hodgepodge made possible by the new age of exploration: belts of Brazilian cannibals embellished with

---

* Rumsey has spent the last decade making many of the 150,000 maps in his collection freely available online via high-quality scans. Dozens of them are now available to peruse as a layer on Google Earth.

† In time, these little cabinets grew into the first natural history museums. Hans Sloane, the London physician called the "last of the universal collectors" (and, incidentally, the inventor of milk chocolate), would invite important guests to his Bloomsbury home to peruse his collection. (During one of these visits, the composer Handel enraged him by placing a buttered muffin atop a priceless medieval manuscript.) When Sloane died, he bequeathed his collection to the Crown, and the British Museum was thus founded.

the teeth of their devoured victims, rhinoceros horns encrusted with rubies, books from Malabar printed on palm leaves, stuffed pelicans, "eighty faces carved on a cherry stone," "an instrument used by the Jews in circumcision." Maps and globes were nearly always part of the display, both to provide context for the wide-ranging collection and because they were valuable items in and of themselves.

This was a watershed moment in the history of cartophilia. For thousands of years, people had drawn maps because they had to: to get from one place to another, or locate taxpayers, or mark the boundaries of fields and pastures. If not for those maps, lives or property would be lost, governments might fall. But here, for the first time, we have evidence of people keeping maps just because they liked looking at them. John Dee, the court astrologer and alchemist to Queen Elizabeth I, noted the fad in 1570, writing that the hobbyists bought maps with three purposes in mind: "some to beautify their halls, parlours, and chambers with," "some other[s] to view the large dominion of the Turk, the wide empire of the Muscovite, and the little morsel of ground where Christendom . . . is certainly known," and "some others . . . to understand other men's travels." Many of the great men of the time were map geeks. During his wild Oxford days, Thomas Hobbes "took great delight there to go to the bookbinders' shops and lie gazing on maps." (Those political philosophers know how to party!) The diarist and secretary of the Admiralty Samuel Pepys had a vast map collection, though he lost his beloved John Speed atlas in the Great Fire of London.

A recent study of old Cambridge records has found that, by 1560, a quarter of all book owners owned maps and atlases as well. Half displayed them proudly on their walls, as can also be seen in many oil paintings of the time. Jan Vermeer was a particular map fan, faithfully reproducing period maps in the backgrounds of more than a quarter of his surviving canvases. In many cases, he seems to have gotten so carried away that his figures are dwarfed by an enormous map: the 1636 Claes Jansz. Visscher map of the Seventeen Provinces of the Netherlands in *The Art of Painting*, for example, or the 1620 Balthasar Florisz. van Berckenrode map of Holland above the *Officer and Laughing Girl*. The fact that early collectors were so proud to display their maps tells us that there may have been some self-interest at play here, beyond just an idle aesthetic or intellectual pursuit. Displaying maps gave you prestige; it was easy shorthand for "See how educated I am!" or "See how far-reaching my business interests are!"* A college sophomore is hoping for the same effect today when he casually adds a German beer stein or a poster of the Montmartre steps to his dorm room decor after returning from a summer in Europe.

The collectors then must have been very different from today's model. Back then, sixteenth-century maps had no patina of age and history, of course—they were contemporary items, hot off the presses. For Leonard and Phil, one of these maps will conjure up a bygone time, but to its first owner, the same map was like a "Breaking News"

---

* Wealthy buyers of the 594-map Blaeu atlas of 1665 could even pay a little extra to have their family coat of arms stamped in gold upon the cover. Compare that with the shoddy way our atlases must live today, crumpled in the backseats of our cars under an avalanche of fast-food receipts (or, if one has kids, Goldfish crackers).

Detail from Vermeer's 1657 Officer and Laughing Girl. *Would you care for a little painting with your map, Mr. Vermeer?*

update on CNN, the first place they could see the latest discoveries about the world outside Europe. It occurs to me that an adult collector then may have looked at maps with an eagerness and curiosity that only children can view maps with today: the joy of seeing an unknown part of the world for the very first time.

Until a wider variety of maps became available in the late sixteenth century, the Cambridge study found, collectors were interested in only two kinds of maps: world maps and maps of the Holy Land. When Leonard decided to focus his collection, he chose Holy Land maps as well. His map library now holds nine hundred such maps, including at least one from every cartographer who ever charted Palestine.

"Why the Holy Land?" I ask.

"There was a lot of stuff that was cost-effective. I'd been to Israel a few times, but the real thing was, I wanted to do something unique, something different." While still a practicing physician, he tells me, he once presented a paper on a rare pregnancy disease. Because there were only thirty-five recorded cases in history, he became the world's leading authority. "In other words, if you're going to specialize, specialize as much as possible."

"And it probably had something to do with your Jewish faith or heritage?" I venture.

"No! Why would I hang pictures of Jesus on my wall?" Sure enough, almost every map on display has a large vignette of the Crucifixion adorning Jerusalem. Many of the great early cartographers were Jewish,* but Holy Land maps were almost always made with Christian devotion in mind. "Once you become a collector"—he shrugs—"you have to keep an open mind."

---

* Jews were, in fact, Portugal's secret weapon in its battle with Spain for cartographic supremacy, as is evidenced by the Hebrew letters so often used as symbols on its maps. Christian mapmakers were constrained by biblical traditions so goofy that even the Texas Board of Education wouldn't touch them today, but in the sixteenth century, they trumped geographic accuracy every time. Take 2 Esdras 6:42, for example, which begins, "Upon the third day thou didst command that the waters should be gathered in the seventh part of the earth: six parts hast thou dried up, and kept them." This text was interpreted to mean that the surface of the earth was only one-seventh water, pretty much the reverse of the actual situation. Medieval maps vastly underestimated the size of the oceans for centuries, with potentially fatal results for mariners.

Leonard knows who his rival collectors in the Holy Land niche are: two in New York and one at the University of Jerusalem. But he avoids most of the cutthroat bidding. "A few maps were too expensive, and I'm happy to have a facsimile. I'd rather have the original, but you have to draw the line somewhere." Not all collectors are so good at drawing that line. Typically, they get off to a fast start, scooping up the low-hanging fruit in their focus area, but the really rare items might come up for sale only once in a decade. Some collectors have spent twenty or thirty years chasing that elusive last map, only to be outbid when one finally surfaces. "Put, in capital letters: FRUSTRATING," Ian Harvey had told me in London when I asked him to describe the lot of the map collector. "HE COULDN'T HAVE WHAT HE WANTED."

The library walls are lined with framed portraits of great cartographers and shelves full of map books. It's clearly a place for scholarly research, not just storage of valuables. "I spend hours in here," says Leonard. "I look at them over and over and over."

"The more you look at them, the more you'll find," agrees Phil. "I spend a lot of time studying maps with a magnifying glass." You can't really say that about any other collectible I can think of. The Rothmans love art as well—there are some Renoir sketches and a small Pissarro framed nearby—but no painting is as inexhaustible as a map.

Two hundred twenty of Leonard's favorite maps aren't in his library at all; they hang in sliding cupboards he's custom-built next to his bedroom closet. It's the world's largest collection of map neckties.

"This is magnificent!" exclaims Phil, who is also an expert on map-emblazoned miscellany (cartifacts, collectors call them). His Marin County home contains the largest collection of map jigsaw puzzles ever assembled by man.

"I'm running out of room," says Leonard. "I need to make another hole in the wall." He never goes anywhere without shopping for a souvenir tie printed with a local map. Sometimes he comes up dry, though—he just got back from Chile, where there wasn't a single map tie to be found.

"That's weird," I respond. "I thought skinny ties were coming back!" Dead silence greets my attempt at South American geographic humor. I see now that the world's largest array of cartographic neck-wear is nothing to joke about.

Many early maps, printed before the dawn of the Industrial Revolution, have survived the centuries in astonishingly good condition. They were printed on rag paper, made predominantly of cotton, linen, or hemp fiber, which is stronger and less acidic than the wood pulp–based papers widely used since. That's why a Jodocus Hondius map of Asia from 1613 might still be bright and pristine, while that yellow *Cathy* comic strip on your parents' fridge looks like it's been through a nuclear holocaust. Most of these older maps will outlive us all.

It's possible they'll also outlive the hobby of map collecting itself. More and more collections are winding up in the bowels of museums and libraries, thanks to well-meaning donors with a scholarly legacy or a nice tax deduction in mind. As a result, the high-quality manuscript maps still in circulation get scarcer every year. "A lot of people, when they die, will their collection to someplace like UC Berkeley," explains Phil. "And it goes into the basement and it disappears forever. It sits in boxes, and they don't even know what they have." The Huntington, a prestigious research library in Pasadena, has such a glut of antique maps that it won't even accept new collections anymore, unless the donor pays to have everything catalogued first.

"So what's the *right* thing to do with an old map?" I ask.

"Sell it back to a map dealer," says Leonard. "Or give it to a friend who will hang it up."

But I wonder how much longer those friends will be around. I saw map lovers of all ages in London, but when you strip away the serious from the merely curious, most collectors fall solidly into a watching-the-History-Channel-under-a-Slanket demographic: sixty and up. "It's graying," Paul Cohen told me. "You get fewer young collectors coming in." Phil has worked hard to recruit younger members into the California Map Society, but with little success. "They join for a year and then don't continue it."

Maybe, I conjecture hopefully, new collectors will continue to take up maps in middle age. "There are no young collectors, period, in anything," Ian Harvey of the International Map Collectors' Society had told me. "When younger, one does silly things like attend to careers. Some people have children, don't they? When I was at university, I was in the pub, not trawling down the Portobello Road looking for antique maps."

But Phil isn't so sanguine. "I think it will decline once this generation is gone," he says sadly, as we exchange good-byes. "I saw it with airline pilots too."

In London, on a whim, I bought my first antique map: a colorful 1850 John Tallis map of Ceylon, with five beautifully decorated vignettes full of ruined temples and palm trees in the corners. It's small and not at all valuable, but I find myself often taking it out to look at. Today the map is wrong in nearly every important respect: Ceylon is now Sri Lanka, it has nine provinces rather than five, and Adam's Peak—now known not to be the island's highest point, as Tallis has it—no longer looms picturesquely above the capital city's "Lake of Colombo," which is now walled by cement high-rises. But, even so, I'd rather look at this map than any modern-day one.

Perhaps all map love is a form of nostalgia. As a kid in Korea, I obsessed over maps of the United States, since they represented the past I was missing. Map collectors just miss a different past: theirs is the nostalgia of the silent-filmgoer, the Civil War reenactor, the chess club fedora wearer. They're nostalgic for a past so distant they don't even remember it. I hope Phil is wrong about the extinction of map collecting. It depresses me to imagine galleries full of perfect little objects like this one winking out of existence one by one all over the globe, like Mayda, like the island of California, like the Mountains of Kong, all vanishing into the past.

Chapter 6

LEGEND

['le-jənd] *n.*: an explanatory list of the symbols on a map

*Most of us, I suppose, have a secret country, but for most
of us it is only an imaginary country.*
—C. S. LEWIS

I n September 1931, Austin Tappan Wright was driving east across
the country, returning from a visit to California at the end of his
summer break at the University of Pennsylvania, where he taught
corporate law. A few miles outside Las Vegas, New Mexico, he was
killed in a tragic car accident, leaving behind a wife and four young children. Wright had grown up in Cambridge, Massachusetts, where his
father, a prominent Greek scholar, was the dean of Harvard's graduate
school. He studied at Harvard and Oxford, practiced law in Boston, and
then turned to teaching, at Berkeley and Penn. But only his family knew
that for most of his forty-eight years, he had also lived somewhere else
entirely: the remote Southern Hemisphere nation of Islandia.

Islandia is a tiny kingdom at the southern tip of the Karain subcontinent, isolated from the rest of the world by the impassable Sobo
Steppes and hundreds of miles of trackless ocean. Its people are peaceful and agrarian and have for centuries resisted the influence of outsiders. In fact, the national assembly passed the Hundred Law in 1841,
limiting the number of foreign visitors to no more than one hundred
at any given time. But that isolation was no obstacle to Wright, who
was able to become the West's foremost expert on Islandia while

circumventing the Hundred Law entirely. You see, he had invented the entire nation and its geography, its people and history and language and culture, all out of whole cloth, as a young boy. Islandia, though intricate and fully realized, is an entirely fictional country.

Wright rarely mentioned Islandia to outsiders, but his family knew about it, and knew that some part of him was always there. "This view looks like Islandia," they would hear him remark at times, as he studied some landscape that must have reminded him of the vivid utopia in his mind's eye. He named the family sailboat *Aspara,* the Islandian word for "seagull."

When he died, he left behind the work on which he'd spent over twenty years: twenty-three hundred longhand pages describing every aspect of Islandian life, from the *sarka* plum liqueur enjoyed by its inhabitants to the candles, shielded from the wind by waxed paper, that light the streets of its capital city. He may never have intended anyone else to read it, but his widow, Margot, taught herself to type and transcribed the entire text. Wright's oldest daughter, Sylvia, who later became a successful humorist and essayist in her own right,* spent the next decade cutting two hundred thousand words (about the length of Dostoyevsky's *Crime and Punishment*) out of the manuscript and shopping the result around to New York publishers in seven thick binders, so heavy that she couldn't carry them all herself.

When *Islandia* was published in 1942, at the height of World War II, it was a sensation. Readers had certainly visited fantastic places before, in day trips to Wonderland and Lilliput and Dante's Inferno, but spending 1,013 pages among the simple, peaceful people of Islandia and their carefully constructed world was an entire vacation—especially at a time when real overseas travel was off the table due to the war. Reviewers clutched for words to describe this brand-new approach to fiction. *Time* called it "perhaps the most sustained

---

* Today, Sylvia Wright is best remembered for coining the word "mondegreen" to refer to an oft-misheard song lyric, like "Excuse me while I kiss this guy" from Jimi Hendrix's "Purple Haze." The term first appeared in a 1954 *Harper's* essay in which Wright described how, as a child, she misheard the final line of a seventeenth-century ballad— "They hae slain the Earl O'Moray, and laid him on the green"—as "They hae slain the Earl O'Moray, and Lady Mondegreen."

and detailed daydream that has ever seen print . . . trompe-l'oeil on a vast scale." The endpapers of the first edition were carefully drawn maps of Islandia, no doubt a crucial part of the illusion.

Today we can still be absorbed in meticulously imagined artificial worlds. In 2010, CNN reported that thousands of viewers of James Cameron's *Avatar* were reporting feelings of loss and depression after watching the 3-D film, even contemplating suicide at the prospect that real life would never be as vivid and impossibly beautiful as the movie's computer-generated moon of Pandora. But Cameron's utopia was the result of hundreds of millions of dollars and man-hours and state-of-the-art digital technology. I prefer the image of the respectable law professor scratching away by gaslight after his children are in bed, trying desperately to record every detail of his little island, the byways and folkways that only he can see but that he has known since childhood. It's the ultimate outsider art.

The creation of geographies must have been in the Wright family genes. As a young boy, Austin Tappan Wright refused to let his younger brother, John, share Islandia with him; John shrugged and created his own island, Cravay. John Kirtland Wright would grow up to gain fame as an influential cartographer, director of the American Geographic Society, and coiner of the term "chloropleth map."* Their mother, Mary Wright, wrote a series of popular novels set in a painstakingly detailed but wholly fictional American university town called Great Dulwich, and the boys learned after their father's death that he too had spent hours mapping an imaginary world of his own devising.

I'm sure we all like to think that we carry within us whole worlds that our fellow humans never glimpse, but few of these worlds, I'm guessing, come complete with their own plum liqueurs and nineteenth-century immigration laws. It's easy to write off the Wrights as a family of dreamy eccentrics, but *many* people invent their own countries and draw maps of rugged coastlines that never were; we call these people "children." The Wrights were unusual only in that they kept summer homes in their childish kingdoms through adulthood.

---

* You may recall from chapter 1 that chloropleth maps are maps that encode information about different territories by coloring them different shades.

Some of the most famous pieces of "unreal estate" in literary history were, after all, inspired by children's maps. Robert Louis Stevenson's *Treasure Island*, with its famous treasure map, would never have been written if not for Stevenson's young stepson Lloyd, who passed a rainy summer painting watercolor maps with his stepfather in their Scottish cottage. The place-names they hand-lettered onto the map, like "Skeleton Island" and "Spyglass Hill," inspired the events of the story.* And when J. M. Barrie dreamed up Peter Pan's home isle of Neverland, he purposefully imitated the cartography of children:

I don't know whether you have ever seen a map of a person's mind. Doctors sometimes draw maps of other parts of you, and your own map can become intensely interesting, but catch them trying to draw a map of a child's mind, which is not only confused, but keeps going round all the time. There are zigzag lines on it, just like your temperature on a card, and these are probably roads in the island, for the Neverland is always more or less an island, with astonishing splashes of colour here and there, and coral reefs and rakish-looking craft in the offing, and savages and lonely lairs, and gnomes who are mostly tailors, and caves through which a river runs, and princes with six elder brothers, and a hut fast going to decay, and one very small old lady with a hooked nose.

When I was in the third grade, my friend Gerald and I were kings of twin monarchies called Oofer and Uffer. (I am now seeing those

---

* Stevenson was a devoted map buff and always connected his love for maps to his childhood imagination. In an 1894 magazine essay on *Treasure Island*, he wrote, "I am told there are people who do not care for maps, and find it hard to believe. The names, the shapes of the woodlands, the courses of the roads and rivers, the prehistoric footsteps of man still distinctly traceable up hill and down dale, the mills and the ruins, the ponds and the ferries, perhaps the STANDING STONE or the DRUIDIC CIRCLE on the heath; here is an inexhaustible fund of interest for any man with eyes to see or twopence-worth of imagination to understand with! No child but must remember laying his head in the grass, staring into the infinitesimal forest and seeing it grow populous with fairy armies."

names written down for the first time in twenty-five years.) I can still picture the maps we drew: Oofer is in orange crayon, Uffer green, and a long narrow strait of cerulean sea separates them, running from east to west. But *why* did we draw the maps? I haven't the foggiest notion. In hopes of refreshing my memory, I pay a visit to Benjamin Salman, a Seattle eighth-grader who is, I imagine, what Austin Tappan Wright must have been like at fourteen.

Like Wright, Benjamin is the offspring of gifted parents: his father, Mark, is a concert pianist, and his mother, Sarah, is, quite literally, a rocket scientist. (She used to be an engineer at the Jet Propulsion Laboratory, where she worked on the *Voyager* probes; now she teaches math at a nearby university.) Their living room is a pleasantly cluttered space full of antique furniture, musical instruments, stacks of books and *National Geographic*s, and papier-mâché masks hung on the walls. Benjamin is crouched on the wooden floor in front of me, spreading out a grid of eighteen sheets of typing paper.

"This is Augusta, one of the largest cities in Alambia," he tells me. "It is a complete, exhaustive map." It's a *Thomas Guide* of the imagination, with thousands of nonexistent streets, parks, and businesses meticulously laid out and labeled. "But this one"—he begins spreading out a map of his entire continent—"will never be finished."

Benjamin's own Islandia is actually a modified version of the real-world continent of Australia, moved northward and tilted at a rakish 30-degree angle, "for geographic diversity," he explains in his offhand, slightly elevated way of talking. He's sitting on the sofa now with his knees around his chin, occasionally chewing on a knuckle. "The actual contents—the geography, the history, the people—they're all completely different." When Benjamin talks about his world, his is not the enthusiastic chatter of the evangelist but the cool, knowledge-able tone of the expert. I wonder if that's part of the appeal of documenting your own alternate world: the knowledge that, despite your tender years, you are the greatest living authority on some subject. More than that, in fact—that you are the unquestioned master of the entire realm. The godlike feeling of dominion that comes when children look at a map must be amplified when they know that the maps

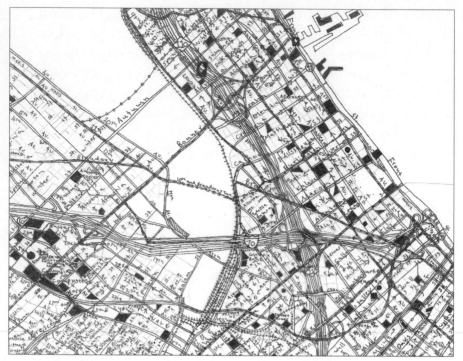

*The mean streets of downtown Augusta, hand-drawn
by Benjamin Salman, the only person who's ever been there*

are entirely their creation, that they can erase cities, raise up volcanoes, and flood river deltas at will.*

"Do you feel like you know your world as well as you know any real place?" I ask.

"Yes. Better! Because I made it up."

---

* Kids probably also enjoy the naughty thrill of tinkering in God's domain; imaginary mapmakers are, after all, the Dr. Frankensteins of cartography, altering natural landforms at whim. Wim Delvoye, for example, is a Belgian artist famous for his shocking installations, like the one where he tattoos live pigs or makes stained-glass windows of medical X-rays of his friends having sex in a radiology clinic. His best-known piece is "Cloaca," a machine that chews up food and digests it into realistic-smelling feces, which he then sells to gallery visitors. But Delvoye is also the artist behind "Atlas," a series of intricately detailed, utterly plausible renderings of imaginary continents. The maps *seem* square in comparison to the rest of Delvoye's outrageous oeuvre, but in a way they represent something just as transgressive: not just a pig reinvented but a world.

Benjamin has been living in his world almost as long as he's been living in ours. Even as a baby, he insisted on speaking a language of his own invention. "We just had to pretend we didn't understand him, and then he'd answer us in English," sighs Sarah. His country was born as a home for his childhood stuffed animals—Blue Roo the conductor, Day-Glo the inventor. The original residents are probably all in attics and thrift shops now, but their homeland has vastly expanded. It's not just the hundreds of neat city and country maps stacked on a bookshelf: Benjamin's Australia is a whole world. Whatever he's currently learning about in his homeschool classes— the Cyrillic alphabet, colonial history, plate tectonics—gets incorporated into the fabric of his imaginary continent. During the 2008 election season, he became so fascinated with the political process that he filled notebooks with his own fictional districts and candidates and their vote totals.

"The Conservative Democratic Party's presidential candidate has just resigned," he announces abruptly, later, as we're chatting over cheesecake. His update doesn't sound like a creative decision he's made but like a genuine news flash beamed in from another world. Time is passing there, just as it does here.

Do Benjamin's parents worry about his unusual dual citizenship? I suspect their concern isn't really their son but the possibility that outsiders (like me) will see him as weird. "It's eccentric, but that's okay," says Sarah. "For us, it's more interesting to have children who are"—she gestures vaguely—"whoever they are." After all, Benjamin's doing just fine. He's an impossibly bright teenager with a wide array of interests— not just maps but history and science and old Marx Brothers movies and classical music. He wants to be a pianist like his dad when he grows up and has just finished composing his first symphony, which he wrote—and orchestrated for fifteen parts—almost entirely in his head, not noodling at the keyboard. (Benjamin has perfect pitch.)

I wonder if Benjamin's Australia will survive adolescence into adulthood, the way Islandia did but Oofer and Uffer did not. Maybe his parents would be relieved, in a way, if the maps and ledgers and histories joined Blue Roo and Day-Glo in the attic, but I can't help thinking it would be a tragic loss, almost like the fall of a real empire.

All that time and knowledge gone forever, without even ruins left to commemorate their passing.

Maps of fictional places are a peculiarity of childhood, but among adults, they're a peculiarity of geek culture as well. Harry Potter's Hogwarts and the starship *Enterprise* have been mapped in more detail than much of Africa, and many kinds of gaming rely on maps, from the beautifully elaborate maps of 1970s "bookcase" games to the quickly sketched dungeons of a fantasy role-playing campaign to the pixel art that maps computer games, both classic and modern.* Even comic books aren't immune: as a kid, I once came across an *Atlas of the DC Universe* in a bookstore and eagerly scooped it up, unable to believe that someone had finally combined my two great loves: (1) atlases and (2) he-men in long underwear punching each other. But I was ultimately disappointed by the book: Gotham City and Metropolis seemed more mythic to me somehow before I knew that they were officially located in New Jersey and Delaware, respectively. C'mon, DC Comics. Superman would never live in *Delaware*.

If most kids grow out of made-up maps around the time they discover girls,† you might think that the prevalence of kiddie maps in geeky pastimes like these is just another sign of arrested development, like eating Hot Pockets and playing *Halo* all night even though you're in your thirties. But fantasy map fans prefer to see a different connection to childhood: a way to recapture the innocence and awe of discovery.

---

* My favorite childhood video games, whether text adventures like *Zork* or shoot-'em-ups like the cult classic *Time Bandit*, all had one thing in common: you had to make a map if you wanted to win. Today's 3-D video games aren't laid out using the overhead map paradigm I grew up on, but mapping is still important to players. When Sony didn't release an atlas of its *EverQuest* online game, players simply went ahead and assembled their own.

† Or boys, for that matter, if the young map fan happens to be female and straight, or male and gay. I know of little work exploring the connections between cartophilia and sexual orientation, but the British travel writer Mike Parker says he has nearly a hundred members in his online discussion group for gay map buffs. The connection between maps and gender has been *much* more exhaustively studied, as we'll see in chapter 7.

"The hallmark of epic fantasy is immersion," says the best-selling genre writer Brandon Sanderson. "That's why I've always included maps in my books. I believe the map prepares your mind to experience the wonder, to say, 'I am going to a new place.'"

Brandon and I were college roommates a decade ago, and in most of my memories of him, he's following one of his roommates around the apartment, reading aloud passages from his latest bulky fantasy manuscript, presumably part three of some eight-volume saga where all the characters had lengthy names full of apostrophes. At the time I was amused by Brandon's antics, but hey, at least it was a pleasant surprise not to be the nerdiest guy in the apartment for a change.

Well, Brandon had the last laugh. In a shocking twist, the epics he'd been writing while working the graveyard shift at a local Best Western were actually, uh, *good*. He sold his sixth completed novel, *Elantris,* two years before graduating, and on the strength of that book and his follow-up trilogy, *Mistborn,* Brandon was chosen ("handpicked," the accounts always say, as though he were a grape-fruit) by the author Robert Jordan's widow to complete *The Wheel of Time,* the megaselling fantasy series that had been left unfinished at the time of Jordan's 2007 death. His first *Wheel of Time* book, the twelfth installment in the series, debuted atop *The New York Times'* best-seller list, knocking Dan Brown out of the number one spot.

A Japanese samurai sword, which Brandon was allowed to choose from Jordan's immense personal collection of historical weaponry, hangs over the fireplace in his Utah basement, where we're talking. Brandon and his wife have plans to remodel the basement into a stone medieval dungeon, complete with torch holders and maybe a mounted dragon head on the wall, but currently it's just an empty bonus room with a navy blue beanbag chair the size of a Volkswagen Beetle sitting in the middle of it. This is where Brandon does most of his writing.

The summer after eighth grade, when Brandon first fell in love with the genre that would eventually pay for his house, maps were a big part of that love. "I started to look and make sure a book had a map," he remembers. "That was one of the measures of whether it was going to be a good book or not, in my little brain. When I first read *Lord of the Rings,* I thought, 'Oho, he knows what he's doing. A map *and* an appendix!'"

J. R. R. Tolkien single-handedly created the epic fantasy genre with his publication of *The Hobbit* in 1937 and then the *Lord of the Rings* trilogy in the 1950s. Tolkien never read *Islandia,* but his own world, which he called Middle-earth, was just as meticulously constructed. He drew upon his day job as an Oxford philology professor to create entire languages for his imaginary races, borrowing some Finnish here, some Welsh there. He designed their calendars and wrote their genealogies. And of course, he drew maps.

Many earlier authors had dabbled in fantastic events and settings, but Tolkien's books were the ones that created a whole new "Fantasy" aisle in the bookstore, one lined with those florid painted covers of dragons and wizards that make Yes album covers look tasteful and restrained by comparison. Why was he so influential? Tolkien's readers were less captivated by his plotting or his characters (which were memorable but, as Tolkien freely admitted, largely lifted from the Anglo-Saxon myths he so loved) than with the bold stroke of his world building, the fait accompli of Middle-earth, already there, as if it had always existed. Other books typically followed familiar characters from "the fields we know" into fairylands, whether through a rabbit hole, a wardrobe, or a chalk sidewalk drawing, but, says Brandon, "*Lord of the Rings* did something very different. It said, 'No, we're not going to transition you into it. We're going to *start you off* in a completely new world where nothing can be taken for granted.'"

Fantasy readers like that abrupt drop into the deep end and the learning curve it takes to keep up. They're not hurrying through the book the way you'd power through a thriller from an airport bookstore. They're taking time to study the rules, to pore over the odd names and arcane histories. Just like Benjamin Salman, they enjoy the sense of being authorities in a whole new realm. "By the end of a big epic fantasy novel, you'll have to become an *expert* in this world that doesn't exist," says Brandon. "It's challenging."

For this very reason, fantasy novels are the kind of reading that comes closest to the way we look at maps. Reading text is a purely linear process. Look: you are reading this sentence. Now you are reading this one. The words from the line above are gone; you are only here, and the words from the line below don't exist yet. But maps tell a different kind of story. In maps, our eyes are free to wander, spatially, the way they do when we study new surroundings in life.* We can sense whole swaths of geography at once, see relationships, linger over interesting details. Fantasies are read a word at a time too, but less propulsively than any other genre. The author is less interested in pulling you through to an ending than in creating a texture, showing you around a new world.

As a kid, I considered C. S. Lewis's Narnia books† to be somehow lightweight, mere fairy tales compared to Tolkien's books, and I realize now that maps were at least partly to blame. Elaborate maps were always to be found in front of Tolkien's books, but my Narnia paperbacks had no maps. Mr. Tumnus's forest in *The Lion, the Witch, and the Wardrobe* was just a bunch of trees, but Bilbo's forest was Mirkwood, between the mighty Anduin River and the wastes of Rhovanion in the east. One forest was just in a story, but the other was in a *place*.‡

It's the importance of place to the genre, not just slavish imitation of Tolkien, that explains why today's fantasy authors still make sure maps are front and center. David Eddings, one of epic fantasy's most popular writers, went so far as to put maps on the *covers* of his books. (Eddings's nation of Aloria was born the same way Stevenson created Treasure Island: he doodled the map first, and the map inspired

---

* The way your eye just wandered down to this footnote.

† Lewis, not surprisingly, was a map fan from a young age. According to his literary executor, Walter Hooper, Narnia itself was named after Narni, an Italian town that Lewis came across in a classical atlas when he was a boy.

‡ Four of the original U.K. hardcovers of *The Chronicles of Narnia* did contain excellent maps by Pauline Baynes, but they didn't make it into the American editions. Baynes was recommended to Lewis as an illustrator by his friend J. R. R. Tolkien, who loved her drawings, but luckily she had some cartographic training as well, having drawn maps for the Ministry of Defence during World War II.

the adventure.*) The maps are certainly functional too; many fantasy novels are episodic quests, and a map is an easy way to plot that course for a reader—it's no accident that the word "plot" can refer to the contents of both a chart *and* a narrative. But Brandon's tried hard to get away from the quest narrative in his own books, most of which take place in contained urban settings, yet he still makes sure his books have maps. His latest novel—the first volume in a projected ten-book series—is called *The Way of Kings,* and it includes no fewer than nine maps.

In fact, maps are so important to Brandon that he's paid nine thousand dollars out of pocket to illustrate the book with full-page maps and other "ephemera." Fantasy fans don't just want maps that look as though they've been laid out digitally on a Mac. They want their maps to be artifacts *from the other world,* maintaining the illusion that it actually exists somewhere. The map in the front of *The Hobbit* wasn't commissioned by a New York publisher; no, it's the very same map the dwarves in the story use to find their way to the dragon's lair. If you're not inclined to believe in dwarves or dragons or their lairs, then burnt edges and water stains on the map can help suspend that disbelief.

Isaac Stewart is the local artist who produces Brandon's maps, and it's no easy job. He's not just producing a nine-page atlas of territory that doesn't exist. He's producing, in effect, a sample page from each of nine vastly *different* atlases from nine different time periods. One map might be a street plan reminiscent of Regency London; the next might be a crude battle plan scraped on the back of a fictional crustacean called a "cremling." Like real maps from the Age of Discovery,

---

* This seemingly backward way of structuring a narrative is surprisingly common in fantasy fiction. Even Brandon has an unpublished "steampunk" manuscript sitting around someplace that was inspired by a map he'd drawn—in this case, a map of the United States with each of the fifty states reimagined as an individual island. The map-first ethos of fantasy novels is also reflected in the genre of fantasy role-playing games like Dungeons & Dragons. At their simplest level, these games consist of one player drawing a map on a piece of graph paper and then everyone sitting down to find out together what adventures the map will inspire.

some are meant to have been drawn by surveyors who actually saw the territory; others aren't.*

"The achievement of a plausible state is not so easy as it might appear," wrote Gelett Burgess in 1902. Burgess was a humorist best remembered today for coining the word "blurb" and writing the poem "The Purple Cow," but he was also an inveterate map geek. "There is nothing so difficult as to create, out of hand, an interesting coast line. Try and invent an irregular shore that shall be convincing, and you will see how much more cleverly Nature works than you."

A video-game designer who moonlights as a fantasy mapmaker, Isaac probably has as much experience testing Burgess's dictum as anyone in the world. A century later, coastlines are still hard. "You wind up doing this seizure thing with your hand, and it doesn't work sometimes," he tells me. Burgess's solution was to spill water on his paper, pound it with his fist, and trace the resulting blotch. Isaac has developed his own tricks of the trade.

"It's funny where I see maps now that I'm looking for them," he says, pulling out his camera phone to show me his library of "found cartography." "Ceiling textures. Clouds. Concrete spills in a road, those are good. They flow out in a way you might not expect." A photo of a rust stain on a wall became an island in Brandon's *Mistborn* series. An aerial view of a vast continent turns out to be a worn spot on a folding chair in a church basement. One picture looks remarkably like the Mediterranean, with verdant green hills and peninsulas surrounding a deep blue sea. It turns out to be guacamole stuck to the lid of a plastic tub. In my mind's eye, I can picture Isaac at his kitchen counter, star-

---

* Our world today is full of oddities that resulted from European surveyors never having visited the territories they mapped. Some are harmless quirks, like Baldwin Street in Dunedin, New Zealand. The world's steepest street, it plunges into the Lindsay Creek valley at a precipitous 35 percent grade—the accidental result of a neat grid laid out by London city planners who had never set foot on the actual terrain. But other colonial relics are less amusing. The nice, straight borders of the new Middle East must have looked lovely on paper when Britain and France carved up the region after World War I, but in practice those somewhat arbitrary lines haven't worked out so well over the last turbulent century.

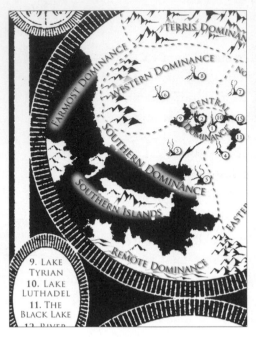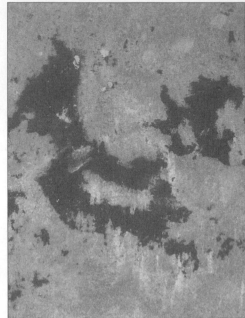

The Southern Islands of the Final Empire . . .
and the rust stain that inspired them

ing dumbfounded at his miniature discovery—like Balboa seeing the Pacific for the first time on that peak in Darien*—and then running for his camera. "Honey, don't put that back in the fridge! *Don't put it back in the fridge!*"

Not every fantasy author feels as strongly about maps as Brandon does. Terry Pratchett includes a map page in every paperback of his popular *Discworld* series of comedy fantasy novels, but the map is always blank. A caption reads, "There are no maps. You can't map a sense of humor." It's true that maps and texts make strange bedfellows sometimes. A map's goal, after all, is to suggest stability and com-

---

* One of the great moments in cartographic history, which John Keats butchered in its most famous retelling. In his sonnet "On First Looking into Chapman's Homer," Keats spends four lines crediting the discovery to "stout Cortez," even though Hernán Cortés never even visited Panama.

pleteness, while literature is all about suggestion, nuance, *not* showing everything.

But that tension hasn't stopped some of my favorite writers from doodling maps of their imaginary settings—and not just in the fantasy ghetto, I'm talking books *without* half-naked barbarian chicks on the cover here. William Faulkner drew his own maps of Yoknapatawpha County; Thomas Hardy sketched Wessex. Even writers who ostensibly create their worlds as philosophical exercises become inordinately fascinated with jots and tittles of cartography. Thomas More's *Utopia* describes the title island in such detail that he's clearly a closet world-building geek, the only canonized Catholic saint I can think of who was so inclined. The first edition even included an addendum on Utopia's alphabet and, of course, a detailed map. Yes, an appendix *and* a map! Epic fantasy readers would be over the moon.

I wonder aloud to Brandon and Isaac if fantasy readers crave immersion as a form of escape because they're dissatisfied in some way with real life. I guess I've wandered a little too close to suggesting that fantasy nerds are all hopeless misfits, and Brandon calls me on it. "Look, I love my life, and I love fantasy. I have no reason to escape my world, but I still like going someplace new. Do people who like to travel hate where they live? When you open a fantasy book and see a map filled with new places, it makes you want to go explore them."

On the flight home from visiting Brandon in Utah, I stare out the window at the Columbia Basin passing slowly beneath me. As the Cascade foothills loom ahead, I see huge trapezoidal holes in the greenery: what looks like virgin forest from the highway is, from the sky, exposed as a patchwork of ugly clear-cuts. I think about what Brandon said about fantasy readers as explorers. Jonathan Swift and Thomas More included maps in their books centuries ago, but fantastic maps didn't really catch on as fetish objects until Tolkien's time, less than a century ago, just as the time of global exploration was wrapping up. The Northwest Passage and the South Pole had fallen by the time *The Hobbit* was released, and Hillary scaled Everest the same year Tolkien drew the maps for *The Fellowship of the Ring*. There were, effectively, no blank spaces left on the map. Maps of the Arctic tundra or Darkest Africa didn't cut it for young adventurers anymore; they had to look elsewhere for new blank spaces to dream about. And so they found Middle-earth, Prydain, Cimmeria, Earthsea, Shannara.

If nothing else, talking to mappers of imaginary worlds has taught me that there's a greater pleasure in maps than mere wayfinding. Austin Tappan Wright never needed to hike his way across Islandia in real life, but that didn't stop him—or his readers—from developing a fanatical devotion to maps of the place. If you never open a map until you're lost, you're missing out on all the fun. As Robert Harbison once wrote, "Nothing seems crasser to a lover of maps than being interested in them only when you travel, like saving poetry for bus rides."

Five or six hundred years ago, there *was* no clear distinction between fantasy maps and "real" ones. As I learned at the antique map fair, medieval mappaemundi regularly depicted fantastic places right alongside real ones: the land of Gog and Magog, from the Book of Revelation, was over by the Caspian Sea somewhere, often surrounded by the wall that, according to legend, Alexander the Great had built to imprison them. The Golden Fleece was drawn near the Black Sea, Noah's ark was in Turkey, and Lot's wife was shown still standing alongside the Dead Sea (as a pillar of salt, of course—you'd think she would have dissolved by now). Paradise was always off to the east somewhere, just over the horizon, surrounded by a ring of fire but still firmly rooted on solid ground.* These maps were expressions of religious devotion, not navigational aids.

Have things really changed that much today? When I browse through an atlas, I'm seeing page after page of places that I've visited exactly as often as I've visited Middle-earth or Narnia: never. Peru, Morocco, Tasmania. Even a road map of my hometown will show me streets that I've never driven, parks I've never visited. I can imagine those places from the map, but that's all it is: my imagination. All maps are fantasy maps, in a way.

---

* In fact, our word "paradise" has a perfectly dull, terrestrial etymology—it comes from the ancient Iranian word "apiri-daeza," meaning a walled garden or estate. Heaven was more concrete then, less ethereal.

A flight attendant announces our descent into Seattle. As the plane dips through a layer of high clouds and the islands of Puget Sound come into view, I find it the easiest thing in the world to imagine these mountains and trees rendered in Tolkien's spidery hand on faded parchment. Or as fractal patches of guacamole on an impossibly blue Tupperware sea.

Chapter 7

RECKONING

['re-kən-iŋ] *n.*: calculation of one's geographic position

Look, the world tempts our eye,
And we would know it all!
We map the starry sky,
We mine this earthen ball.
—MATTHEW ARNOLD

Her name is Lilly Gaskin, and she knows where Turkmeni-
stan and Bolivia and Ghana are. She can point out all these
countries, as well as 130 others, on her wall map of the world,
which probably puts her in the top 99.99th percentile of Americans.
But don't let Lilly's geographical acumen give you an inferiority complex; there are probably plenty of things you can do that she can't.
Like read a book or pee on the potty chair. Lilly is just twenty-one
months old.

Lilly's eight-minute home video has been watched more than five
million times since it was posted on YouTube in 2007. She's the pig-
tailed cutie with big brown eyes who bounces on a crib mattress while
stabbing her index finger confidently at forty-eight different countries
named by her offscreen parents, taking occasional breaks to dance and
clap for herself.

"Where's Mexico?" her mom asks.

"May-hee-coh!" she squeaks happily *en español,* toddling over to
the left side of the map to find it.

She's adorable—cuter than the concentrated extract of a thousand baby koalas, so cute that *Ziggy* and *Family Circus* cartoons spontaneously burst into flame at her mere presence. The wildfire spread of Lilly's Internet video led to appearances on *20/20*, *Rachael Ray*, and *Oprah*. She was a star before even graduating from diapers to pull-ups.

The more suspicious-minded will be asking two questions after seeing Lilly in action. First, what's the trick? And second, what kind of horrific stage parents do this to their little girl?

"We had nothing to do with maps before Lilly did," insists James Gaskin. I've tracked Lilly's family down to Cleveland, Ohio, where her dad is currently working on his PhD in management and information science. Via Skype, I can see the whole family in their living room. Lilly is now four, and she's clambering on the back and arms of the sofa with one of her younger sisters. James and Nikki, their parents, are a young, freshly scrubbed couple straight out of a Clearasil ad or a megachurch youth ministry.

"Once we discovered she could do the things with the maps, she *wanted* to do it," Nikki adds. "It was a game. We would get tired of it *way* before she would get tired of it." In the YouTube video, in fact, you can hear Lilly's parents try to end the game three separate times. "More!" Lilly always insists.

She's always been a prodigious memorizer, say her mom and dad. She's not reading yet, but she knows every word of a hundred or so of her favorite books. But discovering her map ability was an accident. When her beloved uncle Brady headed to Taiwan for two years to serve as a Mormon missionary, Lilly wanted to know where he was. Her parents pointed out Taiwan on a map—and were surprised to find, the next time Lilly saw the map, that she still remembered where Uncle Brady was.

Confirming my intuition that mapheads tend to be gifted spatially, Lilly needs no shortcuts to correctly identify places on the map. "Even when she was just barely two, she could do it on a topographical map, no borders or colors," says James. "She could do it on a tiny globe the size of a golf ball. It's not even the shapes, because she could do landlocked countries like Mongolia."

Lilly's remarkable knack is a powerful argument that geography geeks are born, not made—that some of us come into the world with, in effect, a graticule of latitude and longitude predrawn on the otherwise blank slates of our minds. Her parents have tried the "map game" out on her younger sister, Maggie, as well, but to no avail; their first child was just wired differently. James and Nikki can see why the map game might appeal to Lilly in particular: she's always been a detail-oriented child, prone to noticing—and freaking out—if the power light on the DVD player is left on or the toy cupcakes in her plastic tray are put back in the wrong order. "A little OCD there," admits her dad. "And initially, it was the attention," adds Mom. "She loves the clapping. That really helps her turn on her stuff." Accustomed to just a few pairs of hands clapping for her at home, Lilly seems awestruck in her *Oprah* appearance to have an entire studio full of fans cheering her map skills. Eyes wide, she can barely believe her good fortune.

Lilly will probably grow up to discover, as I did, that such moments of acclaim will be few and far between. As useful and rewarding as map geekery can be, it's rarely honored, or even noticed, by the outside world. But there's one glittering exception that provides a national stage for America's young geography buffs, with millions participating every year: the National Geographic Bee.

In 1988, the National Geographic Society was celebrating its centennial—and, in the wake of the David Helgren–spawned media cycle about map illiteracy, was in the process of refocusing its mission on geography education. Mary Lee Elden, an editor at National Geographic's children's magazine *World,* suggested a geography contest for its readers. The idea snowballed into a nationwide geography competition modeled on the Scripps National Spelling Bee, and the society's board soon approved it as an annual event.

Two decades later, Elden is still coordinating the bee, now a massive event that involves five million participants nationwide. Winnowing a group that size—roughly the entire population of Norway—down to a single winner is a grueling six-month process, of a rigor normally reserved for the selection of Mercury astronauts or Green Berets. Thirteen thousand schools nationwide hold mini-bees each autumn, and the winner of each is given a written test. The hundred top scorers in each state advance to a state-level bee. Finally, the winners from each of the fifty states (as well as the District of Columbia, Guam, Puerto Rico, U.S. Pacific territories, and Department of Defense schools worldwide) are flown to Washington each May to participate in the national bee. They take turns at the microphone through nine preliminary rounds of baffling geography questions, until just the ten highest-scoring finalists remain. These contestants appear in a televised final round ending with the crowning of a lone champion, who receives a $25,000 college scholarship and "lifetime membership in the National Geographic Society." I'm not exactly sure what the latter entails these days, but I bet you get lots of color photos of rain forests and polar bears.

As I step into the Washington Plaza Hotel on a cloudy Wednesday morning, registration has already concluded and the tiled lobby is abuzz with anticipation. Between the koi tank and the closed-off conference rooms that will hold the preliminary matches vibrates a nervous, geographically gifted mass of humanity: fifty-five energetic kids, mostly boys, mostly in striped polo shirts of various colors, mostly heartbreakingly *little*. Each is the nucleus of an excited family unit that doesn't seem to be interacting much with any of the others, beyond sidelong glances. "It sounds like some of the kids have been here many times," one worried-looking grandparent tells her daughter in a low voice. It feels like the mob scene behind the starting line of a marathon. Everyone is waiting for the double doors to open.

Once they do, parents review room assignments and hustle their kids into their respective game rooms. The competitors will be divided into five groups of eleven each for the prelims; each group is asked the same set of questions, and only the top ten scorers overall will advance to tomorrow morning's final. Then I hear a familiar stentorian voice at the end of the hallway, a voice that still makes my pulse rush a little every time I hear it. This isn't puppy love; it's just a mild case of Post-Traumatic Game Show Disorder. My old *Jeopardy!* nemesis Alex Trebek is walking toward me, chatting with bee organizers.

"Hello, Ken!" he says amiably. It's always weird to see Alex out of his usual dapper Perry Ellis getup; today he's wearing a leather jacket and Dad jeans and has a garment bag hoisted over one shoulder. The veteran quiz-show host has emceed the National Geographic Bee finals ever since the event's inception. And he's not just a bored hired gun jetting in for a quick paycheck: Alex is a geography bee *believer*.

"It's not just maps!" he tells me sternly when I tell him I'm writing a book about maps. "That's what we're trying to do here: show people that old-time geography was just maps, but the new geography is all this instead": history, earth science, ecology, economics. He tries on a crazy Jerry Lewis voice to do an impression of U.S. geographic ignorance: "'Uh, France, sure, that's over here, by, uh, Brazil . . .' It would be nice if Americans knew where a country was *before* we went to war with them."

In a downstairs conference room, one group of eleven competitors is meeting their moderator, National Geographic digital media VP Rob Covey. "Work stops at National Geographic every year for the bee," Mary Lee Elden told me. "People gather around monitors to watch." It's a rewarding moment for the society—one of their only chances to see such an enthusiastic young audience for the maps and magazines and TV shows they spend the rest of the year casting out into the void.

"Your first instruction is to relax, if that's possible," Covey says, to uptight parental laughter. The shorter contestants are shown how to lower the microphone stand—there are fourth graders up to eighth graders here, and it's a two-foot swing in height across the great gulf of puberty in some cases. Covey warns them in advance that "England" will not be accepted as a name for the United Kingdom, nor "Holland" for the Netherlands. Oceania is officially a region, not a continent. (This was apparently a point of controversy and protest at a previous bee.) As the eleven boys take their turns at the mike for a practice round, I slip into a folding chair on the room's center aisle. Brian McClendon, who is representing National Geographic's new partner Google at the bee, sits down next to me. He's the VP of engineering for Google's Maps and Earth products, which makes him, among this crowd, something of a sex symbol. There were gasps and whispers of "Yeah!" among the kids in the crowd when he was introduced.

"Okay if I sit here?"

"Sure. This is clearly the fifty-yard line of geography bee seating."

"The Prime Meridian," he corrects me.

"Which country borders more landlocked countries—Algeria or Democratic Republic of the Congo?" Rob Covey is asking the first contestant, Robert Chu of Connecticut. He has fifteen seconds to answer.

"Democratic Republic of the Congo," he replies instantly, with utter confidence. He's correct. My eyebrows shoot up a couple inches. In a heartbeat, he's managed to visualize the borders of two different African nations, *as well as the borders of all their neighbors,* and calculate the answer. The Democratic Republic of Congo beats Algeria by three countries.

The geography bee may have originated as a result of all the face-palm-stupid answers that American students were giving on geography surveys, but the questions in the national bee are far from stupid—they are very, very hard. And fourth graders are acing them. Zimbabwean national parks, Dominican volcanoes, Italian car production statistics, Swazi life expectancy—nothing seems beyond their grasp. "At first you think, 'Oh, that's cute. I bet I can do as well as that,'" says Ted Farnsworth, the father of Arizona contestant Nicholas Farnsworth. "Then you watch the state finals, and you're like—" Here he makes the noise of a slide whistle deflating.

The questions can—in fact, *have to*—be this hard because the kids who make it to nationals are so scrupulously prepared. A few weeks ago I drove out to the exurbs ten miles east of Microsoft's campus in Redmond, Washington, to meet Caitlin Snaring, the impossibly self-possessed high school sophomore who, in 2007, became only the second girl ever to win the bee. But that was Caitlin's second run at the title; the year before, she'd been ousted in the prelims.

"Do you remember the question that you went out on in your first bee?" I asked, knowing she did.

"'What do you call the line of thunderstorms that precedes a cold front?'" she recited verbatim. (Caitlin says she has a "near-photographic" memory.) I didn't know the answer either: a squall line.

"It's not technically a physical geography term," she grumbled, apparently still stung by the loss. "It's just something sailors say. But I was really disappointed. I thought that would be my only chance." After the loss, she cried, briefly, and gave her mom, Traci, a hard time for never having found her a copy of the out-of-print *National Geographic Almanac*, which, it turned out, had included the crucial fact.

"We talked about how hard the questions were going to be, and how hard it was going to be on TV under the pressure," remembered Traci. "I said, 'Do you want to do this again, or don't you?' The next day she had a list of more books she wanted me to buy for her, ready to study. She wanted to do it all over again."

For two years, Caitlin spent six or seven hours a day doing nothing but studying geography. No days off, no weekends off. She always had a book or a map in her lap—in the backseat of the car, on the bleachers at her younger brother's baseball games. She filled ten three-ring binders with lists—mountains, islands, cities on rivers—and used colored markers to mark locations on hundreds of maps. She always prepared two copies: one with labels and one without, so she could test herself flash card–style. Traci remembered Caitlin advancing across the map like Napoleon's army, country by country: "One week she'd focus on, say, India, and we would just check out every book about India in the library, looking for anything new." The phrase "anything new" strikes me as funny: Caitlin's geography knowledge had become so comprehensive that she was literally *running out of new facts to study!**

She studied smarter as well as harder. Her previous year's bee experience had allowed her to analyze National Geographic's question style, and she began to see patterns. So she bought videotapes of every previous bee final and made a database of every question asked. (Having worked out a very similar regimen before going on *Jeopardy!*, I am probably one of the very few people in the world who could nod appreciatively at this story without inwardly thinking, "What a nut!")

---

* There's a confidence that comes from studying a subject so completely. When Caitlin was asked, in her second bee, which country is West Africa's leading producer of bauxite, she didn't even break a sweat, because she'd made a list of the natural resources of *every single country in the world*. (The answer is Guinea, but I'm sure you knew that.)

She made checklists of places and topics that hadn't come up in a while, figuring they had a better chance of appearing next year. She traded tips online with fellow bee veterans: track down an Australian atlas called *Geographica,* they said, or a children's atlas published by Dorling Kindersley. When she realized that lots of bee questions came from *National Geographic* magazine, she began annotating every issue in highlighter. On the plane to D.C. for her big rematch, she came across a mention of the fishing fleet on the Italian island of Lampedusa and neatly marked it in yellow pen. Sure enough, a Lampedusa question popped up in the finals. Right on schedule.

Caitlin breezed through her second bee without missing a single question. In her final showdown against Suneil Iyer of Kansas, the fifth question asked for the capital of imperial Vietnam. She wrote "Hue" and could tell from the time that Suneil was taking that he was writing something much, much longer ("Ho Chi Minh City"). "I'm looking up at Alex, because he's looking at both our answers. He looks at Suneil's, and he's like, hmm." Caitlin mimicked a Trebekian scowl. "Then he looks at mine, and he looks at me . . . and he winks. I was like, *whoa!*"

I was a little jealous. Alex Trebek *never* winked at me.

After themed rounds on current events, wildlife, and medicine, I head upstairs to the Diplomat Room to watch a different cohort of young geographers. Representing Washington State at this year's bee is none other than Benjamin Salman, the boy with a whole country in his head. He's up first in each round and stands at the microphone smiling placidly, with his arms folded. He hasn't missed a question yet—he knows where Dagestan is, where vicuñas live, the largest city in North Africa. (Spoilers: Russia, Peru, Cairo.) Since each player is asked a different question in each round, there's an element of chance underlying the skill. "You'll hear everybody else's questions and think, 'That's such an easy question!'" Caitlin told me. "But then it comes to you, and it'll be the only one you didn't know." One player in this round is asked to identify the country where there's fighting going on in Ramadi and Fallujah (Iraq; you may have heard about it), but the next one needs to locate Hyesan, capital of the Yanggang Province. (Hyesan is a minor industrial city in North Korea, making this a very hard question indeed.) It's the luck of the draw.

Of course, all questions are easy if you know them and hard if you don't. Benjamin knows that Majuro is the capital of the Marshall Islands, which impresses the heck out of me, but records his first miss when he says that karst landscapes are shaped by volcanic activity, not water erosion. But everybody, it seems, has some blind spot here: Eric Yang of Texas misses a question on Japan's Mount Asama, and Henry Glitz of Pennsylvania misses his question in the dreaded analogies round, which contestants shiver and tell ghost stories about. Even for the map-inclined, this round really is a nightmare; imagine if your SAT test was full of questions like

Kafue : Zambezi :: Shyok : _____

Henry says "Mekong," but the correct answer is "Indus." (The Shyok River is a tributary of the Indus, just as the Kafue River flows into the Zambezi.) There are no perfect scores left in the group now; Benjamin might still have a chance.

There's definitely one nerd here who's way out of his league, and that's me. I figured I was a guy with plenty of geolove and quiz-show experience to boot under his belt—surely I could hang with sixth-graders, right? But no, two or three times each round, I'll be stumped by a question that a bee player will quickly answer in a confident little voice that hasn't even changed yet. The Qizilqum Desert is in Uzbekistan! Guanabara used to be a state of Brazil! I feel like Richard Dreyfuss, surrounded by all those superadvanced Munchkin aliens at the end of *Close Encounters.**

After the preliminary rounds are over, there's a logjam at the top

---

* I was expecting this, though. After seeing firsthand the obsessive study tactics of Caitlin Snaring, I proposed a geography contest: her and me, mano a mano, *Jeopardy!* megachamp versus high school sophomore. Despite not having studied geography for two years, Caitlin took me up on it. I gave her a list of the twenty toughest geography questions that I'd been asked on various TV shows, assuming I could give her a run for her money. She didn't just beat me; she demolished me nineteen points to eight.

of the standings: eleven players are competing for the last seven spots in the finals. I hurry downstairs to the tiebreak round so I can cheer on Benjamin Salman—who has history on his side. The Washington champ has won the National Geographic Bee more times than any other state: five overall, one out of every four events in the bee's history. When I asked Caitlin to explain this remarkable track record, she credited the rainy weather. "Kids here are prone to stay inside more," she said, "and if you're inside, you might as well look at a few maps!"—as if this were the most obvious thing in the world. Who would watch TV or play video games when you could look at maps?

An eager crowd has crammed into the hotel ballroom to watch the tiebreaker, wisps of it spilling out into the hallway beyond. I'm craning my neck to try to see the players at the front of the room as the moderator begins the first question.

"Southeast Asia's only member of OPEC, an organization of oil-producing countries, suspended its membership last year because it had become a net importer of oil rather than a net producer. Name this country."

Indonesia! I know this one. I try to beam Indonesian vibes in Benjamin's direction. After fifteen seconds, the contestants reveal the answers they've written. Benjamin wrote "Malaysia," eliminating himself from the finals, but he doesn't betray any disappointment, walking stoically off the stage. But the eleven-year-old from Nevada who also missed the question looks stricken, almost sick. He bursts into tears on the way back to his seat and buries his head in his dad's shoulder.

This boy isn't much older than my own son, so his heartbreak is almost intolerably hard for me to watch. All fifty-five of these kids have put untold hours of preparation into the event. They may be the geographically brightest bulbs in the country, but that doesn't matter: fifty-four of them are going to end up bounced because they missed a question, and they're going to remember that question for the rest of their lives. Is this really a lofty educational exercise? Isn't it more like, well, child abuse?

"Do you ever think, no geography is worth this?" I ask Mary Lee Elden after the match.

"I think they learn something from it," she says. "Yes, they feel disappointed, but they learn to handle their disappointment." The bee, as you might expect, attracts more than its share of kids with Asperger syndrome and other social interaction issues, and these kids are particularly prone to losing control after a tough loss. "I'll be honest with you," says Mary Lee. "As a teacher and a parent, I don't think I'd put my child through it."

But the organizers do what they can to soothe crushed dreams and bruised egos. Contestants eliminated in the finals get to decompress in a backstage greenroom with milk and cookies and staff members telling them how great they were. Children may feel life's setbacks more keenly than adults, but they also bounce back quicker. "It happens every year," laughs Mary Lee. "I have to send somebody back there because they start having a party and they get a little loud, and you start hearing them from outside."

Parents aren't allowed in the cookie room, and that's not an accident. At the start of every bee, Mary Lee sends the students ahead into a reception and asks their parents to stay behind for a moment. "I give them a little talk, saying that they're there to support their children. This is their children's contest, not theirs." The yearly lecture is a result of past run-ins with the atlas-cramming equivalent of high-pressure Little League dads. "I once had a father go up to a young boy after the preliminary rounds and start yelling at him: how could he get this wrong, and why didn't he make the finals? It just tore my heart. I went up and took the boy away from his father and said, 'Let's go over here.' They lose perspective, that their child is just doing the best they can. Just give them a hug and tell them they're wonderful."

That afternoon I hop aboard one of a flotilla of buses parked in front of the hotel. The bee weekend isn't all questions and answers: the day before the prelims, the contestants and their parents get a tour of Washington, and the night before the finals, there's always a picnic. Most of the kids can relax, with the bee finally behind them; for the ten finalists, it's a chance to blow off a little steam before tomorrow's baptism by fire: more of the same brain-straining questions, only now with the added stress of TV cameras and Alex Trebek.

Vansh Jain of Wisconsin and Shiva Kangeyan of Florida, sitting behind me, are among tomorrow's batch of finalists, and they're talking shop. "Is the lowest point in Africa in Djibouti?" Vansh asks. "Yes!" comes a unanimous chorus of replies. The conversation moves on to the tides in the Bay of Fundy.

They all seem lively and relaxed, whether they're finalists like Vansh and Shiva or nearly-made-its like their friend across the aisle, South Dakota's Alex Kimn. They're not sitting with their parents anymore, and the contrast to the high-strung little huddles in the hotel lobby this morning is remarkable. This is band-of-brothers camaraderie, this is furlough from the parental grind.

"So were you guys nervous today?" I turn around to ask.

There is general scorn. "I think being nervous is funny," says Alex.

"What about your parents? Are they more nervous than you?"

"*Oh,* yes." "Yes yes yes!" "Definitely."

I'm sitting next to Doug Oetter, the geography professor who helps run the Georgia state bee. Seeing students *excel* at geography is a pleasant switch for him. "My college students are geeked out to the max," he says—proficient, thanks to AP exams, in genetics, cell structure, amino acids, electron shells. "But you ask them about basic geography or earth science—cumulus clouds or biomes—and they're clueless. I literally have to start with longitude and latitude. They don't know what causes the changing of the seasons, or the tides." Just like ancient civilizations creating legends about pomegranates and things to explain natural phenomena, I think. Except that these kids probably don't care that they don't know.

Academic geographers actually criticized the idea of the bee when National Geographic first announced it, sure that it would hurt the prestige of geography to reduce it to the status of mere facts, spelling-bee fodder. "Rote memorization must be emphasized as the level of competitive difficulty increases," predicted Marc Eichen of Queens College in one geography journal. "The geographic facts would need to become increasingly trivial to produce a winner."

But Oetter disagrees. You can't write without learning the alphabet first, he says, and you can't do sophisticated work in geography if you don't know where places are. "These kids are going to show up in college already knowing that alphabet. They're going to write the geographic novels of tomorrow."

Behind us, tomorrow's scholars are currently trying to figure out which way the bus is headed, with the help of Shiva's compass watch. There is also some disagreement on the identity of the world's leading gold producer. "South Africa! No, China. Yeah, yeah, China."(Correct. China passed South Africa in 2008.)

Encouraged by how quickly the kids on the bus seem to have decompressed, I track down Benjamin Salman's mom, Sarah, at the picnic. She's balancing a plate of barbecue on one knee.

"How'd he take it?" I ask.

"He's okay," says Sarah. "He was disappointed, but now it's okay."

The picnic is held every year at a bucolic farm in rural Maryland. As the sun sinks toward the oak-and-hickory forest to the west of the picnic grounds, gaggles of kids are running around in the grass. When they're not squirming behind a National Geographic microphone, it's easy to believe Mary Lee Elden's contention that "these are normal kids who just happen to be bright." There are games of horseshoes and pickup basketball going on. Kenji Golimlim, a finalist from the Detroit area, might be the shortest contestant in the bee—he barely comes up to my elbow, and I'm not a tall man—but I watch him happily shoot hoops on a ten-foot rim for quite a while. Most of these kids just met a day or two ago, but they seem to be fast friends already.

Beyond the pressure of the competition, it's geography that welds them together. "People here understand what I'm talking about," one boy tells me happily. "They're people I can have geographical conversations with!" In this crowd, you don't have to roll your eyes at Mom when she mentions the geography bee in front of your friends—it's okay to be a maphead. Here, geography can even be an icebreaker. I overhear one of tomorrow's finalists, Nicholas Farnsworth, meeting Roey Hadar, who represents New Jersey.

"Ah, you're from New Jersey! Newark is its largest city. Population 273,000, last I saw."

"High Point in Sussex County is 1,803 feet," Roey replies. This sounds like the beginning of a beautiful friendship.

William Johnston, representing Mississippi, is a sixth-grader with a wide grin and a rite-of-passage bowl cut. "He invents countries where they play this imaginary game called plonk," his mother tells me. "He spends months making up islands." I make a mental note to introduce him to Benjamin. Until this weekend, William's never really fit in with other kids. At his school, students can pass out birthday party invitations in class only if everyone has been invited. "Well, that's the only time he ever got invited to a birthday party," she sighs. "He's just . . . different. But here he's gotten some recognition, and it has been *great*."

Like his fellow competitors, William is a detail-conscious kid, the kind who, even at two or three years old, needed to have all his Matchbox cars lined up just so. "Little things upset him," says his mom. "When Pluto was declared not a planet, he was just devastated."

This is an important clue, I think, into the mind of a map-mad child. When I was young, maps represented stability to me in a turbulent world. No matter how traumatized I felt by starting a new school or moving to a new city or something scary on TV,* all the places I knew still looked the same in an atlas. To this day, I'm thrown for a loop when maps change; I'll expect it to be front-page news when Palau declares independence or Calcutta decides to start spelling its name "Kolkata." In all my old geography trivia books, it was an article of faith that the highest wind speed ever recorded on the planet was 231 miles per hour, during a freak April storm on New Hampshire's Mount Washington in 1934. I was recently shocked to learn that the old record had been shattered by twenty miles per hour during an Australian cyclone in 1996. Appallingly, the reading sat unseen in a computer log for fourteen years before scientists realized they had a new record on their hands! In my view, that cyclone should have been

---

* The terrifying TV of my Reagan-era childhood was all related to nuclear war—*The Day After*, of course, but also this one episode of the sitcom *Benson* in which the cast prepares for Armageddon in a bunker under the governor's mansion. I am the only person in the world who still has nightmares about *Benson*.

breaking news on CNN. How is it that the fundamental parameters of the universe are changing and no one cares but me?*

To young eyes, maps do more than offer a vision of permanence. They also reduce the messy world to something that kids can understand—even, in a way, possess. For centuries, maps have been used as a symbol of human mastery over the world. When I visited Rome a few years ago, I was transfixed by the intricate frescoes of Italian and papal provinces in the Vatican's Gallery of Maps. Each tree in every forest was separately drawn in receding profile, like Tolkien's Mirkwood. I later learned that Renaissance-era popes used the hall as an anteroom—while waiting for an audience with His Holiness, visitors were meant to be pondering the extent of his earthly influence, as well as his heavenly leverage. The round orb that traditionally accompanies the scepter and other regalia in a monarch's crown jewels is a symbol of the globe, reminding subjects that their king or queen *literally* holds the whole world in his or her hands.† In the twentieth century, a newly independent country would proudly publish its own national atlas as a sign that it had shrugged off the shackles of colonialism.

---

* Well, I'm not the only one who feels a little bit of vertigo when maps change, as London transport officials learned in 2009. The "tube map" of the London Underground was created in 1931 by the engineer Harry Beck, who was inspired by diagrams of electric circuits to create a map that was schematically but not geographically accurate and was paid all of five pounds for his troubles. The map has become part of the fabric of London life, appearing on countless T-shirts, coffee mugs, umbrellas, and so on, and in 2006 was voted the second best design in British history (the Concorde came out on top). The last time the city revised the map, it decided it could do without the pale blue line representing the Thames River—do you really need to know where the river is when you're riding a train?—and erased it. It was thoroughly unprepared for the resulting outcry, as Londoners reacted as if the actual river itself had been dammed. A BBC News editor compared the move to "removing the smile from the Mona Lisa." London Mayor Boris Johnson, in New York on business when the change was made, was furious. "Can't believe that the Thames disappeared off the tube map whilst I was out of the country! It will be reinstated," he tweeted to his constituents. Maps change, of course—the globe in my office doesn't have Yugoslavia on it, let alone Pangaea—but we rely on them to pretend at all times that they don't.

† The Swedish crown jewels, however, are the only ones that include an orb with *actual continents* enameled on it, perhaps a signal of Sweden's secret desire for world domination.

Whether you're King Louis XVI or a bewildered modern-day seventh-grader, maps provide that same sense of confidence and ownership, that God's-eye vantage on the world. Lilly Gaskin likes playing with maps, but she doesn't really know yet that they represent places. These kids do know, and that's what sharpens their enthusiasm. "On a map, you can see the whole expanse, even though you're only in one part of it," Caitlin Snaring told me. "You know where you're going next." Mary Lee Elden has noticed that the best geography bee contestants often come from small towns. The kids from Manhattan or L.A. or Washington already think the world revolves around them; it's the ones from Minocqua, Wisconsin, or Flagstaff, Arizona, who are so ravenously driven to connect to the faraway places they see on maps.

At the picnic, the light is almost gone, the cookies are almost gone, and the bee parents gather up their kids. The last thing I see before I board my bus back to D.C. is William Johnston and Benjamin Salman, the two architects of imaginary nations, walking together in the twilight, their heads down, talking seriously and animatedly to each other. I have a feeling that the game of plonk is about to arrive on the shores of Alambia.

I expect to hear the familiar National Geographic TV trumpet fanfare the next morning as I walk through the doors of the society's headquarters between L and M Streets. That's how "National Geographic" the lobby is: big wise yellow rectangles looming above me on the window glass like the monolith in *2001,* a bathysphere and a sculpture of a silverback gorilla on exhibit to my right, Egyptian hieroglyphics and coral reef photos on the elevator doors. The hall outside Grosvenor Auditorium,* where the finals will be held, has a ceiling pricked with artificial stars, re-creating the constellations as they appeared on the night of January 27, 1888, when the society was founded.

I take a moment to chat with the parents of Eric Yang of Texas,

---

* Named for Gilbert Grosvenor, the son-in-law of Alexander Graham Bell, who was the first editor of *National Geographic* magazine.

who made an early mistake in Benjamin Salman's room during the prelims but bounced back to make the finals. A decade ago, the Yangs emigrated from Singapore, where, I tell them, my family once lived. His mom, Aileen, takes the opportunity to brag about her evidently well-balanced son: he plays jazz piano, earned a 2200 on his SATs at age thirteen, and made the state swimming team. He reads cookbooks obsessively, she says, but doesn't like to cook much. He dreams of someday going to Belgium. Eric stands by impassively while his litany of accomplishments is paraded before me.

"Your son seems pretty calm," I tell Aileen.

"We say he's a cucumber!" she agrees, presumably in the "cool-as-a" sense, unless this is some Singaporean vegetable metaphor of which I'm unaware.

"Are you all nervous about the finals?" I ask Aileen.

She shakes her head. "He says, 'Mom, I don't have to be a winner. Winning is a blessing.'"

As I make my way to my seat, I'm stopped by another proud finalist parent, Lorena Golimlim, whose son Kenji was the four-foot-nothing basketball player I'd watched the night before. "Kenji! Can you recite the first two hundred digits of pi for Ken?" He does, with relish.

Apart from Nicholas Farnsworth of Arizona and Kennen Sparks of Utah, all today's finalists are Asian American, mostly of South Asian descent. This isn't unexpected; Indian American culture so values this kind of educational success that a nonprofit called the North South Foundation has organized an elaborate farm system for Indian bee nerds, holding mock spelling bees, geography bees, and math Olympiads through its seventy-odd chapters nationwide. A more troublesome demographic challenge for National Geographic is the fact that all ten finalists—and fifty-three of the fifty-five national contestants this year—are boys. Only Alaska and Wyoming, the two least populous states in the last census, are represented by girls.

At the picnic, I asked Wyoming's Kirsi Anselmi-Stith about the disparity, which she chalked up to the social pressures of her age. She shrugged. "The girls are in makeup by now," she said. "It's not cool to be a geographer."

"Is it hard being one of the only girls?"

She grinned. "No, it's more entertaining. When we walk in the room, everyone gets quiet." An athletic seventh grader with long blond hair, Kirsi certainly seemed to be getting her share of attention at the picnic. All night she was orbited by five or six boys a head shorter than her, a nervous jumble of orthodontia and Adam's apples.

The "map gap" between men and women is, of course, a staple of gender debate in our culture, the focus of countless unfunny stand-up routines and syndicated columns about men who refuse to ask for directions or women who can't find the right highway on the road atlas.* But in recent years the issue has moved from the Ray Romano/Erma Bombeck sphere into the laboratories of cognitive psychology, with real scrutiny being given to the question of whether (and why) women and men navigate and read maps differently.

In 1995, after boys had won six of the first seven geography bees, National Geographic commissioned two Penn State professors, Lynn Liben and Roger Downs, to study the reasons girls were underperforming. They hoped to find the usual anodyne reasons for a performance gap of this kind: that boys were more competitive or girls more anxious or the questions somehow biased. Instead, the results were a little more troubling.

"Boys as a group *do* have a little more knowledge about geography than girls as a group," admits Liben. She hastens to add that a field of fifty-three boys and just two girls does *not* mean that boys are twenty-six times better than girls—just that "very tiny" differences tend to get magnified by the bee format of slicing off the top finisher at each of several tiers.

My immediate assumption is that the root of the achievement gap is spatial ability. Tests on gender and navigation have found that women tend to navigate via landmarks ("I turn left when I get to the gas station") whereas men use dead reckoning ("I still need to be north and maybe a little west of here"), which ties in nicely with the evolutionary perspective: early men went out on hunting expeditions in

---

* The author Deborah Tannen says that this is the topic she's most often asked about from her 1990 best seller on intergender communication, *You Just Don't Understand.*

all directions and always needed to be good at finding their way back to the cave, developing their "kinesic memory," while women foraged for edibles closer to home, developing "object location memory." Simply put, men got better at finding places, while women got better at finding things. Fast forward twenty thousand years, and I exasperate my wife by not being able to see my car keys even when they're sitting on the dresser right in front of me. Meanwhile, I laugh at her tendency to turn a map upside down if it's not facing the "right" way. "Mindy, turning the map doesn't actually rearrange the symbols on it in any way," I will say, rolling my eyes, while she ignores me and silently ponders what a divorce settlement would look like now that we live in a community-property state. But many, many other people are map-turner-upside-downers just like she is. In 1998, John and Ashley Sims invented an upside-down map that would make southward travel easier for non–mental rotators like Mindy. A series of male map executives turned the idea down before a woman heard about it, immediately saw the appeal, and signed on. Three hundred thousand upside-down maps have since been sold.* I wonder if the same factors account for the sudden omnipresence of GPS navigation in cars and smart phones: finally, ladies, a map that will turn itself upside down automatically while you turn! I tend to switch our GPS to the other map view—you know, the one where north actually stays north while you drive—which annoys my wife when she next hops into the car. It's the cartographic equivalent of leaving the toilet seat up.

The biological gap "is not huge, but it's there," Liben confirms. "It's maybe *the* only remaining cognitive difference between boys and girls." But she cautions that any number of societal factors could be causing those small differences to snowball. "We know that boy babies are tossed around more than girl babies. Boys are allowed to ride their bicycles farther than girls are—we know they explore more. These are the kinds of things that are going to increase your environmental knowledge, the chance that you can look at a map and figure out how to get somewhere." These little environmental nudges can last all

---

* Ashley Sims went on to invent "Jellyatrics," a popular British variety of "gummi"-type candy in which the sweets look like—you guessed it—old people.

through life. Liben points out that even in an age when two work-ing spouses are often equal partners in cooking, shopping, and house-keeping, the family car is the last bastion of 1950s gender roles: men nearly always drive. This isn't true in our car—when we go someplace together, Mindy often ends up behind the wheel. Of course, that's only because she'd rather be the driver than the one stuck with reading the map, so I haven't exactly disproved Liben's point.

For her part, Mary Lee Elden thinks the aptitude gap is small enough that it can be closed with outreach. "It's a matter of interest level," she says. "How can we get more girls interested?" She points to the campaign, twenty years ago, to attract women to medicine. "Fifty-one percent of medical school students are now women. The big push was 'Girls, you can do it.' Well, I think the same thing for geography. We just need to tell the girls they can win it too."

The ten finalists, now all dressed in matching blue shirts with a National Geographic Bee logo, are seated in two tiers at the left side of the auditorium stage, which has been decorated for the occasion with a dramatically lit map of the seven continents set against a grid of blue translucent squares reminiscent of the *Jeopardy!* set. Out strides Alex Trebek to complete the game-show illusion. "These ten finalists," says the forty-year quiz veteran, "are about to dazzle everyone with their knowledge of the Earth and everything on it and in it." Besides the $25,000 giant check, this year's champion will also win a cruise—not the fun, frivolous *Wheel of Fortune* kind of cruise, of course, but a soberly educational filmstrip of a cruise: a visit to the Galápagos Islands with Alex Trebek himself aboard! But National Geographic has judged its target demographic correctly: the ten finalists bounce excitedly in their seats at this announcement.

After the first round, Alex takes a minute to chat with each of the contestants in turn. The mini-interviews on *Jeopardy!* are so cringe-inducing that many viewers TiVo right through them, but these ten kids are charming and genuine. Alex, a father of two himself, seems perfectly at ease and much warmer than usual as he chats with them. There are some signs of nerves—Vansh Jain's little cheeks puffing in and out, Zaroug Jaleel rocking from side to side—but for the most part, the kids seem remarkably poised, with none of the unpredictable, outsized personalities I remember from National Spelling Bee coverage. All seem to have charmingly old-timey hobbies: stamp collecting, chess, archery, ballroom dancing. Arjun Kandaswamy of Oregon, the most mature-seeming of the boys, describes his Eagle Scout project, and Shiva Kangeyan blithely banters with Alex about models of World War II–era planes.

The second round opens with a National Geographic employee wheeling out a Chinese mime made up as a terra-cotta warrior, so that Alex can ask a question about China's Shaanxi Province. Caitlin Snaring had warned me about this.

"At nationals, they bring out objects to distract you! 'This is the tool they use to fork out people's brains in Fiji!' So you don't pay attention to that." The visual aids range from ancient artifacts to live animals—penguins, maybe, or armadillos. Last year, a nervous kookaburra caused some excitement by leaving a little souvenir onstage during its brief appearance.

"Well, they use them to entertain the audience," her mom had explained. This less sinister explanation hadn't even occurred to Caitlin. Anything that interrupted her laserlike focus *was the enemy*!

Kennen Sparks of Utah and Zaroug Jaleel of Massachusetts both misidentify the major river of Shaanxi Province as the Yangtze (it's the Yellow). Then, two rounds later, they both miss questions on archaeological sites, making them the first two finalists to be eliminated. I notice, during this round, that the questions the kids struggle with aren't always the ones you expect. Shantan Krovvidi of North Carolina earns a strike for not knowing that Salisbury is the closest city to Stonehenge, while Kennen goes out for guessing that the largest city in the West Bank is Jerusalem. (It's actually Hebron.) These are reasonably well-known bits of cultural literacy, but the kids blank on them, even as they nail much harder questions about the Turkish city of Izmir or the islands of Vanuatu. Their knowledge has come from a firehose blast of atlases and encyclopedias, not a lifetime of travel and media. It isn't lived in, like ours.

A Smithsonian curator enters, holding a gorilla skull for the kids to ignore while they're asked for the name of the East African chain of volcanoes in which mountain gorillas live. Four boys fail to come up with the name of the Virunga Mountains, including Siva Gangavarapu, who—heartbreakingly—wrote "Virunga Mts" on his card, then crossed it out and began to write "Rwenzori" as time expired. Each time someone walks offstage, the pace of play accelerates, the next round becoming just a little bit shorter. Suddenly, half the seats are empty.

The next three rounds of questions eliminate one contestant apiece, in the orderly manner of a children's counting rhyme. ("Ten Little Indian Americans"?) Kenji's little Auto-Tuned chirp of a voice, so reliable in earlier rounds, is unable to identify Mexicali, Mexico, in his allotted twelve seconds, and then there were four. Ten-year-old Vansh doesn't know that Clew Bay is in Ireland, and then there were three. Finally, in the tenth round, Shantan is stumped on the name of a Bulgarian port city. After his incorrect guess, he looks to his left: Eric Yang hasn't missed a single question, but Arjun and Shantan each entered the round with one strike against them. If Arjun misses his question as well, Shantan will get a new lease on life and could still make the finals.

"Arjun, which South American country has phased out its former currency, the sucre, and adopted the United States dollar as its official currency?"

Arjun bites his lip. "Ecuador?" he tries.

"Ecuador is right!" announces Alex. Arjun lowers his head and pumps his fists quietly. Shantan has just won the third-place prize, a $10,000 scholarship, but he still looks awfully unsatisfied as he turns off his mike and rises to walk into the wings. He was so close.

The two finalists, Eric and Arjun, switch seats for the finals. Alex will stand at a lectern between them on the lower tier as they each use paper cards to write answers to the same questions. Whoever answers more of the five final questions correctly is the champion.

"The so-called winning question every year is actually a *losing* question," explains Anders Knospe, sitting in the audience next to me. Anders signed quite a few autographs in his Bozeman, Montana, middle school after winning the 1994 bee; he's returned fifteen years later to reminisce and say hi to Mary Lee Elden and other bee organizers. He came down on the train from Yale, where he's finishing up a PhD in physics.

"Look how calm they are," I say. Grown men have been known to faint dead away from the stress of competing on *Jeopardy!*, but these middle schoolers have come through the quiz crucible with flying colors. Eric, on Alex's left, has stayed perfectly poker-faced—aloof, even—through the entire finals. The cucumber, just like his parents said. Arjun has been more antsy throughout, a little more the awkward adolescent than the other nine finalists, exhaling visibly with relief in the tenth round when he stayed alive with a wild guess of Bogotá, Colombia, as the home of Plaza Bolívar. But now he too is staring at the paper in front of him with stony concentration.

Anders shakes his head. "I'm sure they're very nervous," he whispers, remembering his own final matchup. "I don't know why I remember this, but there was a bead of sweat running from my shoulder all the way down my arm."

"If you're ready to go, here is question number one," Alex begins. "Slavonia and Dalmatia are historic regions located in which present-day country?"

It's one of the former Yugoslav republics, I know, but which one? Serbia? Croatia? Bosnia?

"Put your cards up," prompts Alex. "The correct response is the one you have written down, Croatia. You are tied, one apiece. Here's the next question. What is the local name given to the katabatic winds in southern France that can cause damage to crops in the Rhone Valley?"

Eric and Arjun both wrote "mistral." "You are right once again," says Alex. "This is going to be fun, isn't it, folks? You can tell already."

Sure enough, the round ends with neither finalist having missed a single question. They know that Kandy is in Sri Lanka; Zaragoza, Spain, on the Ebro; and Sochi, Russia, on the Black Sea. Alex pulls out a sheaf of tiebreaker questions. The first wrong answer now will end the bee.

"Located northwest of Qatar, Sitrah is a port city in what oil-exporting island country?" Eric's parents are sitting in front of Arjun's in the audience to my left. The Yangs seem as tranquil as their son.

The Kandaswamys are also motionless, but they're sitting up ramrod straight with wide eyes, as if slightly aghast at the proceedings.

Eric pauses a moment before writing his answer, but both come up with "Bahrain," so the final extends to a seventh question. "Akimiski Island is the largest island in a bay that also marks the southernmost extent of the territory of Nunavut. Name this bay." Neither boy is suckered into answering "Hudson Bay"; both know that it's James Bay.

The auditorium is silent; never before have so many people been so interested in the waterways of Nunavut. "You still have enough cards there?" asks Alex, smiling. "Yes? Good."

Question eight. "Timiș County shares its name with a tributary of the Danube and is located in the western part of which European country?" There is a long pause this time before the Sharpies begin squeaking. Is it Hungary? The finalists seem just as unsure as I am.

There's a low buzz from the spectators as the answers are revealed. "We notice that the boys have not come up with the same response this time," says Alex dramatically. Arjun's card says "Hungary," which was my guess. Eric has written "Romania."

Arjun is staring up at Alex as if he were about to impart some secret religious truth; Eric is staring fixedly ahead. "The country is Romania!" announces Alex. "Eric Yang, you are the 2009 National Geography Bee champion!"

The crowd erupts in applause. Arjun shakes his head bitterly into the palm of his right hand. "What a final!" marvels Alex. "What a final. Yes indeed." Eric makes the smallest fist pump I've ever seen, a matter of millimeters, and then rests his chin on one knuckle, allowing a secretive smile to cross his face for the first time all day.

Aileen Yang is still crying fifteen minutes later, as I come up to congratulate them through the throng of newspaper reporters hoping for a quote from the champ.

"Eric, did you know Romania?" I ask.

"It was an educated guess," he admits. He tried to picture the terrain of central Europe—where tributaries of the Danube were likely to arise, which way they might run. I'm impressed. He wasn't just regurgitating place-names, as the bee's critics have claimed. He had a very deep knowledge of the region.

"How did it feel to win?" I want to know.

"It was pretty big," he says quietly. "A major milestone." Understated to the last.

I didn't realize how badly I needed to meet the fifty-five bee kids until I watched them in action. After decades of news stories about young people stymied by simple maps, I had generalized their message into this not-unreasonable conclusion: all Americans suck at geography. It was therapeutic for me to see firsthand that some kids are still as map-crazy as I was, that the future might actually be in pretty good hands. "That's what I like about the bee, that it's the good news about education," says Mary Lee Elden. "A lot of what you read in the paper is so negative. We need to reward kids who are doing well in academics. These kids aren't going to get the football trophy or the basketball trophy, but they have something to offer the world, a lot to offer the world. And we should reward them."

Success at the National Geographic Bee is a surprisingly accurate way to predict kids who will go on to do extraordinary things. Anders's particle physics work at Yale is only the tip of the iceberg. Susannah Batko-Yovino, the first girl to win the bee, is now a doctor doing cancer research at the University of Maryland. Kyle Haddad-Fonda, who won in 2001, is studying Chinese-Egyptian relations at Harvard, and just earned a Rhodes scholarship. Caitlin Snaring's goal is even loftier: she's going to be secretary of state someday, she announced on the *Today* show. An autographed photo of Condoleezza Rice arrived in the Snaring mailbox in short order, as did a congratulatory letter from the president.

"But the spelling bee kids got to *meet* President Bush," Caitlin's mom tut-tutted as we looked at her framed souvenir. That was the first but not the last time I became aware of the uneasy inferiority complex that geography bee people have regarding the Scripps National Spelling Bee. They tend to get upset that a contest of *spelling*, of all things, gets more prestige and attention than geography, a subject that—unlike spelling—is actually taught beyond the fifth grade, important in adult life, and unable to be easily automated by your word processor or e-mail client.

At the postfinals luncheon, even Alex Trebek reveals his secret spelling bee envy. "No one's asked me to speak, but I'm going to speak anyway," he says, leaning back in his chair. After a few glasses of Chardonnay, he's expansive, telling the room about his basement full of *National Geographic* magazines, which he rereads endlessly. "I don't mean to put down the spelling bee, but if the spelling bee can get prime time on ABC, we're better than they are. We're more interesting and broader in scope. My gosh, we should have a prime-time show like that."

But whether the public ever catches on or not, Alex's plans are to host the bee in perpetuity. "I'll keep doing it till they have to wheel me out like the terra-cotta man," he vows.

In ten years, who knows? Maybe he'll be handing the giant check to YouTube's Lilly Gaskin on national television. Just imagine the applause she'll hear then.

Chapter 8

MEANDER

[mē-ˈan-dər] *n.*: a sinuous bend in a river or other watercourse

You have to fly around the world all day
to keep the sun upon your face.
—STEPHEN MERRITT

The oldest surviving road atlases were designed to keep people from having to go anywhere at all. When a medieval cartographer like Matthew Paris drew beautifully illuminated maps of holy places and the roads that led there, he was largely targeting an audience of his fellow monks, who would pore over every step of the journey without ever leaving their monasteries. They were believers in *peregrinatio in stabilitate*: pilgrimages of the heart, not of the feet. Armchair travel was fine—not that any of these monks would have been allowed anything as comfy as an armchair—but if you actually undertook the trip, just think of all the seductive and licentious temptations that might await you on the road! Well, don't think about them too much, brothers. Let us pray.

Even if you didn't have ecclesiastical reasons to stay close to home, a map of Rome would have been about as useful as a map of Mars. During the Middle Ages, most people lived, worked, married, and died without ever going farther than twenty miles from their place of birth. If you were that rare ambitious soul who actually did dream of travel beyond your home county, your lifetime checklist was probably a single pilgrimage: Canterbury, say, or Santiago de Compostela, or Jerusalem.

That was it. If there had been a travel best seller in the fifteenth century, it might have been called *One Place to See Before You Die.*

That was pretty much the state of travel for the next five hundred years. When Lord Castlereagh founded the Travellers Club in London in 1819, its membership was limited to gentlemen so well traveled that they had to have been—can you believe it?—five hundred miles from London. Yep, five hundred miles. A single ski trip to St. Moritz, and you too could sip cognac in the oak-paneled Travellers Club library alongside the Duke of Wellington and explorers like Sir Francis Beaufort and Captain Robert FitzRoy of the *Beagle.*

A transportation revolution—mass rail transit in the nineteenth century and then air travel in the twentieth—changed all that. For the first time in human history, it's possible to go virtually everywhere. And so people have. The north face of Mount Everest, one of the least hospitable places on the planet, was completely untouched by human hands until 1921. It's now so overcrowded that climbing teams send up Sherpas weeks ahead of time to grab primo spots, like teenagers camping out overnight to snag concert tickets, and international cleanup efforts have been needed to remove trash from the cluttered slopes.

The jet age has given birth to a new kind of connoisseur: the geographically inclined *collector.* These are not collectors of things, of baseball cards or Fiestaware or *Happy Days* action figures, but of places. You can't go every place on Earth, of course, not even with twenty-first-century technology. After all, the playing field is 200 million square miles in area. So the completist traveler will specialize: visiting not every place but the highest point on every continent, or every U.S. county or state capital, or every Denny's, or . . . the possibilities are endless.

There are tens of thousands of these place collectors wandering the globe, but they all have something in common: they all pretend that the checklist is incidental to the journey, but they all know deep down that's not true. The list is crucial.

Louise McGregor is a quiet, gray-haired woman in her sixties who looks like your grandma. Unlike your grandma, she *really* had her heart set on a trip to Somalia. "They wouldn't let me off the plane in Moga-dishu!" she is complaining to a gaggle of women in the noisy bar of a swanky Beverly Hills prime rib restaurant. "All the Somalis got off, but when we tried, 'Where do you think *you're* going?'" Somalia has been a chaotic no-man's-land of anarchy and bloodshed for years, but Louise seems genuinely miffed at the slight. She was able to cross off Djibouti and Yemen on her recent trip to the Horn of Africa, but not Somalia.

"Have you ever been someplace where you felt like you were genu-inely in danger?" I ask.

"Of course! I've lived in New York and L.A."

Come on. I wouldn't really stack smog and traffic up against sui-cide bombs, beheadings, and pirates.

She shrugs. "The most fun places just aren't safe. My friend and I look at the State Department list of dangerous places, and that's how we choose where to go."

The modern-day American version of the Travellers Club is the Travelers' Century Club, founded in 1954 in southern California by Bert Hemphill and Russ Davidson, who worked together in an elite L.A. travel agency catering to people looking for very posh trips to very unusual destinations. "Century" refers to the club's exclusivity rule: you must have visited at least one hundred different countries to join. The idea was that this would be a nearly insurmountable goal, but forty-three charter members had qualified by the time the decade was out. "It turns out one hundred wasn't all that difficult, even back then," says Klaus Billep, club chairman for the past twenty years.

Today the club boasts more than two thousand members, and this holiday prime rib luncheon is its biggest annual shindig. I was look-ing forward to hobnobbing with these modern-day explorers, spiri-tual descendants of Francis Beaufort and Robert FitzRoy—preferably someplace with a roaring fire and wildebeest heads on the wall. But my safari fantasy was rudely interrupted when Klaus filled me in on the club's regular luncheons. "They used to be dinner banquets, but then some of our members heard about freeway shootings in L.A. Most of them don't really like to drive at night."

So let me get this straight: these intrepid explorers have been to Kamchatka and the Galápagos, but they won't brave the 405 after dusk? That's when I first realized who has the time and money to visit one hundred countries: the very rich and/or (usually "and") the very old. Looking around the restaurant, you'd be forgiven for thinking that the "Century" part of the club's name might refer to its members' ages. There are plenty of the Orange County furs, pearls, and face-lifts that you'd expect.*

And yet . . . most of these senior citizens have probably been to more cool places in the last year than I have in my whole life. Sixty-something Louise McGregor just drove across Ethiopia on a twelve-hour bus trip and apparently caused a bit of a ruckus on a Mogadishu runway. You can't say they're not adventurers.

"How many countries have *you* been to?" she asks me, having ascertained that I'm merely a curious interloper and not a club member.

Uh-oh. I'd been doing a mental count in the car on the way here. I feel like a reasonably well-traveled guy, having lived on three continents. And yet my total is a dispiriting twenty-four—and that's counting a ninety-minute layover in the Taipei airport, as well as the time I stuck my foot across into the North Korean side of a conference room during a high school field trip to the DMZ.

"Twenty-nine," I lie, rounding up to the nearest, uh, prime.

Louise is taken aback. "What are you doing writing a book about geography if you've only been to twenty-nine countries?"

Touché. In this room, at least, I'm freakishly provincial. But I wonder if Louise isn't onto something: could America's infamous lack of map savvy have something to do with our reluctance to travel overseas? After all, it's hard to care much about a place you've never visited and know you probably never will, and a shockingly small slice of America even has a passport.† Sarah Palin made headlines for not owning a passport as late as 2006, when she needed one to visit U.S.

---

* Some members, though, have managed to see all the continents before hitting the age of, well, incontinence. The TCC's youngest member is Lani Shea, who visited her hundredth country at the tender age of two years, eight months. Her parents, of course, are also club members.

† The number hovered around 20 percent before the laws were recently changed to require passports for visits to Canada, Mexico, and the Caribbean and has risen only slightly since.

troops in Kuwait and Germany. When Katie Couric asked her why not, she boasted that she wasn't one of those idle, privileged college students who got whisked off to Europe with a backpack. "I've worked all my life," she said. "I was not a part of, I guess, that culture." Is this what we've become, a country where an interest in occasional travel is a *culture*—and a suspiciously un-American trust-fund kind of culture at that—rather than a familiar part of middle-class life?

At lunch I'm the youngest person at my table, by an easy forty-year margin. Eighty-seven-year-old Bill Crawford, buttering a roll to my left, just got back from Greenland. ("How was it?" "It was cold!") He's a dapper fellow in tweeds, a turtleneck, and a trim white beard. His interest in faraway places was born at age fifteen, when he saw Clark Gable in *Mutiny on the Bounty*. "I said, 'Someday in my life I'm going to visit Pitcairn Island'"—where the *Bounty* mutineers wound up—"'and get to know the people.' Well, last year I bought a house there."

When Bill was seventy, he celebrated by buying a Harley and putting 65,000 miles on it, crisscrossing the continent. His plan is to travel until he's 110—"When you rest, you *rest*!" he says, implying with grim emphasis that the second "rest" is of the "rest in peace" variety—but his eyesight, failing from glaucoma and macular degeneration, is starting to slow him down. He's philosophical, though. "What will be, will be, but I'll muddle through. I'm not going to worry about it. If it happens, it happens." He grins and elbows me, winking one clouded eye. "Like going out on a date, right?"

Klaus Billep, the chairman, is taking care of some club business at the front of the room. ("Hold the microphone closer to your mouth!" one hard-of-hearing oldster in the back exhorts him.) The award for traveling the farthest to get to today's luncheon is given to a band of hardy club members who have just returned from Wake Island. This tiny coral atoll between Hawaii and Guam is a heavily guarded U.S. missile site, and the military clearances involved in planning a visit make it one of the hardest-to-reach places in the world. In fact, of the 141 visitors who made the trip, five were TCC members crossing off the very last item on their checklist of destinations. Excited gasps and a spontaneous ovation rise from the room.

Klaus also gives honorable mention to "a gentleman eighty-six years young who drives all the way from Fresno every year." Rod Ritchie, sitting on the other side of me, raises his hands high above his head to greet the applause. "Still among the living!" he crows.

"Age is in your mind," Rod tells me. "When you're my age, you realize that most of your friends and colleagues are dead. And I didn't want the trailer behind my hearse to be filled with money; I wanted to spend it! So I started traveling." A friend told him about the TCC, and they started comparing country counts. "That was like a disease he gave me," he chuckles ruefully.

There certainly does seem to be something addictive about the disease of country collecting—some practitioners call themselves "country baggers," as if entire nations were elusive prey to be stalked and mounted like gazelles. This table is full of men pushing eighty and ninety, but they're eagerly sharing their latest stories of adventure and peril. Bill took an Amazon trip from Cuzco, Peru, to Manaus, Brazil, through anaconda-infested swamps that are the heart of the South American cocaine trade. Rod was trapped in Fiji during the 2000 coup. "Aw, the problem was in Suva," he says dismissively. "I was way over in Nadi on the other side of the island." And still the road calls: Bill wants to see Attu, at the tip of Alaska's Aleutian islands, the westernmost point of the United States.* Ninety-seven-year-old Alfred Giese, the oldest Traveler present, will be going around the world on the *Queen Mary* next month. There's a reason why we call the travel bug "wander*lust*," not "wanderwhim" or "wanderhobby." It's an urgent, passionate thing.

These wanderers seek each other out because no one else understands them or wants to see their vacation slides. "We've all got this crazy obsession," says Christopher Hudson, the English-born book publisher for New York's Museum of Modern Art who is currently serving as TCC president. "I find that when I talk to my other friends

---

* Because the most remote of the Aleutians lie across the International Date Line, they are also, paradoxically, America's *easternmost* islands as well—by a certain pedantic definition.

about travel, either their eyes glaze over or they think, 'Oh God, why's this guy dropping all these names?'"

The club also provides its members what Chris calls "a good source of information for going to all of these obscure places." The TCC publishes, at last count, 483 different "info files" on far-flung destinations containing the kind of travel advice you won't get from Fodor's. (If you go to the disputed enclave of Nagorno-Karabakh, get your visa stamp on a separate piece of paper, or you won't be allowed back into Azerbaijan! Prepare for mud if you're hiking to Taki Falls, the highest waterfall in the Micronesian nation of Palau!) Every luncheon ends with a travelogue lecture from a recently returned club member—right now, as Chris and I talk at the back of the banquet hall, a slide presentation on Papua New Guinea is beginning; many members are taking notes. I look up just in time to see the phrase "Penis gourds" appear on a PowerPoint bullet list. Then comes the photo—yup, penis gourds are exactly what you think they are. It's a little hard to keep eye contact with someone when there's a gigantic penis gourd hovering right behind his head.

As a member of the Travelers' Century Club executive board, Chris has a vote on which destinations will or won't make the official TCC list of destinations. This is trickier than it sounds: there are only 192 member states of the United Nations, but the TCC recognizes a whopping 319 different "countries," including any territory that's somehow removed from its parent nation. This seems sensible in some cases (surely Paris and Tahiti shouldn't count as the same "country" to world travelers just because one still administers the other) but leads to absurdity in others (Alaska is a separate country by TCC rules, while Indonesia somehow counts as eight different countries). "Even though we have these slightly strange rules, we take them very seriously," says Chris and, unbidden, starts patiently explaining to me why the board recently voted to make Abkhazia—but not South Ossetia, another breakaway Georgian region—a TCC "country." This is evidently not the first time he's had to go through this with angry club members. I nod sagely as he runs down the *obvious* differences between Abkhazian and South Ossetian infrastructure, a little nervous that there might be a quiz later.

Many people took up country collecting because they heard about the TCC, but the reverse is more often true: these were people who were already obsessive checklist travelers before they knew there was an organization collecting dues for it. Every few years, someone writes in to *The New York Times*' travel column asking if there's a club for people who count countries, and the editor dutifully runs the TCC's mailing address. The same process of accretion built the Highpointers Club, whose three thousand members are dedicated to visiting the highest elevation in every U.S. state. The club was founded by Jack Longacre, an Arkansas trucker who enjoyed visiting state high points and started noticing the same names recorded in all the peak registers, some boasting about their personal counts. "My God!" he remembered marveling. "There must be others out there with no more sense than myself!" In 1986, the editors of *Outdoor* magazine let him run a short item looking for like-minded collectors; thirty replied. The following year, nine of them met atop Mount Arvon, Michigan's highest point, and that became the first of the club's annual "Konventions."*

I suppose I also started highpointing before I knew there was a club. A few years ago, my wife and I hiked Mount Greylock in northwest Massachusetts to admire the fall foliage in the Berkshires from above. It was an easy hike—at only 3,491 feet, Mount Greylock is less than half the elevation of Flora Mountain, the *hundredth* tallest peak in my home state of Washington—but somehow I felt very rugged and manly knowing I was standing atop the *entire state* of Massachusetts. After discovering online that as many as ten thousand like-minded people share that rush, I track down Craig Noland, official Highpointers "membership guy." He's manning the club's sign-up table at a Smoky Mountain wilderness show in Pigeon Force, Tennessee, when I call him up.

Craig's been to forty-six of the fifty state high points and come within a thousand feet of two more. "I got blown off Mount Hood [in Oregon] in a snowstorm once," he tells me in a thick, friendly southern

---

* The odd spelling of "convention" and of the club's "Keep Klimbin'!" motto aren't signs of latent Klan sympathies. Rather, the famously thrifty Longacre liked to tell people he owned a used typewriter with a broken C key.

accent. "I doubt if I'll get Alaska. I'm older now, and I'm more decrepit, and I've got too much steel in my back."

But most U.S. high points aren't the forbidding peaks you're picturing, like Hood or McKinley.* Only five require real mountaineering; the rest are doable even if you're a rookie like me who thinks a crampon is something you might buy in *that pink aisle* of a drugstore. Some are even less rugged than Mount Greylock: Delaware's highest point, for example, is in a trailer park. Ohio's is a vocational school flagpole. The highest point in Florida is Britton Hill—at 345 feet, the lowest high point in any state and considerably lower than many Florida skyscrapers.† It's a rest stop. "Watch out if you use the restrooms there! There are copperhead snakes," Craig says helpfully.

It's a strangely arbitrary pursuit, visiting places with no inherent interest just because the capriciousness of manmade borders has put them on your checklist. George Mallory said he wanted to climb Everest "because it's there," but what brings three hundred people a year to a slight rise in an Iowa cornfield? There's really nothing to see; Mallory might say they're visiting "because the map says something's there, but there really isn't." The quest is even more puzzling in the cases of collectors like Peter Holden, who has eaten at more than twelve thousand McDonald's restaurants, or "Winter,"‡ who has vis-

---

* For many years, the least accessible U.S. high point wasn't the icy, 20,000-foot McKinley but rather 812-foot Jerimoth Hill in Rhode Island. That's because the only approach to the high point was the driveway of Henry Richardson, a local curmudgeon who would threaten highpointers with physical violence whenever they knocked at his door. Richardson died in 2001, and the Highpointers Club was successful in opening the once-impenetrable summit to visitors.

† State high points must be natural elevations, not manmade ones. Otherwise highpointers would be hiking the stairs of Chicago's Willis Tower (the former Sears Tower) and One Shell Square in New Orleans, each of which is taller than any hill in its respective state.

‡ Winter was born Rafael Lozano, but gets annoyed when the media refers to him by anything else but his self-selected one-name moniker. For many years, Starbucks was opening stores faster than he could visit them, but the recent economic collapse closed nearly a thousand Starbucks, putting his goal within reach. But every closure hurts him, he told *The Wall Street Journal*. If a store closes without him visiting it, "I would lose another piece of my soul." Ask not for whom the bell tolls; it tolls for Winter.

ited all but twenty of the 8,500 Starbucks locations in North America. They *never* get to check off a Mount Shasta or a Tahiti from their lists. Their travel goals are dull, ubiquitous, and nearly identical. They are voyagers of the suburban strip mall, pathfinders of the parking lot. But they take their obsession no less seriously. Holden once ate at forty-five Detroit-area McDonald's in a single day (his standard order is two Big Macs, but on marathon days, he'll settle for a diet soda or a packet of McDonaldland cookies to save for later.) A documentary about Winter's lonely crusade shows him living out of his car and even sucking spilled coffee out of his grimy cup holder at one point, because he'll check off a Starbucks only once he finishes the drink he buys.

Dr. Alan Hogenauer, a former airline executive and tourism marketing consultant, has coined the name "systematic travel" for this kind of geographic completism and teaches the concept to his travel and tourism students at Loyola Marymount. There's no question that he practices what he preaches. His website lists no less than 396 different checklists he's either working on or has completed. He's most famous for being the first person ever to visit every site in the national park system,* but he's also visited all eleven parishes of Barbados, all thirty "Historic Houses of Worship" in the city of Philadelphia, all fifty-one weather stations in Thailand, and every U.S. presidential birthplace. At this point he's resorted to inventing new things he can count, as I learn when I track him down days after a weekend jaunt to Casablanca. "That gave me Africa in January," he explains proudly. "Now I have all seventy-two 'continent-months': visiting some point in every continent in every calendar month."

Two maps hang in Hogenauer's office at Loyola, neatly displaying his travel history with pushpins and intricate webs of string. The

---

* Hogenauer completed his national park quest in Alaska in 1980 and says that twenty-five years went by before anyone else took credit for the same feat. "Which is obscene!" he exclaims. "They're fabulous places to visit, and you and I are paying millions a year to maintain them, and twenty-five years go by before someone else sees them all?" Today the National Park Service runs a "passport" program in which visitors can stamp a little booklet at every park site, an attempt to turn every American into a "systematic traveler."

tangle is so dense over much of the world, like North America, that he can't add new routes anymore. He insists that checklists are just a means to an end, an excuse to explore. "Look, if I'd helicoptered into every national park, I wouldn't have enjoyed it. But by *going* to each one, and finding out how to get there, and linking it to everything else, and seeing things along the way, they seem much more real."

But I'm accustomed by now to place collectors protesting, methinks, a little too much. They all downplay the appeal of the checklist itself, but having a system is clearly a very real source of pleasure for these people. Otherwise, why wouldn't you chuck the list at some point and just go wherever the hell you felt like? Part of it is simply the universal smug thrill of crossing something off a to-do list, of course. And Hogenauer says that *finishing* a checklist is even better. "You recognize things in their entirety. If you can say you've got one hundred percent of something in your background, you don't have to worry that you missed out on something."

The checklist ensures novelty and breadth of experience as well. The specter of mortality, the awareness of limited time, seems always to be with these systematic travelers, especially the older ones. Hogenauer tells the story of working at his first job, for Ma Bell, with an older coworker who had elaborate plans to finally see the world with his wife upon retiring. She died the very day he retired. "The look on that guy's face!" he remembers sadly. "It was such a momentous realization. You've got to do things when you can." So why go back to Cancún if you've never seen Tierra del Fuego? Why put off seeing Laos if you're right next door in Thailand? Gather ye visa stamps while ye may! Old Time is still a-flying!

The Travelers' Century Club has expanded the world's list of "countries" to 319, but even that is too limiting for some collectors, forever hungry in a shrinking world for the next place, the new thing. And so a TCC member named Charles Veley created MostTraveledPeople.com, a website where his loyal globetrotter readers can vote on an even longer list of legit destinations. They've currently inflated the count to a whopping 872. All fifty U.S. states are now separate "countries" on the list. So are the twenty-two regions of France, even if they're all about the size of Vermont. It's the rare spot that *doesn't* make the cut, in fact. Point Roberts, Washington, a tiny bit of the United States that dangles down from Canada just a few hours northwest of my house, is currently on the vetoed list, with only 40 percent approval.

No one's been everywhere yet, but the competition is intense. "I get a lot of e-mails from people claiming that other people are cheating," Veley tells me, his unfailingly mild, affectless voice betraying no irritation whatsoever. "Some people just like to tattle." We've met near his home, a converted colonel's residence in San Francisco's decommissioned Presidio. He looks exhausted, not so much from last week's four-country swing through Europe, during which he was able to cross off the tiny North Sea island of Heligoland, but from a subsequent stop that sounds even more grueling: taking his three young children to Disneyland.

Though Guinness doesn't have a category for it anymore (too subjective, too contentious), Veley is, by the universal acclamation of international newspaper headlines, the world's most traveled man. He's been mugged in Buenos Aires and peed on by Costa Rican tree frogs. He's had his canoe overturned in the hippo-infested waters of the Zambezi River. But in photos of his journeys, he's always smiling placidly, usually in a neat Oxford blue shirt and khakis, whether he's hanging out with Nepali holy men, Ethiopian village children, or Rio's Carnival showgirls. The overall effect is like that prank where a stolen garden gnome turns up in odd places all over the world, always with the same wide eyes and benign grin.

At thirty-seven, Charles became the youngest person in the history of the Travelers' Century Club to polish off the club's entire checklist. He and some friends had founded the software company MicroStrategy, and the dot-com boom of the late nineties had made them millionaires many times over. Charles decided to retire early and see the world. All of it.

He traces his wanderlust back to a childhood fascination with geography. Not all systematic travelers love maps—TCC chairman Klaus Billep confided to me that "when we add Abkhazia or Tokelau to our list, people have no idea where they are. They have to call us or look them up on our website." But Charles is a map nut after my own heart.

"I remember visiting my mother. My parents were separated, and my mother lived on a farm way out in remote West Virginia. And I would sit in our Land Rover in the driver's seat. I'd lay the road atlas down beside me in the passenger seat and look down and pretend that I was driving. When the road on the map turned to the right, I'd turn the steering wheel to the right. And I pretended that I was driving to the Pacific Ocean."

It's no accident that, in his garden-gnome travel photos, he's always swarmed by grinning locals. Charles is scrupulously social when he travels. People are as important to him as places are. More important, maybe. "I like understanding where people are from, how they think, and seeing how that relates to geography too. There's a real power in meeting someone and knowing something about them, just because of where they're from." I tell him I've noticed that my trivia background can do the same thing, but he disagrees—his brand of travel gets you something more. "It's a real bond. The first step is knowing the trivia, just knowing the name of the place, but the second is having an emotion tied to it. Trivia is secondhand at best, but once you've been there, you can feel their situation, you're able to relate."

But as with Alan Hogenauer, the checklist, the system, is a big part of his travel compulsion as well. One of the first concepts I ever studied in my computer science classes was the TSP, or traveling salesman problem, in which programmers try to find the shortest route a traveler can take to visit every city in a given list. This seemingly simple problem is actually an incredibly rich and complex one, and even fast modern computers can take years to solve it exhaustively when a few hundred cities are added to the list. The traveling salesman problem is a theoretical exercise, but Charles Veley has spent the last decade working on solving it in real life.

"I love it. I'm a computer guy, and when you have an algorithm you're working on, you find that the more you work it, the more it improves. So I was working constantly on around-the-world tickets. You want to be efficient. Let me make sure I'm not going to be stuck in a place I don't want to be for seven days. If I just research a little more, maybe I can find a way to make this trip more efficient and more enjoyable."

I nod eagerly—I'm an efficiency nerd myself. My wife's idea of a successful date is one where she likes the movie or the play or the restaurant, but I'm content if I can just find a great parking space, ideally the *optimal* parking space. What a rush.

"But does that kind of rigid efficiency take away from the spontaneous fun of travel?" I ask. "The freedom of the open road, all that?"

"Well, that's the challenge," says Charles. "To do both. My philosophy is always to plan every minute accounted for—but be prepared to throw the plan out the window." In 2005, Veley mounted an expedition to Rockall, a ninety-foot-wide skerry in the North Atlantic. It's so hard to get to that the number of recorded visitors at the time—twelve—was the same as the number of men who have landed on the moon. Charles's attempt failed due to high swells, and his crew had to settle for reaching over the side of the boat and literally sticking Post-its to the island's sheer cliffs. Three years later, he returned, and once again the twenty-foot swell was too high for the inflatable Zodiac to land. But, ready as ever to improvise, Charles donned a wet suit, jumped into the seething Atlantic, and splatted against the side of the rock. "It's slippery, covered with algae and kelp and bird guano," he says, but he "clung to it long enough to call it a landing." He remembers it as one of the great triumphs of his life.*

But why? Why the risk and the time and the money just to spend a few seconds on a barren dead volcano, poking seventy feet above the sea four hundred miles from anywhere? Mallory knew: "Because it's there."

I came of age with the sickening certainty that everyone else on the planet had confidently mastered the adult world and I was the only one who felt clueless and a little out of my depth. For many years,

---

* I wonder if Veley will ever get the chance to visit the island of Ferdinandea, a submerged volcano that occasionally rises out of the Mediterranean south of Sicily only to subside or erode again. The last time it emerged, in 1831, it led to a wave of tourism, as well as diplomatic arguments over who owned the territory. Ferdinandea last made news when the United States bombed it in 1986, mistaking it for a Libyan submarine, but scientists predict that recent volcanic activity could lead to a reappearance sometime soon.

I had no idea that *everyone* feels this way, at least from time to time. Charles Veley, though, is a man comfortable with the amenities. He can get his bearings and feel competent anywhere on Earth, whether he's clinging to the kelp on Rockall or ordering his namesake drink at the famous Hemingway Bar at the Paris Ritz (the "Lemon Charlie," a favorite of Kate Moss).* He speaks five languages fluently and has flown fighter jets. He knows to feign anger when government officials give you a hard time in Saudi Arabia but to smile wider when the same thing happens at an African roadblock.

That's the dream for most people, who don't feel totally comfortable anywhere but think that everyone else magically does. Charles is like a superhero to me, but he confides that maps are part of his secret. "The more you know about a map is power," he says. "Take a look at someone who's lost and someone who's not. The person who's not is a little bit more in control."

If you're a *schadenfreude*-seeker, though, know this: the NASDAQ collapse and an accounting scandal caused Charles's start-up stock price to plummet in the first years of the new millennium, shortly after his early retirement. In one trading day in March 2002 alone, his shares lost 61 percent of their value. To pay the bills, he has recently returned to his old job as vice president of corporate development at MicroStrategy, but he's traveling more than ever. He says he has no regrets about his decade of globetrotting, which he reckons cost him more than a million dollars. "I got to travel as a young, healthy person with fewer ties. If I'd had kids first, I couldn't have done it at all. I'm pretty pleased with it."

The money is the elephant in the room, I suppose, as it so often is in American life. Was Sarah Palin right? Is world travel a perk of birthright and privilege, only for those who have never in their lives flown coach or eaten at a chain restaurant? Or can normal people be supertravelers too?

---

* The Lemon Charlie was the result of the Ritz bartender's five-year attempt to duplicate a limoncello cocktail that Charles and his wife had once tasted on the Amalfi Coast. Moss is actually the one who named the drink, when she inadvertently mangled the word "limoncello."

Chris Guillebeau thinks so. Chris is another one of those who made a personal goal to visit every nation on Earth, even before he knew there was a club of über-rich "Greatest Generation" types doing the same thing. Like Charles, he's a guru of travel efficiency. Unlike Charles, he's not a dot-com millionaire. In fact, he's a thirty-one-year-old high school dropout who now earns a living via his "lifestyle design" blog, selling self-help guides on inexpensive travel and starting microbusinesses. After 9/11, he and his painter wife, Jolie, felt they should be doing more in the world somehow, and they decided to spend four years volunteering for a medical nonprofit in Sierra Leone and Liberia. Traveling across Africa, he began racking up countries: twenty, then thirty, then forty.

"This is awesome! What would it take to get to one hundred?" he tells me he remembers thinking. We've met for lunch in a brewpub in Portland, Oregon, where he now lives. I order a burger, rare, then feel a little guilty when Chris asks for the vegan special, something virtuous with tofu and quinoa. I wonder if the waitress can guess which one of us is an expert on the clean-water crisis in developing nations.

He did some back-of-the-envelope math, leveraging his growing skills at sniffing out cheap travel deals, and realized he could do it for $30,000. That's still a lot of money, of course; most people don't have $30,000 between the couch cushions that they can, on a whim, drop on around-the-world travel. But Chris saw it as a bargain. "That's cheap!" he marvels. "That's so cheap! What else could I buy for thirty thousand dollars? A lot of people might buy a car for that, and I can see *one hundred* different countries?" It was no contest. Off he went. He's since expanded his quest to the entire world—his current total is 149 countries, with the hard goal of finishing by April 7, 2013.

Chris is driven by the same things that guide the other super-travelers I've met: the love of logistics and novelty, a near addiction to setting and achieving ambitious goals. But you won't find him on MostTraveledPeople.com, voting on whether or not Point Roberts, Washington, should count on some Official List. "I don't care about that," he says simply.

"They're very serious about it."

"I know they are, and I don't care. I wish them well. I'm concerned about their motivation, but I hope they're happy. If they're happy, that's great."

"What's the danger?"

"The danger is relying on external reward, because there isn't any." He's right. Winter has explained his Starbucks count by saying, "I want everyone in the world to know my name," but his eccentric quest will never make him genuinely famous. When *The Guinness Book of World Records* dropped its "Most Traveled Person" record, Charles Veley lamented that "It was like finishing a marathon only to discover that all the officials had gone home . . . very frustrating."

"And he spent a million dollars on it," marvels Chris, sighing. Chris has spent a tiny fraction of that on his own adventure, proving his point that almost anyone can travel, and extensively—it's just a matter of how badly you want to.

The checklist may drive the addiction, but for most of these globe-trotters, the journey quickly becomes its own reward. Early in his travels, Charles let his yen for efficiency get the better of him, making token stops in countries just so he could cross them off. Now he can't wait to go back and *really* see them: Bulgaria, Iran, Honduras, Tunisia. "There is no finish line," he says. It's not about completion anymore.

And highpointers know that their collection isn't about the climb so much as it is getting off the beaten path. "It's a vehicle that takes you places you never would have thought about going to," Craig Noland says. "Have you ever been to Kenton, Oklahoma?" Oddly enough, I haven't. He explains that it's the panhandle town nearest to Black Mesa, the Sooner State's highest point. "You can go there and see dinosaur tracks and the country's longest mesa. There's a three-state border that's changed places five different times. You can see the wagon ruts from the old Santa Fe Trail. It's the only town in Oklahoma that's in the Mountain Time Zone. You can spend the whole day there, in the middle of nowhere! But you'd never say, 'Hey, let's go to Kenton and check it out.'"

I don't really have a list of my own, though I admire those who do. I respect finishers, people who won't settle for doing *most* of something. I like knowing that tens of thousands of compulsive travelers are crisscrossing the globe right now, elevating the most mundane of human endeavors—getting from one place to another—into a kind of performance art.

As recently as a century ago, people who wanted to see the entire world knew that could never happen, so they would sit with atlases and idly daydream of the places they saw mapped there. In our age of casual travel, it surprises us to remember that no sitting U.S. president *ever* left the country until 1906, when Teddy Roosevelt wanted to find out how the Panama Canal was coming along. For the first time in history, jet-age transportation has put essentially the entire Earth within the reach of these insatiable travelers. They can now dispense with the atlas, having visited every single one of its pages. They've *become* the atlas.

And in at least one case, they've literally become the territory as well. In 2002, Jack Longacre, the founder of the Highpointers Club, learned that he had terminal cancer. "I want to be on the mountains," he told friends as he prepared his will. "That's where I belong." So he collected film canisters, labeled them with the names of the fifty states, and distributed them to club members. When he died nine months later, they honored his last wish by scattering his ashes on the United States Geographic Survey markers atop all fifty high points, the peaks and the trailer parks, the mesas and the rest stops, every single one. One final checklist.

Chapter 9

TRANSIT

['tran-zət] *n.*: a piece of surveying equipment used by mapmakers:
a theodolite with a reversible telescope

*There are map people whose joy is to lavish more attention on the
sheets of colored paper than on the colored land rolling by. I have
listened to accounts by such travelers in which every road number
was remembered, every mileage recalled.*

—JOHN STEINBECK

It's a spectacularly beautiful day for a drive in the Pacific Northwest. Mount Rainier looms above the blue waters of Commencement Bay so big and clear that it looks like a special effect. Behind it tower summer banks of golden cumulus clouds straight out of a Maxfield Parrish painting. But the two men I'm driving with seem oblivious to nature's wonders. They're interested in a different kind of scenery.

"That bridge we just crossed was built in 1928. It was widened ten years ago, but the plaque there is still stamped with the original date," says Mark Bozanich, who is behind the wheel. He's a slow, thoughtful talker with a slightly scraggly white beard, the prerogative of the wise old geek in virtually any field. "And that bridge we're going under now still has the old Milwaukee Railroad logo, did you see that?"

John Spafford, in the passenger seat, is a somewhat younger guy with frosted blond hair, still clipped as short as it must have been during his eight-year career in army intelligence. He's been explaining the snarled traffic caused by a state route that essentially dead-ends to our southeast. "There's a missing link between Tacoma and the 167, the Valley Freeway. It comes down into Puyallup, and now you're connecting with the 512 that'll take you south to I-5, but there are plans to expand it all the way up to the port!" Visions of a six-lane limited-access bypass from Tacoma all the way north to the Seattle suburbs dance in John's eyes.

Mark and John are self-confessed "roadgeeks," as these amateur highway scholars prefer to call themselves.* Just as Britain's oft-ridiculed "trainspotters" have made a science of ticking off locomotive numbers in little notebooks, so have roadgeeks appointed themselves the guardians of America's road network, from its mighty interstates to its tiniest country lanes. They can tell the difference between a Westinghouse streetlight and a GE one and are the only ones who notice when the lettering on interstate signage is switched over from Highway Gothic to the new Clearview font. (Hint: Look for the curved tail on the lowercase "l"!) They follow road construction projects with a regularity and fervor that others might reserve for a favorite soap opera or sports team. They know why there's one I-76 in southern Pennsylvania and another one in northeastern Colorado,† and how to interpret West Virginia's odd, fractionally numbered county routes.‡

Scratch a roadgeek, and you'll find a maphead; virtually all their stories begin with a road atlas, scrutinized for long hours during one of the endless driving vacations of childhood. Mark grew up carefully tallying the traffic signals on Highway 99 between Seattle and his grandparents' house in Portland every summer and still has a voluminous collection of old gas station maps. John inherited his family's navigator position at the tender age of nine, when a road atlas got thrown at him in the backseat after Mom misread the map once too

---

* There are kinder variants, like "road buff" and "roadfan," but more elaborate coinings, like "odologist" and "viaphile," have yet to catch on.

† The western I-76 used to be numbered I-80S until 1975, when officials began removing the letter suffixes from highway designations.

‡ Visitors to the Mountain State take note: the top number is the main route from which the county route branches, and the bottom number tells you which branch.

often. For years, a buff like Mark or John would study the highways with the sad conviction that he was the only person in the world so fascinated with cloverleafs and control cities.* The phenomenon didn't get a name until the dawn of the Internet, when these lonely "roads scholars" were surprised to discover thousands of like-minded enthusiasts all over the world. "Great," Mark's daughter likes to tell him. "All fifty people that are interested in highways can now find each other."

Even better, the Internet gave roadgeeks a place to "publish" their work. Photography is a huge part of roadgeek travel; when test-driving a new car, the dedicated buff will always check to see how a camera would fit up front, the better to take dashboard photos of every mileage sign and junction of their future expeditions. Buffs might feel a little silly keeping thousands of these snapshots in shoe boxes under their bed, but on the Web, they can be shared with the public: a permanent record of their journeys, even if no one ever looks at it. Every roadgeek website includes pages of these nearly identical photos, an endless stream of green rectangles and "Exit Only" arrows and the taillights of semitrucks. These aren't rare findings, like a bird-watcher's photos; after all, millions of motorists see the exact same views every year. But central to the roadgeek urge is the certainty that these journeys must be documented—collected, even. Roadgeeks often boast of how many routes they've "clinched"—that is, driven every single mile of.† It's a very specific—and attainable—form of systematic travel.

And maybe the very banality of these driver's-eye slide shows is their real value. Though the rest of us may take it for granted, the U.S. Interstate Highway System is one of the most remarkable engineering feats ever conceived. Its origins date back to 1919, when a young army officer named Dwight D. Eisenhower, missing his family in California, agreed to join a cross-country convoy of military vehicles heading for the West Coast. Part of the company's mission was to find out

---

* A control city is the likely destination listed on freeway signage. On a junction where one lane is marked as continuing I-380 north toward Cedar Rapids, while the right-hand lane is marked as exiting to I-80 west and Des Moines, the control cities are Cedar Rapids and Des Moines.

† Not every single mile *in every lane*, though. That would just be silly.

if these trucks and staff cars—which had just won a grueling trench war in Europe, mind you—were even *capable* of surviving the trip. In 1919, driving from sea to shining sea wasn't the leisurely five-day tour we know today. Paved roads largely disappeared outside major American cities, so the convoy had to contend with mud, dust, ruts, unstable bridges, and even quicksand. Their "successful" entry into San Francisco came sixty-two days after starting out (an average speed of six miles per hour!), and the convoy lost nine vehicles and twenty-one men* in the 230 accidents they suffered along the way. Eisenhower never forgot the ordeal, especially when compared to the expansive and well-maintained autobahn network he saw in Germany during the Second World War. In 1956, as president, he signed the Interstate Highway System into law, authorizing 41,000 miles of superhighways with a combined land area the size of the state of Delaware and using enough cement to build eighty Hoover Dams. It was the greatest peacetime public works project in history.

And yet, unlike the Hoover Dam or the Golden Gate Bridge, tourists don't line up every day of the year to ooh and aah over the interstate system. In fact, we literally grind it underfoot in our haste to arrive at, and photograph, far less impressive bits of roadside construction (the Corn Palace; the world's largest rocking chair; Branson, Missouri). Roads are like maps in that we think about them only when they *don't* do their job and we wind up lost or stuck or sidelined. If not for roadgeeks, who would appreciate the lowly highway? Mark pauses for a moment in our route to point out the road construction connecting Sprague Avenue to state highway 16; a new westbound viaduct is being built because the unique design of the existing one—four-legged piers, each leg weighing almost four hundred tons—means that it can't be widened. It's true: the tapered legs of the old viaduct are quite distinctive, even beautiful. I don't think I've ever really *looked* at the supports of any elevated highway, though I'm sure I've driven on thousands.

Maybe roadgeeks can find something to fascinate them on just about any highway in America, but they also have their own special

* To injuries—no deaths were reported, thankfully.

landmarks and pilgrimages. Some of these oddities are so bizarre they'd be spotted even by amateurs like me. There's the traffic light in Syracuse's Tipperary Hill where the green signal is on the *top* (a nod to the neighborhood's Irish roots). Or 1010th Street west of Eau Claire, Wisconsin, believed to be the nation's highest-numbered road. Or the strange vortex that is US-321 through Elizabethton, Tennessee—it enters town signed as south–north but reverses the signage when it hits US-19E: now the two directions are north–south, respectively. No matter which way you leave town on US-321, you're headed south!

Breezewood, Pennsylvania, an unincorporated hamlet of only two hundred people, is perhaps the most notorious destination. "Most people would say, 'What's in Breezewood?'" Mark tells me. "But mention it to a roadgeek, and they'll shudder." When I-70 was built through the area, funding disagreements with the Pennsylvania Turnpike Commission meant that no ramps could be built connecting the new freeway to the turnpike. As a result, there's still a gap of less than a mile in the freeway there, and drivers on I-70 are puzzled to see traffic signals suddenly appear *on the interstate*. Local gas stations and fast-food franchises love the anomaly, of course, and have opposed any attempts to build a real interchange. Roadgeeks now use the term "breezewood" to refer to any place where stoplights unexpectedly interrupt highway traffic, and some darkly blame former Pennsylvania congressman Bud Shuster for the original imbroglio. Shuster is still well remembered even in the real world for spearheading an array of pork-barrel transportation projects in his district, but in the roadgeek world, he's a scheming supervillain of Fu Manchu proportions. In 1991, Shuster insisted that a new highway through Altoona be signed as Interstate 99—in violation of national guidelines—despite the fact that it lies between I-79 and I-81. The numbering was out of order! To roadgeeks, with their sometimes Asperger-like insistence on order and constancy, this was an unforgivable sin.

But the road buff's eye for detail often performs a public service as well. We all rely on the design of the nation's highway system every day, whether we're commuting to work or buying a head of lettuce shipped to us straight from California on I-80, but how many of us actually follow proposed improvement projects or monitor new road signs to make sure they're right? Roadgeeks are the only ones writing huffy e-mails to their state transportation departments when they notice confusing signs or misnumbered shields, and time and again, from Kanab, Utah, to Pensacola, Florida, they've been pleased to see the errors they reported fixed the next time they've driven by. We may not know it, but we are all in their debt.

The patron saint of these highway watchdogs is Richard Ankrom, an artist fed up with the confusing interchange between the Pasadena Freeway and I-5 near his downtown Los Angeles home. Instead of waiting for the state to replace the unhelpful overhead sign, he conceived of an art installation he called "Guerrilla Public Service," to be performed before an audience of 140,000 motorists every day. Ankrom crafted a perfect replica of a regulation California Department of Transportation directional marker and I-5 shield marker, and, early one morning in 2001, he armed himself with an orange vest and hard hat, some safety cones, and a fake invoice in case he was challenged. Twenty minutes later, the "art" was successfully installed on the sign—so seamlessly that nobody even noticed the fix for nine months. When a free weekly paper finally broke the news, Caltrans roundly

A time-lapse view of Ankrom setting up his "installation"

condemned the project as vandalism but, unable to argue with progress, left the homemade sign in place for the next eight years, where it helped millions of Angelenos and tourists navigate downtown successfully. In 2009, Caltrans finally replaced Ankrom's sign with an official one—but the new one still incorporates Ankrom's improved design.*

"Where are we now?" I ask. We're driving down a rather dreary commercial strip between Tacoma and neighboring Lakewood, and, though I'm trying to think like a roadgeek, I can't possibly see why this particular road is on our itinerary.

"This is the old U.S. 99," says Mark in unusually reverent tones. The West Coast's Route 66 (only upside-down!), Highway 99 once ran from the Canadian border all the way to Mexico, but it was decommissioned in 1968 when I-5 was completed, and much of it is now anonymous and unsigned. Roadgeeks are archaeologists as well, finding history in the modern urban ruins. They see the ghosts of Esso stations and motels shaped like tepees where now there's only a wasteland of pawnshops and adult video stores.

The last stop on our itinerary is another historic spot: the famed Tacoma Narrows Bridge, recently twinned with a new span heading west to the Kitsap Peninsula. The original bridge across this strait was the famous "Galloping Gertie," which collapsed in a 1940 storm. If you were ever in an introductory physics class, you've probably seen the famous footage of the bridge wobbling and warbling terrifyingly due to harmonic resonance before it crashed into Puget Sound. The new bridge is reassuringly sturdy.

"Being a roadgeek is definitely something the rest of the population doesn't get," sighs John Spafford as we turn around and head back toward downtown Tacoma. "It's not genetic—even my kids don't have it. I'm a little disappointed." He prefers vagabond family vacations straight out of his childhood, but his college-aged daughter wants a *real* vacation like her friends get: a week by the pool in Orlando. "We

---

* The old sign, to Ankrom's chagrin, was crushed in a bale of scrap metal and sent off to China. Just like Gustave Courbet's *The Stone Breakers* and William Blake's *A Vision of the Last Judgment*, another priceless work of art lost to the ages.

never stay anyplace more than a night," he says, shrugging. "She's tired of seeing cornfields."

Even if his own kids never learned to enjoy the fabled wonders of roadgeek America—the sixteen-lane stretch of I-285 near the Atlanta airport or the record thirty-six times that I-91 and US-5 cross each other through New England—John has still managed to jump-start a new generation of young roadgeeks. Since leaving the military, he's taught elementary school, and his fourth graders begin every school day with a little geography exercise, tracing highway routes with dry-erase marker on a state map at the back of his classroom. "By the end of the year," he boasts, "my sharp ones can tell highways just by the shape of the shield. 'Aha, this is U.S. 12!'"

Mark, on the other hand, has landed the roadgeek's dream job: he works for the Washington State Department of Transportation, in charge of the state's official highway map. Back in Tacoma, we say good-bye as he drops me and John off by our respective cars. The last I see of him as he pulls away is the personalized license plate on the back of his Ford Taurus: "MAPPER," with a surround that reads, "I'm not lost / I'm a cartographer."

Driving home to Seattle, I pass the stadiums where the Seahawks play football and the lowly Mariners play something not entirely unlike baseball. Just a block east from the sports fields, I realize, is the western terminus of Interstate 90. I remember once driving past that on-ramp with my son, Dylan, after a ball game. "If you got on that highway there," I told him, "the road wouldn't end until you got all the way to Boston Harbor. It stretches all the way from the Pacific Ocean to the Atlantic."

Dylan was transfixed by the idea and begged to drive to Boston *that very night*. (It was getting kind of late, so we just got ice cream instead.) I remember having my mind blown by the same notion as a kid, that all roads were essentially connected and that our driveway was the start of a continuous river of asphalt and Portland cement that might end at Disneyland or the Florida Keys or Tierra del Fuego. Today I can't see the same mental picture without wincing at some of the uglier results of America's century of road and automobile culture: suburban sprawl, rush-hour traffic, air pollution, those bumper stickers where Calvin from *Calvin and Hobbes* pees on the Chevy logo. But as a child, my romance with the roads in my atlases and stretching out from my front door was unclouded by any real-life complications. They were only space and potential.

The size of America makes our national fascination with maps different from cartophilia in other parts of the world—Britain, for instance. As you might expect from a nation so geeky that it once put the Daleks from *Doctor Who* on a postage stamp, the British are second to none in their love of maps, and their government Ordnance Survey's "Explorer" maps, with their iconic orange covers, still sell in the millions every year. But there is something cozy and fiddly about map love across the pond. The British take pride in creating scaled-down versions of the countryside in exhaustive detail, as if it were a model railroad landscape or miniature Christmas village in a shop window. In his book *Notes on a Small Island*, the American travel writer Bill Bryson remembers sitting down on a stone bench while hiking in the Dorset hills and pulling out a map to get his bearings.

> Coming from a country where mapmakers tend to exclude any landscape feature smaller than, say, Pike's Peak, I am constantly impressed by the richness of detail on the Ordnance Survey 1:25,000 series. They include every wrinkle and divot of the landscape, every barn, milestone, wind pump and tumulus. They distinguish between sand pits and gravel pits and between power lines strung from pylons and power lines strung from poles. This one even included the stone seat on which I sat now. It astounds me to be able to look at a map and know to the square meter where my buttocks are deployed.

The immensity of the New World landscape, with its postcard-ready canyons and cataracts and mesas, has bred a different kind of map love. Not all of its footpaths have been thoroughly trod by centuries of apple-cheeked old men with plus fours and walking sticks. There's still the illusion, at least, that there's too much to see, that the land dwarfs our puny attempts at cataloguing it. You can see that difference when you compare American road maps with, say, Michelin maps of Europe, which are still full of beautiful details that drivers couldn't care less about: relief lines, railroads, hiking trails, forests, wetlands. The difference is one of heritage. British and European road maps are descended from generations of topographical walking and cycling maps. Americans, on the other hand, adopted road atlases only after they'd adopted the automobile—which was quickly. Because of the vastness of the distances to be covered, cars suited us to a (Model) T.

In fact, our roads changed to suit the maps, not the other way around. Map historians love to claim that the decisions of cartographers can have drastic real-life effects on the territories mapped—Weimar-era maps that emphasized all the territory Germany lost in the Treaty of Versailles may have led to Hitler's rise to power and the Second World War, for example—but the tangled feedback of cause and effect in such cases makes it hard to point to a single smoking-gun map. Not so in the case of the American highway system as we know it, which was largely dreamed up in one fell swoop by Rand McNally & Co.

Rand McNally dove into the automobile navigation business in 1907, but not with maps. Instead it acquired a competitor's line of "Photo-Auto Guides," which displayed a driver's-eye view of landmarks and intersections along popular routes, just like a roadgeek's dashboard photos. Arrows overlaid on the road showed drivers exactly where to turn, anticipating Google's popular Street View tool by almost one hundred years. The Chicago-to-Milwaukee photos were actually taken from the front of Andrew McNally II's Packard, as he and his new bride drove north for their honeymoon. These photo books were a practicality, not a novelty, back then; in fact, they were more useful than maps. That's because there was still no consistent, widely used system identifying American roads. Rand McNally had to tell drivers "Turn left at the red barn" instead of "Turn left at Highway 15," because Highway 15 probably wasn't numbered and it certainly wasn't marked.*

The map firm held an in-house contest seeking a solution to the mapping problem, and a draftsman named John Garrett Brink proposed a jaw-droppingly bold solution: the mountain would have to come to McNally. Instead of figuring out better ways of drawing America's messy tangle of roads on a map, Brink thought, the company should unilaterally designate a system of routes across the country and choose symbols and numbers for them. Then Rand McNally teams would drive across the country, relabeling *every single route* by painting colored stripes and highway logos on telephone poles, like Indian scouts marking pioneer trails across the Old West. In fact, Rand McNally called the work of these early Richard Ankroms its "Blazed Trail" program. By 1922, a fifty-thousand-mile network of numbered, well-marked highways stretched across the country, and state and federal agencies began to follow suit with their own numbering schemes. The modern American road atlas was born, and so was its free cousin, the oil-company road map. Eight billion of these gas-station maps were printed between 1913 and 1986, the biggest promotional giveaway of the twentieth century.

The road atlas has become inseparably tied to that uniquely American ritual of liberation: the road trip. When I think about driving a route across town, I picture the actual landmarks involved, but when I plan a trip any longer than an hour, my mental imagery is plucked straight

---

* Companies like Google are still facing these issues as they develop driving directions for parts of the world without widely used addressing systems. Their solution has been similar to Rand McNally's: base directions on landmarks, not street names. Instead of being told, "Head south on Bannerghatta Rd, then turn left on Hosur Main Rd," a driver in Bangalore, India, might see, "Head south toward the hospital, then turn left at the end of the road." Even landmark-based driving isn't foolproof, though. Google GIS specialist Jessica Pfund told me about a Pakistani user of Google Map Maker who had always used the bright blue wall next to his house as a handy navigational landmark. Last week, he complained to her, the wall had been painted gray, and now nobody could find him.

from Rand McNally. In my mind's eye, highways aren't black striped with yellow. They're bright blue ribbons with red borders, stretching across a landscape white with absence: literally the open road. National forests are mottled blobs constructed, if I think hard enough about it, not out of trees but out of a lime-green cerebral cortex of tiny, winding convolutions. There are trees too, of course: one evergreen apiece in every state park, right next to a little green triangular tent.

In fact, road atlases have become such a Pavlovian bit of shorthand for travel and independence that some mapheads can satisfy their wanderlust without ever leaving home, just by opening a Rand McNally road atlas. Meet the participants in Jim Sinclair's annual St. Valentine's Day Massacre, a contest by mail that he's held every February for more than forty years. They travel a circuitous course across America from the Golden Gate Bridge to the Statue of Liberty (or the reverse route in odd-numbered years) all without ever leaving their armchairs or kitchen tables. The journey is made entirely on maps.

The Massacre (like Jim's other yearly map events, the Circumglobal Trophy Dash and the Independence Day Fireworks) was born out of the faddish road rallies held in the mid-1960s by clubs like the Chicago-based Concours Plains Rallye Team, of which Jim was a member. These sports car buffs weren't racing for speed, as they do at Monte Carlo. In these "TSD" (time-speed-distance) rallies, teams navigated a complicated set of driving directions on public roads at preset speeds, with the aim of passing a series of checkpoints at the precise seconds required. During the long midwestern winters, when icy roads left the drivers housebound, someone suggested a map-based version of a road rally, and in 1964 the first Massacre was held. Jim took the event over in 1968 and in 1980 quit his chemical engineering job to run the contests full-time.

Just as it was then, Massacre HQ is still the Sinclairs' sixties-era rambler just north of Pasadena. It's a rainy, misty day in the foothills of the San Gabriel Mountains when Jim and his wife, Sue, invite me inside to what I can immediately see is a grandparents' house straight out of central casting: public radio classical music playing quietly somewhere, shelves lined with Garrison Keillor and Agatha Christie hardcovers, grandkid photos on every flat surface. The only difference is Jim's home office, which has metastasized to cover the whole living room. The pool table is now piled deep with boxes, envelopes, and stacks of reference books. "We have paper boxes for end tables now," sighs Sue, who sits across from us on the plaid sofa, near her quilting basket.

"I liken the Massacre to skiing, in that when somebody tries it, they'll either get it right away and like it, or they'll say, 'What's this for?'" says Jim. He's a serious, professorial-looking man in his late sixties with white whiskers and a deep, gruff voice. "I've given up feeling that anybody would like it, because I know that most people don't have that kind of mind."

I know that Jim means that *not just anybody* can get into his contests, but you could be forgiven for wondering if he meant that *not anybody* is capable of understanding them. See, map rallying is a strange and byzantine pursuit, even harder to describe than it is to master. As a kid, I would see regular ads for the Massacre in *Games* magazine, and I imagined the event as a freewheeling scavenger hunt through the atlas—exactly the kind of thing I would have loved at that age, though I never actually signed up. The reality of the event, I see as Jim and I peruse last year's contest booklet, is very different.

Here's a sample step from the third of the rally's eight legs, this one between Paris, Ontario, and Eden Park, Ohio:

> **8.** After having gone through U.S. 24 shield on page 51, turn on highway whose number comprises two digits and that is upon a limited-access highway in the direction that's toward nearest other unnumbered interchange.

If you can parse and negotiate that instruction correctly, you must then answer a multiple-choice question about your chosen route:

> **Q27.** Which among these do you see first?
> a. Bowling Green
> b. Ohio Tpk.
> c. Pemberville
> d. Scotch Ridge

Questions like these are the equivalent of the manned checkpoints at a real road rally: they test whether or not you've followed the course successfully. Jim and his collaborators cleverly "fail-safe" each step of the way, so that even when you miss a turn or a trick, you generally get looped back onto the correct route without ever realizing your misstep.

The devious traps built into each step typically rely, in equal parts, on careful observation and hair-splitting interpretation of the contest's rules. You might think a "road" is the same as a "named highway," for example, but not in the Massacre: here, they're very different. (A road is the line on the map, and it may carry one named highway, like "Interstate 25" or "Iowa 42," along its path, or several at the same time, or none at all.) "Course following"—how to navigate the road between the end of one instruction and the beginning of the next— seems like a simple concept, but in practice it requires a set of four tiebreaking rules of decreasing priority, each so complex that even the word "on" comes with its own Clintonian three-paragraph definition. Even punctuation matters: a place-name without quotation marks refers to the place itself, but with quotation marks, it refers to the map text *labeling* the place. And so on.

This level of precision can sometimes make the Massacre seem airless and technical to clueless newbies like me, but Jim insists that's not the goal. "We try to make the rules correspond to reality," he tells me. "We try to keep as much verisimilitude as we can, to have people actually feel like they're on the road, going from this point to that point. They're seeing landmarks along the way. They're watching for turns." For longtime participants, much of the fun lies in the in-jokes and regular "characters" that pop up en route, adding some color to the otherwise legalistic proceedings. The most beloved such regular is the Old Maltese, a grizzled coot often spotted near his cabin in Malta, Montana. The Maltese is Jim's alter ego in the yearly contest, and the Sinclairs still get phone calls at home every February asking if "the Old Maltese is there." (Participants are encouraged to call or write if they don't understand the rules.) "I always say, 'He's not in, but can *I* help you?'" says Jim.

These recurring traditions have kept the same players coming back to his contests for decades. They are a devoted bunch. Nancy Wilson, a retired ER nurse from Petaluma, California, has been playing in the Massacre for more than thirty years. She once scheduled a trip to Liechtenstein just so that she could postmark her Massacre answer sheet from the tiny Alpine country. (Jim makes sure to recognize the top score submitted from each state and country.) Bart Bramley is a professional bridge player from Dallas (the American Contract Bridge League player of the year in 1997, in fact) and a four-time winner of the Massacre. His nearsightedness has been getting worse of late, but he's put off getting the LASIK surgery that would cure his myopia in minutes. Why? Because now, without contacts, his vision is clearest when he's looking at objects practically touching the tip of his nose—the perfect distance for map rally purposes. "I can examine the map from about one inch away and see everything," he says. "If I got LASIK, I wouldn't be able to do that anymore."

But time has winnowed away the faithful. Around three thousand players entered the Massacre each year at its early-nineties peak; last year fewer than five hundred sent in answers. It's tempting to point to this decline as another apocalyptic sign of How Americans Hate Maps, but instead Jim blames the death of road rallying, the sport whose fans made up his core audience. "We used to ask them their age," he says, "and in the seventies the answer would come back in their midthirties. Then the next year it'd be late thirties. Then it would be close to forty. It was obvious that we were keeping the same cohort."

"Every once in a while we'll hear from somebody saying their father or their mother has passed," Sue adds. "I think they're letting us know, not only to stop the mail but to say their late parent really enjoyed it."

"It's bittersweet," Jim agrees.

"Or we'll hear from someone who says, 'My eyesight's not good anymore.'"

"We don't dwell on it."

"But it is sort of nice, that somebody thought enough of us to take the time to write."

Sometimes a caller will even tell the Sinclairs how much they enjoyed finishing the contest with Mom or Dad one last time. Most solvers play alone, but others evidently make the Massacre a February family tradition. As a map lover, this sounds like an idyllic way to spend quality time with the kids. I imagine three or four generations of delighted faces crowded around an open road atlas. There are steaming mugs of hot chocolate in my mental picture, and for some reason everyone is wearing sweaters. That's for me, I decide. This year, the Jennings family will be driving its first annual map rally!

Not long after I return home from California, a big white Priority Mail envelope shows up from the Sinclairs' address. I eagerly rip it open and find a Rand McNally road atlas (with a "St. Valentine's Day Massacre" logo custom-printed on the cover) and a route booklet. The introduction is signed by both Jim and "the Old Maltese," who wish me luck.

That evening I gather Mindy and the kids together and explain that we're going on a cross-country drive . . . *through the atlas!* The reaction I get is excitement before the ellipsis and a suspicious scowl afterward, as though I'd just told a room full of kids that I was going to show them some awesome magic tricks . . . *using science!*

We open the atlas to northern California and find the Golden Gate Bridge, our starting line. "Go right at Interstate 580 in San Rafael," I read aloud. "Which among these do you see first? (a) Berkeley, (b) San Francisco, or (c) London."

"There's Berkeley," says Mindy. We all agree, and I circle the first "a" on the answer sheet. Five steps later, by the time we get to Sacramento, the kids are already getting edgy.

"This is boring!" Dylan complains. "When are we going to be done?"

"Most people take twenty or thirty hours to finish the course."

"Thirty *hours?*" he groans theatrically.

"Wow," says Mindy. "This is just like being on a *real* car trip with Dylan!"

Twenty minutes later, the mutiny is growing. Caitlin is singing to herself on the floor under the table; Dylan is making loud explosion noises and playing with a toy army man wearing a parachute. I'm squinting at a map of southern Oregon, trying to count the lakes I'm passing along U.S. 395. From a car this would be easy; in the atlas, it's surprisingly headache-inducing. For one thing, I've resorted to a ruler to measure the distance from each lake to the highway. (By Massacre rules, I can "see" only things that are less than a quarter inch from the road). Also, I've just realized that instruction 16 placed me "upon" this highway—not *on* it. This is apparently a crucial distinction. I leave one finger to mark my spot on the map while flipping through the rules to try to understand the subtle differences between "on" and "upon." Suddenly Dylan launches his paratrooper into the air and it lands right on the atlas where my finger was carefully tracing.

"Dy-*lan!*" I bellow, in full-on Dave-from-the-Chipmunks mode.

"Wow," says Mindy. "This is just like being on a *real* car trip with Dad!"

Thus ends my ill-advised attempt to try a thirty-hour map exercise with two small children. Perhaps, like John Spafford, I'm doomed to be the last map geek in my own gene pool. I grouchily scoop up my road atlas and my grievances and head off to my office to continue my virtual road trip in silence.

For the next few weeks, I doggedly spend an hour or so every night on the Massacre. (Now I know what it massacres: your free time.) My kids learn to leave me alone when I'm hunched over the road atlas muttering things like "Go left on 191, then go right on unpaved road when you see '191' in Wyoming" and moving my finger slowly across the paper as if all the highways were Braille. It turns out that, despite my fascination with maps of all kinds, I am really, phenomenally bad at map rallying. At one point during the second week, I find myself in west Texas when I can infer from the directions that I'm still supposed to be in Colorado. When I finally figure out where I went wrong and get back to the Rockies, it takes me a full hour to inch my way from

Cañon City, Colorado, to nearby Pueblo. That's longer than it would take me to actually *drive* those forty miles.

I begin to secretly hope the whole thing will turn out to be a prank, like those elementary school tests in instruction-following that begin with "Read all the instructions before beginning," then march you down a list of pointless, labyrinthine directions only to end with something like "Ignore all the previous steps. Leave your page blank except for your name at the top, and hand it in." But as the days stretch into weeks and I wind my way through Kansas and Nebraska, my hopes dim. So does my vision. Every time I go back to recheck my answers, I somehow wind up following the same deterministic instructions onto different highways entirely. Theoretical physicists take note: the Massacre instructions appear to occupy some kind of nexus of quantum-level uncertainty. Schrödinger's Road Trip.

On a road trip, when you start to lose it, you should pull over for the night. Jim allows rookies like me to mail in answers after completing only four of the Massacre's eight legs, and in the end that's what I do. Stranded in South Dakota, doomed never to "see" the Statue of Liberty at the finish line, I admit defeat and mail in my answer sheet.

Three weeks later, I get an e-mail from "the Old Maltese," letting me know that I finished in first place! Well, I finished first among first-time contestants who, like me, wimped out halfway. All six of them. Still, my final score of sixteen isn't bad—that's sixteen missed questions out of forty-eight. As in golf, the lowest score wins. Bart Bramley is one of six entrants this year with a perfect score of zero, handing him his fifth Massacre win. Maybe the LASIK will have to wait one more year.

When the complete answer sheet arrives in the mail, I notice with a groan that one of my sixteen goofs was the very first Massacre question: do you see Berkeley or San Francisco first driving east across the Richmond–San Rafael Bridge? How did we manage to blow that one? Reopening the atlas, I see my mistake. In my careful perusal of the teensiest map text, I'd managed to miss a much bigger feature: San Francisco *County*, stretching almost all the way across the bay.

I should have listened to Edgar Allan Poe. Way back in 1844, in his classic mystery story "The Purloined Letter," Poe has his detective, Dupin, say the following:

> There is a game of puzzles which is played upon a map. One party playing requires another to find a given word—the name of a town, river, state or empire—any word, in short, upon the motley and perplexed surface of the chart. A novice in the game generally seeks to embarrass his opponents by giving them the most minutely lettered names; but the adept selects such words as stretch, in large characters, from one end of the chart to the other. These, like the over-largely lettered signs and placards of the street, escape observation by dint of being excessively obvious.*

In my conversations with roadgeeks and map rallyers, I marveled at their endless compulsion for precision, which struck me as the polar opposite of the kind of Kerouacian freedom that the American road has come to symbolize. On a *real* road trip, I sneered, you wouldn't worry about the typeface of the interstate signs or the history of their numbering. You certainly wouldn't limit your sightseeing to places within a quarter-map-inch of the road you were on. Or even *upon*.

But maybe Dupin was right: by focusing on these tiniest, geekiest details, I've been missing the big picture about roadfans. If this hobby were just about *arbitrary* detail, Jim Sinclair could mail out a copy of *The Betty Crocker Cookbook* to his players every year and have them follow circuitous and confusing directions to bake Lemon Chiffon Cake. Roadgeeks could obsess about anything with a nice regular number-

---

* Billy Wilder used the same gimmick in his underrated 1943 war movie *Five Graves to Cairo*. The titular "graves" are actually materiel caches scattered across the Sahara. Their locations turn out to be hidden on the map in exceedingly simple fashion: they were left at the spots where the letters E, G, Y, P, and T stretch out across the desert, spelling "Egypt" on the map.

ing system: baseball cards or tornadoes or Mozart sonatas. But instead they chose maps as their vehicle. Roadgeek photography and the St. Valentine's Day Massacre are just ways to get as close as possible to the atlas, like zooming in endlessly on Google Earth. That's how compelling maps are to us cartophiles. We want to enter them.

"You know how most people can't walk past a mirror without looking?" Bart Bramley asked me. "I feel the same way about maps." While I was working on the Massacre this year, it felt like aversion therapy: a dose of maps so strong that even I couldn't handle it. But if so, it didn't work—I have a feeling I'm going to be entering the rally again next year. Look out, Bramley. I'm gunning for you!

Maybe I'll even invite the kids along again. But next time we'll run it like a real family vacation: they'll be in a separate row of seats, kept away from the adults by a clever safety system of straps and buckles, and plugged into a portable DVD player at all times. Family togetherness! Next year, we might even get farther than South Dakota.

Chapter 10

OVEREDGE

['ō-vər-ˌej] *n.*: the portion of the map that lies outside the neatline border

Look for the secrets half buried like trinkets in a field,
Hope that the hidden things someday will be revealed.
—JOHN DARNIELLE

At midnight on May 1, 2001, some unnamed hero at U.S. Air Force Space Command, located on the high plains just east of Colorado Springs, pressed a button, and it affected millions of people all over the world. Most of the things the government can do at the push of a button *don't* immediately improve our quality of life, but this action, ordered by the president himself, made life ten times better for map nerds everywhere. Just like magic, the Global Positioning System—an array of twenty-four satellites in medium Earth orbit—could now tell you where you were standing, anywhere on the surface of the planet, to within just a few meters of accuracy.

A cynic might point out that the only reason the military had the power to make the system so much better at the touch of a button was that it had been lying to us all along. The first GPS satellite had been launched way back in 1978, but only government users had access to the real data. Civilian owners of GPS receivers got a scrambled signal that introduced random error, so that most of the time their location information would be off by hundreds of feet. Giving citizens the wrong answers to important questions is nothing new for the U.S. government, of course; the IRS has been doing it for years. But in this case, the error was intentional, baked into the signal for reasons of national security.

But by the late 1990s, this scrambling, euphemistically called "selective availability," was becoming obsolete. The military had figured out how to localize its GPS jamming in places where secrecy was an issue, and a new ground-based technology called Differential GPS was allowing civilians to improve on satellite data anyway. So President Bill Clinton ordered "selective availability" to be turned off altogether, and in the spring of 2000, White House science advisor Neal Lane announced the big moment. "All the people who've bought a GPS receiver for a boat or a car, or whether they use one in business or for recreation, will find that they are ten times more accurate as of midnight tonight," he told reporters.

In Portland, Oregon, that night, a computer consultant named Dave Ulmer stayed up to watch the change on his GPS receiver, a clunky Magellan 2000 that he'd bought back in the mid-1990s, when the year "2000" appended to a product name still sounded sleek and futuristic. "It was really quite a momentous thing to see happening," he says. "I still have the track logs that I recorded during that event." One minute he had a three-hundred-foot radius of inaccuracy on his screen, the next—hey presto!—he had only thirty. That difference, he knew, would have meant a lot to him two months previously. In March, he'd been snowmobiling to the peak of Mount Saint Helens, trying to follow a trail he'd taken once before. But selective availability led him one hundred yards off course, and he shot out over an ice ridge he wasn't expecting. "I slid down one side of the mountain on my back, and the machine went down the other side of the mountain, end over end, and got demolished. It was quite an eye-opening experience about what three hundred feet can do to you."

Seeing his signal converge on his home that May night was like putting on a pair of eyeglasses after enduring a lifetime of astigmatism. Later, lying in bed, he was too excited to sleep. The scrambled GPS of the 1990s could tell you that you were in a football stadium (which, if you *were* in a football stadium, you probably already knew) but the new technology could tell you exactly which yard marker you were standing on, and that opened new horizons. What wonderful things can we do now with GPS? he remembers thinking. There's got to be something that human beings have never done before until this moment in time. "And that," he says, "is when I invented geocaching."

The next morning, Ulmer began gathering supplies. On a woodland turnout by the side of a winding hillside road a mile from his home, he pulled over and half buried a five-gallon bucket containing a notebook where finders could sign their names, four dollars in cash, *George of the Jungle* on VHS, a Ross Perot book, mapping software, the handle of a slingshot, and a can of beans.* Then he posted the latitude and longitude of that spot on an Internet newsgroup for GPS users. That first announcement was startlingly prophetic, envisioning in detail not just a single celebratory stunt but an ongoing international treasure hunt in embryo:

> Now that SA [selective availability] is off, we can start a worldwide Stash Game! With non-SA accuracy, it should be easy to find a stash from waypoint information. Waypoints of secret stashes could be shared on the Internet, people could navigate to the stashes and get some stuff.
>
> Make your own stash in a unique location, put in some stuff and a logbook, and post the location on the Internet. Soon we will have thousands of stashes all over the world to go searching for. Have fun!

The next day, a Vancouver, Washington, GPS buff named Mike Teague drove across the Columbia River and found Ulmer's stash. He signed his name and left some cigarettes, a cassette tape, and a pen. That weekend, like a carrier of a virus, Teague created two new

---

* This historic first geocache is long gone by now, but a new cache, complete with commemorative plaque, was placed at the site by "Team360" in 2003 for the convenience of cachers making a pilgrimage. The Original Can of Beans, or OCB, was found nearby by Team360 on that occasion and has become an honored relic, unveiled to hushed silences at geocaching gatherings as if it were the finger bone of a saint or a splinter of the True Cross.

stashes of his own, on the slopes of Mount Saint Helens. Within just two weeks, there were stashes hidden in a half dozen states, as well as Chile, Australia, and New Zealand, and Teague put up a simple website to keep track of the growing list of stash coordinates. It was becoming clear that Ulmer had tapped into something primal—not just the boredom of gadget gurus but some neglected part of our hunter-gatherer hindbrain that *needs* to look for elusive things and rarely gets the chance in a modern world where everything we really need (food, water, heat, reality shows) gets served up to us instantly while we sit by passively.*

Up the freeway three hours in Seattle, a newlywed computer programmer named Jeremy Irish returned home from his honeymoon to find that SaviShopper.com, the retail dot-com he worked for, was failing. "It was kind of depressing," he tells me. "I was looking for distractions." His wife had given him permission to buy a GPS device, and when he typed "gps games" into Yahoo!, the first site that came up was Teague's "stash hunt" list. There was one just fifty miles from his home, he saw, and an hour later, he was bouncing along a boulder-strewn logging trail in his less-than-rugged Saturn SL2. At the end of the trail, he continued on foot through a sunbaked clear-cut, on the hottest day of the summer. "I had very limited water with me," he says. "It was horrible. A horrible trip." But the thrill of finding the stash—an index-card box hidden behind a stump—made the whole ordeal worth it. "Walking down the hill, I thought, well, the first thing I need to do is prepare people, so they're not as inexperienced and unprepared as I was."

Ulmer and the other early GPS scavenger hunters had already decided that "geocache" was a better name for their treasures than "GPS stash"—drug mules and potheads have stashes, but old-timey explorers and French-Canadian trappers have caches!—and Irish decided to begin a successor to Teague's site under the name "Geocaching.com," which came online with just seventy-five caches

---

* If true, this would explain virtually every hobby ever concocted by man, from golfers to stamp collectors to those frightening old people you see running metal detectors over the dirt at parks and beaches.

listed. A *New York Times* article outed geocaching to the general public in October, and the Web server in Irish's guest bedroom could barely keep up with demand. Maybe, he thought, Geocaching.com could become a real company.

Together with two other castaways of the e-commerce collapse, he began raising money, but found that venture capital options in those post-Internet-bubble days were few and far between. "Can you imagine going into a VC and saying 'Hey, we've got this idea—we're going to create a listing service for plastic containers in the woods'? 'How are you going to monetize that?' 'I don't know! You never asked that back in 1998!'" Instead, their first source of funding was a gross of donated T-shirts that they slapped with geocaching logos and sold via the website. The following spring, they started selling "premium memberships" to Geocaching.com as well, so they could quit their day jobs and work on improving the site full-time. That decision turned Geocaching.com into a robust, user-friendly site, the first place a curious consumer would go after getting a GPS receiver as a Christmas present, and it made geocaching into a mass-culture phenomenon. There were only three hundred caches listed when 2001 began; by the end of 2002, there were more than ten thousand.

That transition didn't come without growing pains, though. The early geocaching community was an outsider one, an odd mix of techie hackers and tie-dyed outdoorsmen,* and many were skeptical about an Internet company—from Seattle, no less, just like big bad Microsoft!—swooping in to systematize and commercialize their guerrilla pastime. "Some felt uncomfortable with a small group of people making money off of all their work," says Ed Hall, who ran another website called Buxley's Geocaching Waypoint, the first to display geocache locations on maps. "What are they bringing to it? Why are they trying to assert ownership over *our* game?" Irish and his partners made missteps as well, sending legal warnings to Hall's site (for

---

* The geocaching community still sits at a unique Venn-diagram intersection between indoor and outdoor types. The early GPS units all had rugged model names that sounded like SUVs—Venture, SportTrek, Oregon—despite the fact that many of them were being bought by bookish gadgeteers.

mining Geocaching.com data to draw his maps) and Quinn Stone's NaviCache site (because his logo used the word "geocaching," which Irish had attempted to trademark). After Dave Ulmer himself got into a dust-up on Irish's message boards, his name was removed from the site's "History of Geocaching" page, which for a time credited the placing of the first cache to an anonymous "someone."

The old scuffles are water under the bridge these days. Jeremy Irish is now more savvy about the court of public opinion, and the old guard has come around to the idea of a more centralized, newbie-friendly version of their hobby.* Even Dave Ulmer, not a fan for many years, has mellowed. "I don't mind them making money off of it," he tells me. "Geocaching.com is an excellent website. The guy has put incredible hours into developing the site. He deserves a reward for that." Irish's little start-up has grown into Groundspeak Inc., which employs more than forty-five "Lackeys," as they call themselves, at its Seattle headquarters, all in cubicles festooned with lime-green shades reminiscent of a forest canopy. On March 8, 2010, the geocache count on its website hit one million.

One million geocaches! To be more precise: 1,385,781 active caches at the moment I write this, with more than a thousand new ones appearing each day. That is an astounding number. By comparison, here is a partial inventory of other things there are in the world: 6,230 wide-body jets; 32,000 McDonald's restaurants; 663,000 zebras; 40,000 Segways; and 15,900 synagogues. You've seen all those things, but despite their comparative ubiquity, most people have never knowingly seen a geocache; Groundspeak cofounder Bryan Roth recently called geocaching "the biggest hobby in the world that nobody knows about." That's the whole point of the game: the caches are hard to find if you're not expressly looking for them and sometimes even if you are.

---

* For evidence that Irish's site was crucial to geocaching's growth, look no further than some of the other GPS games that have appeared more recently, like Geodashing (essentially geocaching to randomly chosen points), Shutterspot (geocaching from photo clues), and GeoVexilla (a global game of capture the flag). All are well-designed games, but they're still played by dozens or hundreds worldwide, not geocaching's millions.

But they are everywhere, on all seven continents. There's a geocache hidden in a stone wall at the Vatican, and one in a high temple niche at Angkor Wat, and another in the crook of a tree by Victoria Falls in Zimbabwe. Run your hands along the bottom of the front gates at Las Vegas's Bellagio casino, and you'll find one magnetically attached. There are six on the slopes of Colorado's Pikes Peak and two at Antarctica's McMurdo Station.

Geocaches have changed a little since Dave Ulmer's day. In fact, his historic first cache would be quickly rejected today by the network of Geocaching.com volunteers that vets all new caches, since it breaks several of their cardinal rules: no buried caches, no food, no money. But the essentials of the game are still exactly what he proposed in his 2001 Usenet post. A container is hidden somewhere in the world—the container might be big or small, elaborately camouflaged or just a simple piece of Tupperware. In addition to a paper log, the cache may contain "swag"—cheap trinkets that finders can swap. The latitude and longitude of the hide are posted on the Web, and anyone with a GPS receiver is free to find it and sign the log with their name (or, more often, their geocaching "handle"). Most will return to Geocaching.com and post a log there as well, describing their experience.

Never having found a geocache myself, I'm a little skeptical—can something that sounds so much like a Boy Scout merit badge actually be any fun? The only GPS device in the Jennings home is "Daniel," the low-end Garmin navigator suction-cupped to the windshield of our car. Daniel is actually the name of the English-accented voice we've selected the device to speak in; the factory default was "Jill," a high-maintenance-American voice that we can't stand. When you make a wrong turn, Jill's error message of "Recalculating!" is an aggrieved sigh. Daniel's "Recalculating," by contrast, is in the calm, silky tones of an old family chauffeur. He never judges you. (Actually, our Daniel hasn't said "Recalculating" since I figured out how to hack into his text files. He now says, "You turned the wrong way, dumb-ass. Just do what I say," which is a source of endless delight to the backseat.) The kids treat Daniel like a member of the family. A few months ago, as we were walking through a science museum exhibit about GPS, Dylan said wistfully, "I wish Daniel was here. He'd *love* this."

We don't have a handheld GPS, but I remember what Jeremy Irish told me when I visited his office at Groundspeak: "Geocaching is a trick to get kids to go outside. That was our original mantra." I'd love to see Dylan out exploring the woods behind our house, following ants and building forts and damming streams on a sunny afternoon, but despite our best efforts, he's a true child of the twenty-first century: send him outside, and he'll just *stand there* for twenty minutes with his nose pressed against the sliding glass door, like the world's saddest garden gnome.

But nerdy kids are often big geocachers. Imagine: a treasure hunt just like the ones in books, only there are hundreds of them within a few miles of your house! To an adult, the search is its own reward, but for a child, it seems too good to be true that the search's end is often a trove stuffed with green army men, Happy Meal toys, plastic jewelry, and other priceless treasures.

My wife thinks it's worth a shot. "Dylan will do anything if you give him a twenty-five-cent toy at the end," she says. "That's why he's always asking when we can go back to the dentist."

"Apparently it's totally catching on now that so many people have GPS devices in their phones," I tell her. "Look at this list of famous people who geocache. Mia Farrow, Wil Wheaton, Ryan Phillippe. The drummer from Poison."

Mindy actually seems interested for the first time. "Wait, he goes geocaching with only one arm?"

"From Poison, not Def Leppard!"

A week later, Dylan and I drop sixty bucks on a kid-friendly Geomate.jr, which comes covered in pale green rubber and preloaded with a quarter of a million cache locations. We slip in a pair of batteries, and thirty seconds later its little digital-watch screen is telling us there's a cache exactly 0.17 mile southeast of our front door. Maybe I shouldn't be surprised, but I am. "It's only nine hundred feet that way," I say as we strike out down the driveway, with Dylan waving his GPS back and forth in front of him at arm's length, like it's Fisher-Price's My First Dowsing Rod. "It must be on the back of that hill across the road."

Geocachers always talk about how the joy of caching is in the journey, in the chance to stop and see the unexpected places right under your nose that you otherwise would have driven right past. In fact, it's so axiomatic that geocaching will reveal the hidden secrets of your neighborhood that there's even an acronym in the trade for it: YAPIDKA, meaning "Yet Another Park I Didn't Know About." This is the lasting appeal of the game to Dave Ulmer, who now spends the entire year motoring around the West in an RV. (When I spoke to him, he was camping in the Bradshaw Mountains just south of Prescott, Arizona.) He doesn't log his finds anymore, but, he says, "The minute I get the slightest bit bored, I'll bring up Geocaching.com and see what's in my area. I don't care about the box full of trinkets, but I might find an Indian corral or a fabulously unusual geologic site or lava caves or a beautiful forest viewpoint. You're not going to stumble on that on your own. But with geocaching, you just walk right up to it."

I'm not expecting the woods across the street from my house to hide any mysteries greater than a few broken beer bottles, but once Dylan crests the hill I hear him yell, "Whoa, Dad, come check this out!" The Douglas firs on the hillside—the same ones I can see out my office window every day—conceal an elaborate network of wooden boardwalks and ramps winding through the forest, sometimes as high as ten feet in the air. We've been living across the street from an Ewok village for three years and never knew!

"Some older kids built this to jump their BMX bikes," explains a neighborhood girl, cutting through the woods with her friends. I'm trying to listen politely without taking my eyes off Dylan, who is running up and down the ramps making rocket-ship noises and—hopefully—not getting tetanus from anything rusty and pokey. "But they left and went to college, I think. Nobody uses them now."

I look down at our toy receiver. My coordinates have "zeroed out"; I'm now standing on a uniquely specified point on the Earth's surface, right down to one-thousandth of a minute of longitude and latitude. I'm unexpectedly awestruck at something I take for granted when I use GPS to navigate in the car: every time I take a few steps, the numbers change on the toy in my hand, and that's because it's listening to machines *in space*. A $20 billion array of sophisticated military satellites is helping me find Tupperware in the woods. Truly we are living in the future.

But where's the cache? I have yet to develop what cachers call "geosenses," the seemingly extrasensory ability to get inside the head of the hider, to look at a landscape and spot the likely hiding places of the "geojoy."* No GPS locator is correct down to a single foot, of course. My readings are dependent on the time it's taking signals to bounce off a constellation of six overhead satellites, and if signals start bouncing off of other things—these tall trees, for example—rather than traveling into space in a straight line, small errors will creep in. I know the cache is somewhere in a tight radius around these coordinates, but Space Command can't actually tell me, "It's in that hollow log, dummy!"—I have to look. I kick through leaves, I lift up rocks, I reach under tree roots. It's exactly as much fun as looking for your car keys or searching for your retainer in a cafeteria garbage can. People do this for fun?

But then comes the epiphany. I'm standing at the base of the highest dirt-bike ramp when I realize: geocaching coordinates include only latitude and longitude. What about the Z-axis? What about height? I inch my way up the rickety wooden track. Dylan wants to come too, until he gets halfway up and then realizes he liked it just fine on the ground. At the highest point, where the teenagers used to turn their bikes around, I reach my hand under the platform, and there's something square and metallic. "I got it! I got it!" I shout, euphoric with the unexpected endorphin rush of *finding*. Aha. *That's* why people do this for fun.

Dylan opens the little box and it's love at first sight: a Cracker Jack carton without any of that stupid popcorn or peanuts, just cheap toys. To a six-year-old, it might as well be diamonds and rubies. He spots a plastic sheriff's badge he wants, so he digs around in his pocket until he finds an unused Chuck E. Cheese token and leaves that in its place. I sign the log, carefully replace the cache in its perch, and we head for home as Dylan babbles cheerfully. "Dad, when can we come back and

---

* Yes, some cachers annoyingly append the prefix "geo-" to every other word. The effect is a little like characters in a 1950s science-fiction movie who eat "space fruit" for "space breakfast" in their "space kitchen."

play on the ramps? Dad, are there any more geocaches on our street? Dad?" Score: geocaching 1, video games 0.

Somewhere in the vicinity of five million people are active geocachers, and the rules of the game are scanty enough that no two people play it quite alike. The vast majority are casual cachers, who might occasionally spend a sunny afternoon driving around town with a spouse or kids in tow, looking for a few easy grabs. On a road trip, or with time to kill before an appointment in an unfamiliar part of town, they might think to pull out their smartphone to see if there's a geocache nearby. They are sensible, temperate souls, not prone to crazy obsessions of any kind, and so they are deeply respected by their neighbors and community. Let us speak no more of them.

But some geocachers are more obsessive and their quarries more elaborate. "Extreme cachers," for example, literally risk life and limb for no other reward than an elusive "smiley"—the happy-face icon that signifies a successful find on Geocaching.com. They're not going to waste their time on any cache that's not hidden over a cliff or in an abandoned mine shaft, up a forty-foot oak tree or at the bottom of the Great Salt Lake. They speak in hushed whispers of great white whales like Psycho Urban Cache #13, a legendary West Virginia cache that was dropped via helicopter atop a seventy-foot pylon in the middle of the Potomac River.* Some of these caches are so extreme that they've *never* been found, like Gokyo Ri, left on one of the highest peaks of the Nepalese Himalayas in 2004, or Rainbow Hydrothermal Vents, left by a Russian Mir submersible at the bottom of the Atlantic Ocean in 2002.†

"Puzzle caching" is extreme caching for the mind, and its devotees

---

* The first team to recover Psycho Urban Cache #13 used an elaborate system of ropes, lines, and magnets to snag and replace the cache without ever leaving terra firma; the second team managed to place an anchor on top of the tower with a bow and arrow and then scaled its sheer stone sides.

† This cache was actually left by none other than Richard "Lord British" Garriott, the video game developer whose *Ultima* series I spent much of my childhood playing (and mapping). Garriott, the son of a former NASA astronaut, has also been to space: he was the sixth "space tourist" to board the International Space Station.

forgo scuba or rock-climbing gear in favor of a simpler piece of equipment: the sharpened pencil. A puzzle cache is suggested by a tantalizing blue question mark on the Geocaching.com maps, because it's the only type of geocache that *doesn't* come with a latitude and longitude. Instead, would-be finders must outwit some kind of diabolical puzzle—crack a code or answer an un-Google-able quiz or riddle—to decipher the correct coordinates. With its high per capita density of software engineers and other pasty computer types, Seattle is a hotbed for this kind of cache, and soon I'm hooked. No matter how esoteric the subject—backgammon, twentieth-century earthquakes, Chinese characters—I'm willing to dive into it for a "smiley." One cache requires me to master the matrix that transforms the RGB colors on my computer monitor into the YIQ system used by color TVs. For another, I have to calculate the "geographic centroid" of Seattle—the point at which you could balance the city on the head of a sufficiently sturdy pin. At one low point, I even rent the Uma Thurman movie *Prime* in order to derive a set of coordinates from the MPAA registration number at the end of its credits. I feel a vague kinship with extreme-caching daredevils whenever I find one of these caches—I may not have rappelled down a sheer cliff face, but I did have to face *some* grueling ordeal, whether it was matrix algebra or a lousy Uma Thurman rom-com. Signing each log, it feels as though I've *accomplished* something.

Extreme cachers and puzzle cachers might take hours or even days to notch a single geocache; they prize quality over quantity. Power cachers, on the other hand, are the bottomless gourmands of the geocaching world. Their dictum is to cache as much as possible for as long as possible. On September 27, 2010, a two-person team from Malibu calling themselves "ventura_kids" set a new world record by finding 1,157 caches in a single day.* Do the math: that's a new cache every minute and fifteen seconds . . . for twenty-four hours. By comparison, Dylan

---

* Ventura_kids first took the world speed record in the summer of 2009, notching 413 smileys on the roads around the Denver Airport to celebrate the fiftieth birthday of fellow cacher "EMC of Northridge, CA," who, along with "f0t0m0m," accompanied the Kids on their record-breaking run. EMC is actually Elin Carlson, an accomplished soprano whose nerdiest claim to fame, aside from her prolific geocaching career, is the fact that she sings the ethereal "oo-*wooooo*" vocals for the latest incarnation of the *Star Trek* theme.

and I spent more than an hour finding that BMX cache, and that was just a stone's throw from our front yard. The key to this kind of brutal efficiency is planning. The ventura_kids' entire route was charted in advance, in an area with no traffic or stoplights. Their Jeep was stocked for any eventuality, including ten gallons of gas and headlamps for each cacher. At each stop, team members would scramble like a pit crew, typically uncovering the cache before the driver even had his GPS device unmounted from the dashboard. (They used preprinted stickers instead of signing in ink, which saved precious seconds.) "Pace yourselves," Steve O'Gara of ventura_kids advised anyone on the Geocaching.com forums who might want to follow in his team's footsteps. "Try not to get any injuries near the beginning. Keep drinking water. Stop for a picture now and then. Watch out for scorpions, and cactus."

Even so, this amazing marathon was possible only because of the venue chosen: rural roads in the high desert of south-central Nevada. Many of these highways are "power trails," in which easy-to-find cache containers have been placed every 528 feet (by Geocaching.com rules, no two caches may be closer to each other than a tenth of a mile) along the side of a road, usually at the bases of electrical poles. Why

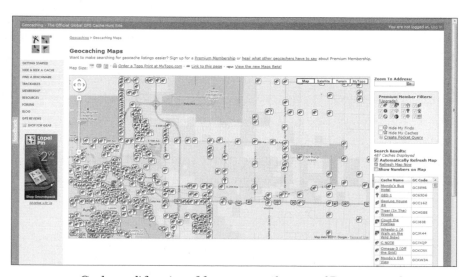

Cache proliferation: fifty square miles east of Denver, with its Malthusian swarm of little geocache icons placed along "power trails"

leave a trail of geocaches along an ugly highway, rather than in some scenic nature spot? To encourage feats of speed like this one, of course.

The artificial abundance of a million-geocache world has soured some old-school cachers on the game. Originally, the rarity of geocaches was part of their allure; you had to venture to a remote mountaintop or deserted beach to find one. By definition, how can it be special anymore to find something so ubiquitous? Purists call the new glut of low-quality caches "micro-spew," and heap scorn on their most typical delivery system, the 35-millimeter film canister. "Film canisters are to geocaching what spam is to e-mail," they will tell you, or "Every time you hide a film canister, a fairy dies." Ed Hall once made it a point to find every cache in his neighborhood but finally gave up when a cache—a film canister, natch—showed up a quarter mile from his house in the least exotic spot imaginable: the drive-through of his nearest Burger King. "It was at that point," he says, "that I realized geocaching had probably jumped some kind of shark."

But other geocachers thrive on the density. They won't rest until there's a pill bottle Velcroed to the metal skirt at the base of every parking lot lamppost and a magnetic key container beneath every picnic table. The more the merrier! I think this is a telltale clue to what's driving geocaching's sudden popularity: the urge to fill an otherwise overexplained universe with mysterious secrets. Children intuitively believe that our gray everyday existence must conceal beneath its surface another world, brighter and more interesting, like the one in storybooks. But then they get older and gradually come to terms with the sad truth that there *is* no hidden world—no Confederate gold behind the bricks of the old fireplace, no genie in any of the glass bottles washed up by the surf. Geocaching restores those lost treasures by the thousands. It's a way for acolytes to make the world feel a little more magical, one camouflaged Altoids tin at a time.

The Harry Potter books have sold six jillion copies by trading on this same fantasy: a secret world known only to a small coterie of insiders. In J. K. Rowling's series, just as in geocaching, seemingly ordinary places and objects conceal numinous secrets: a blank brick wall might open onto a magical secret alley, an old boot or a newspaper might be an enchanted teleportation device in disguise. It's no

surprise, then, that geocachers have borrowed the word "Muggle"—
a clueless nonwizard in Harry Potter's world—to apply to clueless
nongeocachers. This reflects both the satisfaction cachers take in their
secret knowledge (they can walk along a busy trail with the confidence that they know something about that particular tree stump that
nobody else knows) and the very real threat posed by outsiders. Cachers
will go to great lengths to avoid being spotted while hiding or retrieving a geocache, because all it takes is one too-curious onlooker and
the secret spot might be "Muggled" (plundered) and thereby ruined
for future seekers. So there's a clandestine thrill to the sport, almost
reminiscent of Cold War–era double espionage: lots of long, chilly
waits on park benches pretending to feed birds and cautious drive-bys
of prearranged "dead drops" on lonely country roads.

Geocachers develop their own tricks to avoid suspicious looks (followed, quite often, by 911 calls—police interrogations are a rite of passage for prolific cachers*) as they lurk in shrubbery and poke around
utility boxes. Some swear by a fluorescent orange vest and clipboard:
you can apparently act as fishy as you like as long as you're dressed like a
city employee. Others, like David Carriere of Ottawa (geocaching handle "Zartimus") go caching only by dead of night. "It was the only time
I could find to go, with the kids and all," he tells me, but I'm not entirely
convinced by his innocent explanation. Zartimus, you see, is best known
in caching circles for his eccentric uniform: a Batman cape and cowl
accompanied by a ten-foot bullwhip. If Muggles approach, he says, "I
kill the light by pulling the cape over my head and I just sit there. You
can't see me with that thing on because the cape breaks up the shape." I
prefer daylight caching (and don't own a single superhero vigilante cos-
tume), so I develop a strategy of talking loudly into my GPS receiver as
if it were a cell phone while searching, and I avoid caches near schools
and playgrounds unless I have my kids with me. You may laugh, but if
you're a middle-aged man, just try spending twenty minutes carefully
rubbing your fingers over every inch of a playground's chain-link fence
and see where you end up spending the night.

---

* Scubasonic, whom we will meet in a moment, has been questioned by police no fewer
than twenty-five times.

Geocaching and the law have had something of a checkered relationship. The creepy lurking isn't the most serious problem; since 9/11, hiding weird-looking packages in public urban places has become an increasingly bad idea, and hardly a month goes by without news reports of a geocache-sparked mass evacuation, which typically ends in a bomb squad dutifully detonating a small box of gumball-machine toys. Often these hides have been placed, in violation of Geocaching.com guidelines, too close to infrastructure: bridges, railroads, or monuments. And it doesn't help that one of the most common kind of geocache container is the most suspicious-looking one possible: a green military-surplus ammunition can. You might as well hide your logbook in a round black ticking sphere with a sizzling fuse on top and the word "BOMB" written on the side. In Arabic. "I use Tupperware now, because it doesn't look dangerous," says Ed Hall. "An ammo box: not so much."

Cache containers in the wilderness can cause problems of another kind: once you attract hundreds of people to some out-of-the-way spot, it's not an out-of-the-way spot anymore. Visible "geotrails" tend to form as vegetation gets trampled and soil compacted.* The National Park Service banned geocaching from national parks and wilderness areas early on, seeing it as a perversely elaborate form of littering. But in a time of declining park attendance, many wilderness managers are privately sympathetic to geocachers, who are model visitors in other respects: avid, knowledgeable nature lovers who often organize cleanup events as they search, using the motto "CITO"—"cache in, trash out." In October 2009, the park service "clarified" its policy by giving park superintendents leeway to allow geocaching where appropriate, and in 2010, caches finally returned to some national parklands.

Just three months after finding my first cache, I'm officially addicted. I don't go out on twenty-four-hour power-caching runs like the

---

* Six weeks after placing the first cache, Dave Ulmer predicted this very problem, becoming so alarmed at the eco-Frankenstein he'd created that he posted on June 17, 2001, "OK, OK. I Give Up! All development on the sport of Geocaching should cease." It was too late.

ventura_kids, but I do get a little twitchy if I haven't grabbed a cache for a day or so. I try to pretend that my habit is "just research," or I drag Dylan along with me as a sort of beard, so that I can blame it all on his insatiable appetite for plastic toys, but he typically gets bored at least an hour or two before I do and I have to string him along with the promise of doughnuts so that he'll come with me for *just one more, I swear.* I schedule errands around the locations of puzzle caches I've solved. I switch out my Swiss Army knife for one that has tweezers (for removing stubborn log papers from tiny cache containers) and a ballpoint pen for signing. In fact, I've signed my caching handle in so many logbooks that I actually catch myself endorsing a check with it once.

It's not unusual for geocachers to rearrange their lives around the game. "Viajero Perdido," an Alberta geocacher, became so obsessed with a single cache on Nicaragua's Mosquito Coast, one that had sat in the jungle for five years without a single find, that he flew all the way to Central America just to log it and tacked on a Caribbean vacation so that friends and family wouldn't think he was crazy. (He and his native guides spent hours blazing trails with machetes, but with no luck; he returned home with nothing but a "DNF"—"Did Not Find"—to his credit.) "Hukilaulau," from Long Island, says he took a temp job in Phoenix just so he could stop in Kansas along the way to log "Mingo," the world's oldest active cache.

Dave Ulmer claims that geocaching's addictive properties were all part of his master plan. "Geocaching is a new application program for your brain," he tells me. "It's like getting a new game for your computer and installing it. When you learn about geocaching, you're installing a new game in your brain." Ulmer has spent the last decade working on *Beyond the Information Age,* a manifesto on information theory that he's convinced will change human history, if he could only get someone to read it. From my perusal of the manuscript, I become convinced that it's either completely crackpot or completely genius; I'm just not smart enough to tell the difference. In Ulmer's parlance, geocaching is an "ISSU"—a self-replicating "intelligent system specification unit." "It's a very complicated system, when you think of all the millions of people that are involved in it. That's how I put it together, and that's why it worked so damn well. It was engineered to be that from day one."

"So you see the whole activity as a life-form that spreads on its own? Are we all little neurons in this big brain?"

"That's right!"

But for all my absorption into the geocaching hive-mind, there's one coveted caching honor I don't have: an FTF, or "First to Find." Some cachers specialize in finding *virgin* caches—being the first to sign a newly placed hide. If twenty-four-hour power cachers are the marathoners of the geoworld, then First-to-Find hounds are its sprinters. Bryan Fix, a Portland, Oregon, native who caches as "Scubasonic," has a near-superhuman FTF track record: more than nine hundred FTFs notched, fully 14 percent of his finds. He once bagged ten in a single day, which is remarkable, since the Portland area sees only ten or fifteen new caches in a typical *week*.

Back in the day, when there weren't many geocachers, the FTF was an achievement within the reach of mere mortals; even casual cachers would stumble upon one from time to time. But this is the steroid era. "Premium" members who pay Geocaching.com $30 a year can choose to receive instant notifications the second a new cache is published, and the hard-core types make sure those messages find them on their phones or PDAs.

"I actually sleep with my BlackBerry," Bryan tells me from behind the desk of his Vancouver, Washington, real estate office. He's a strikingly youthful-looking forty-nine-year-old, with a high, gleaming forehead that somehow makes him seem boyish, not balding. "I have it on the vibrate mode, and if it beeps, I jump up and I'm gone. I always have my clothes laid out next to the bed. I'm out the door in a minute, and I enter the coordinates on the way."

"So you're like a doctor."

"Well, I don't get the money."

The FTF junkies are often the most social of geocachers, since they're the only ones who so often converge on the same cache at the same time. Bryan knows and likes his nemeses, even though he's not the most beloved figure on the local circuit. "I've been accused of cheating," he sighs. "I guess they're bothered that I get so many, but if you want to get 'em, get up off the couch and go get 'em! There's nothing stopping you." He's seen cars squeal up to new cache locations only to have their angry drivers scowl at him or slam their fists on the car roof in frustration when they see that there are already flashlights combing the forest. No one, after all, remembers the *second* team to climb Everest.

He's also learned over time where his rivals live, based on which geocaches they've beaten him to—FTFers, like street gangs, develop "turf." So Bryan decided to broaden his turf by analyzing where new geocaches would appear and at what time of day. "I started seeing a pattern," he says. "So I would actually drive over and sit centrally located, where I thought they were coming up." He still spends some nights at his favorite spot, the Foster Road on-ramp to I-205, camped in his car like a cop on a stakeout, waiting patiently for new prey to appear on his BlackBerry or laptop. Most nights, sooner or later, one does. "And then I take off. I'm out of there."

I don't get instant notifications of new geocaches, so in my short geocaching career I've never even come close to an FTF. Then, one drizzly afternoon as I'm walking out of the grocery store, I idly pull up the geocaching app on my phone and select "Find Nearby Geocaches." I'm just blocks from home, and I motored through all the caches in my neighborhood months ago, so I'm not expecting to see anything close by. But there sits a blue question mark at the top of the list: a mystery cache I don't recognize, just a mile or two away. I bring up its full listing, and it looks like a simple logic puzzle. Even better, it was published less than two hours ago and the user log is still empty. I race home and spend ten minutes scribbling away at the problem with a pencil, and finally produce some likely-looking coordinates. When I bring them up on Google Earth, they turn out to be the end of a biking trail just five minutes from my house. Is a local "Scubasonic" type already en route, or do I have a chance? I grab my car keys and take the stairs down to the garage three steps at time, adrenaline-infused blood throbbing in my ears.

"Hey, are you going out?" calls Mindy from the kitchen. "Dylan forgot his piano books. Can you drop them off at Janetta's before his lesson starts?"

Is she serious? How can she not know what's at stake here? *"No!"* I bellow, slamming the garage door behind me.

In the car, I stare at myself in the rearview mirror for a moment. What have I become? I'm yelling at my family and sabotaging their piano lessons, and for what? So that my signature will appear maybe one centimeter higher on a piece of paper that practically no one will ever see? I dutifully trudge back upstairs and grab Dylan's piano books. Then I race back to the car and peel out.

It's pouring rain when I arrive at the bike trail, and the spot seems deserted. The cache is now exactly four hours old—surely it's been found once or twice by now. I'm drenched by the time I finally see the tiny pill bottle hidden in the tall grass at the base of a wooden post. I unscrew the top with shaking fingers, and I'm not sure if that's from the cold or not. For some reason, I find myself thinking of the explorer Robert Scott. When Scott journeyed to Antarctica in 1911, he had high hopes of being the first to reach the South Pole. But on January 16, 1912, his team spotted a rock cairn on the ice ahead of them, and dog sled tracks heading north. The Norwegian expedition of his rival Roald Amundsen had beaten him to the Antarctic FTF by a matter of weeks. "The worst has happened," he wrote in his journal. "All the day dreams must go; it will be a wearisome return."* I'm expecting to read the name of some GPS-toting Amundsen inside the cache, but instead I find something I've never seen before in my geocaching career: a completely blank log sheet. It's unspoiled territory, just like the white fringes on the edges of maps during the Age of Discovery, and I do feel like a pioneer as I proudly make my mark with the tiny ballpoint in my Swiss Army knife.

If geocaching really is a video game downloaded into our skulls, then the initials atop its high-score list are undoubtedly LVB, for Lee van der Bokke, a retired telecom engineer from San Francisco's East Bay. In his eight years of caching, van der Bokke, aka "Alamogul," has racked up a staggering 53,353 finds, more than anyone else in the

---

* In fact, Scott and his entire party were lost in a blizzard on the return trip. Geocachers, thankfully, generally face much lower stakes.

world and almost 15,000 more than his nearest rival. That number is almost certainly on the low side, in fact; he's probably logged three or four more finds while I've been typing this paragraph. He cached for many years as "Team Alamo" but grew tired of skeptical cachers assuming his unlikely numbers were being churned out by some massive conglomerate. "The 'team' is me and my wife," he insists. "And she hates geocaching!"

Van der Bokke began as a casual cacher; he was stuck at home all day with a grumpy eightysomething father, and geocaching was a way to pass the time while walking his golden retriever, Casey, in the local hills. As his numbers grew, so did his intensity; he began to strip his caching runs of nonessentials: the dog, the wife, even left turns.* "I don't cache every day," he tells me. "I'll normally go a couple days a week, somewhere with high numbers."

"So you plan in advance? 'Here's the area we're heading for, here are the thirty caches we're going to get'?"

He laughs dismissively. "Oh, no. We don't go *anywhere* for just thirty." This must be the geocaching equivalent of Linda Evangelista's famous dictum that supermodels "don't wake up for less than $10,000 a day." Thirty sounds pretty good to me—it would be at least triple my own daily record—but hundred-cache days aren't unusual for megacachers like Alamogul. "Sometimes it's a chore," he concedes. "More than twenty-five caches in a day, and it starts to get boring. But if you've driven a long ways to go somewhere, you want to get it done."

So megacachers will cache long past the point of pleasure, because they know the withdrawal would be worse? It's hard not to see at least a smidge of compulsion in their devotion to the game. When van der Bokke discusses caching, he has an almost Howard Hughes–like propensity to use the word "clean"—he's motivated, he says, by the desire "to clean out an area. I wanted to keep a ten-mile radius around my home *clean*." This very morning, he and a friend had been out "clean-

---

* That's right: when you're caching for numbers, says van der Bokke, "Left turns in urban environments are absolute killers. You're sitting at the light. You're sitting, you're sitting, you're sitting. Then you have to make another left turn to get back out!" "Wait, *that's* the secret of your success?" I ask incredulously. "No left turns?" "That's one of them."

ing up" some new caches that had appeared within this ten-mile safe zone—and were unable to find just one. "That's frustrating, because now it's sitting there. I'll sit at my computer being frustrated. It's still there on my map." You scrub and scrub and that nonsmiley just won't go away!

But I understand that compulsion now; it bothers me too when I look at my neighborhood on Geocaching.com and there's the little green box of an unfound cache tucked in amongst the smileys, taunting me. Oddly, the idea of unlogged caches doesn't bother me much in real life; I'm fine driving past them and saving them for another day. But something about seeing them on a map makes their presence almost unbearable. I wonder if this is the dark side of maps, if their orderly authority can gull us into believing in the rightness and importance of all kinds of iffy propositions. In 1890, for example, the diamond magnate Cecil Rhodes was lobbying hard for Britain to connect her two territories in Africa. Think how great it would look on a map, he argued, if British imperial red ran all the way from Cape Town to Cairo! Luckily, Lord Salisbury, the foreign secretary, was no map buff. "I can imagine no more uncomfortable position than the possession of a narrow strip of territory in the very heart of Africa, three months' distance from the coast, which should be separating the forces of a powerful empire like Germany and . . . another European Power," he told the House of Lords. "I think that the constant study of maps is apt to disturb men's reasoning powers." Similarly, the maps made by the great Serbian geographer Jovan Cvijić after World War I showed the ethnographic divisions of the Balkan peoples in neat stripes and soothing pastels. But in practice, that beautiful map helped inspire a century of brutal ethnic cleansing, an attempt to make the region's real-life ethnic borders as clear cut as they seemed on the map.

Whatever you think about van der Bokke's obsession, there's no denying the scope of his achievement. When friends or family scoff at the time he puts into his global Tupperware hunt, he asks them, "Do you know anybody that's number one at *anything* in the world?" There was, perhaps, only one other geocacher who was ever in his league. Alamogul's predecessor atop the caching leaderboard was one "CCCooperAgency," the world's most prolific cacher for most of the last decade. CCCooperAgency was Lynn Black, an insurance agent from the Harrisburg, Pennsylvania, area—by all accounts a popular and extraordinarily energetic geocacher but to me a total enigma. She walked away from the game in 2009 and now refuses to discuss the geocaching world she once ruled.

Most prolific megacachers are retirees with limitless free time, but Black was a busy business owner and mother of three. She hauled her family around on power-caching runs all over the eastern seaboard, but none of them quite had her boundless stamina for the game. She soon became aware that her geocaching obsession was becoming a problem. "I don't do anything besides geocaching," she told a newspaper in 2005. "You need to set up a clinic for Geocachers Anonymous," her husband, Kevin, concurred. She tried to quit several times, telling an interviewer in 2006, "I started to miss my kids. They're sick of geocaching. It's just too selfish, you know what I mean?"

But each time she thought she was out, like Michael Corleone, she'd get pulled back in. Her rival Lee van der Bokke had been about fourteen hundred caches behind Black from the time he started and couldn't gain any ground on her no matter what he did. In 2005, he heard from a mutual friend that she'd quit caching once and for all, in order to see more of her family. "Two days later," van der Bokke marvels, "she hops on a plane and heads to Germany without her family for six weeks' caching! That got me so upset." In late 2008, she finally called it quits after her 25,000th cache and retired her CCCooper-Agency account for good. But within a week, she was caching again—though not as avidly—under a different handle. Finally, on the last day of 2009, at a cache near a Lancaster County lake just off the Pennsylvania Turnpike, she left the following log:

> Was out enjoying a nice walk with my husband and he was the one to find it. Very nicely done. Last cache.

And with those two words, "Last cache," she was finally done.

The saga of CCCooperAgency, as I come to understand it in fragments, from interviews and message board postings and geocache logs, is a cautionary tale for me. Some people are born with a genetic predisposition to addictions like alcoholism, but, like Lynn Black, I seem to have been born to geocache, and to geocache obsessively. My deepest loves—maps, exploring places, solving puzzles, space-age gadgetry—make me a perfect-storm candidate for GPS rehab.

After-school specials have led me to believe that "bottoming out" stories from *real* addictions often involve back alleys and Dumpsters, and in the end, mine does too. I'm nosing around the Dumpster behind a Discount Tire one afternoon because my GPS receiver seems convinced that there's a geocache hidden somewhere in the rockery there. I've been searching for less than a minute when I realize that a jump-suited "tire specialist" is watching me with the kind of sour, victorious expression you'd expect from someone who just caught a strange man examining his garbage.

"Uh, what are you doing back there?" he wants to know, and I have to admit I can see his point.

I clamp my GPS to my ear. "Oh, sorry, I had to pull over and take this call. I sort of wander around when I'm on the phone."

He stands watching me with arms folded until I'm back in my car and out of his parking lot.

What *was* I doing back there? Geocaching is supposed to be an excuse to explore the world's hidden beauty spots, but I've made it from a means into an end. And because I'm a city dweller, most of my caching has been of the decidedly unscenic urban variety: "microcaches" dangling down manholes, magnetic "nanocaches" no bigger than Tylenol pills stuck to bike racks and garbage cans and ballfield bleachers, even one disguised as a wad of chewing gum and stuck under a table on a sub shop's patio. I decide to broaden my horizons: I need to get out of the city.

Browsing the Groundspeak website, I discover a cache just two hours north of me that comes highly recommended. It sits above a little-known waterfall on the Nooksack River not far from the Canadian border. Only a handful of brave souls have found the cache: its Geocaching.com terrain rating is the maximum five stars, which would be a first for me. "THIS IS A VERY DIFFICULT SLOPE," warns the hider's description in stern capital letters. "DO NOT

ATTEMPT THIS CACHE ALONE." He also reminds me that I'm under no obligation to seek his cache, that he assumes no liability in the event of my untimely death or mangling disfigurement, etc. No more Dumpster diving—this is the cache for me!

That weekend, I dig out my hiking boots and some old work gloves and drive up to Hard Scrabble Falls. I've never been on this highway before, so I've brought some printouts of other nearby geocaches I might pass along the way. But the five-star cache is the first order of business. The bottom of the falls is a short, easy hike up a dry creek bed from the trailhead, and the morning is soul-scrubbingly beautiful. It's early spring in the Northwest, the kind of day that seems gray and wintry until the sun breaks through the clouds for a moment and reveals that the seemingly dead black trees are actually covered with a million specks of the clearest, most limpid green. January to June in just seconds.

This is no Psycho Urban Cache #13, but by my standards, at least, it's pretty extreme. There's no trail up the steep slope south of the falls; instead, some thoughtful local has left a system of tree-anchored ropes to help visitors up the more vertical sections. I make it up the 430-foot zigzag with much huffing and puffing but no life-threatening scrapes, and I count the stair steps of roaring water as I pass them: six, seven, eight. By the time I finally make it to the ninth cascade, where the cache is hidden, my arms and legs are sore. That's what I came for, I tell myself—after all, you can't spell "geocaching" without "aching"! Here I locate the ammo box without any trouble, as expected: the cache is listed as a five-star climb but only a two-star hide. A means, not an end.

I walk to the rocky edge of the ninth waterfall and look across the valley to the Cascades on the other side. It's everything the Discount Tire parking lot was not: grandiose, inspiring, entirely free of used prophylactics. I feel a moment of kinship with Dave Ulmer, the grandfather of geocaching. He still sends me near-daily e-mails full of nutty Ayn Rand quotes and gorgeous photos of sunsets and cacti, and it's comforting to know that he's still wandering the West somewhere like David Carradine in *Kung Fu*, following his GPS receiver to ghost towns and cliff dwellings and abandoned gold mines. GPS buffs often use the acronym POI to refer to the "points of interest" to which the technology has taken them. In fact, I think, geocaching makes the whole planet into one big POI—a richer, more compelling place to live.

Standing on the edge of the cliff, I unfold my printout listing nearby geocaches. I still have a few more hours of daylight; I could probably find eight or nine roadside caches on the drive home. *Or* I could keep following this trail up past the geocache; apparently there's a tenth waterfall and then ropes down to the punch-bowl valley on the other side. It won't pad my count, but then again, that's not really the point, is it? I put the paper back into my pocket, slip on my gloves, and continue up the side of the mountain.

Chapter 11

FRONTIER

[frən-'tir] *n.*: a line of division between two countries

*Our age today is doing things of which antiquity did not dream . . .
a new globe has been given to us by the navigators of our time.*
—JEAN FERNEL, 1530

In Lewis Carroll's final novel, *Sylvie and Bruno,* a mysterious traveler called "Mein Herr" tells the two titular children that his faraway world has advanced the science of mapmaking well beyond our puny limits. He scoffs at the idea that the most detailed map available should be six inches to the mile. On his world, he boasts, "We very soon got to six *yards* to the mile. Then we tried a *hundred* yards to the mile. And then came the grandest idea of all! We actually made a map of the country, on the scale of *a mile to the mile!*" But, he has to admit, this ultimate map has never even been spread out, because the farmers protested that it would block their crops' sunlight due to its amazing size.

Carroll's notion of a map exactly the size of its territory, in perfect one-to-one detail, inspired Jorge Luis Borges's short story "On Exactitude in Science" and was further explored by Umberto Eco in a remarkably thorough 1982 essay. Eco straight-facedly enumerated the logistical problems that such a map would entail: the armies of men required to fold it, for example. He ponders making it transparent, to address the objections of Carroll's farmers, but realizes that any markings on the map would have to be opaque, thereby blocking some local sunlight, which could affect the ecology of the territory beneath. And if it did, the map would then become incorrect!

Obviously, Carroll, Borges, and Eco weren't proposing such a map as a serious cartographic innovation.* Their giant maps are whimsical thought experiments on the tricky relationships between maps and the territories they describe, and affectionate send-ups of map buffs and their love of endless detail. Consider how little the maps these men knew had changed over the centuries: a map in 1870 or 1970 looked more or less like a map in 1570. It was a piece of paper with dark lines standing for coastlines, pastel borders for political divisions, and labeled dots for cities. North was probably up; a grid of thin lines probably represented latitude and longitude. Except for the sad dearth of mermaids or cannibals engraved in the corners, little had changed in five hundred years.

But we live in a strange, shifting time for maps. The sudden onslaught of digital cartography and location-based technologies has changed, for the first time in centuries, our fundamental idea of what a map looks like. Twentieth-century map buffs absorbed in an atlas may have envisioned the page as a window into another world, but today's maps literally act like windows, not pictures: we peer into them. We can scroll them and rotate and zoom them. We can switch them from road maps to terrain maps and back again or overlay them onto jewel-like, cloudless photographs of our planet from space. Perhaps they even move when we do or show us nearby friends traipsing across them in real time, a children's fantasy idea when it appeared in a Harry Potter book just a decade ago but now a commonplace reality. It will take a generational shift to complete this definitional shift—after all, my Pictionary doodle of the word "telephone" still has a twisty receiver cord and maybe even a rotary dial, to the bewilderment of my

---

* In the same chapter in which he invented the life-sized map, incidentally, Lewis Carroll went on to invent the modern sport of paintball. No, really. "Mein Herr" tells the children of a planet on which, when war was waged, "The bullets were made of soft black stuff, which marked everything it touched. So, after a battle, all you had to do was to count how many soldiers on each side were 'killed'—that means 'marked on the back,' for marks in front didn't count."

cell phone–drawing children—but the change is well under way. For better or for worse, maps aren't what they used to be.

And Carroll and Borges would be flabbergasted to see that the biggest game changer has been an actual implementation of their impossible life-sized map. Geobrowser globes like NASA's World Wind and Microsoft's Bing Maps platform may be virtual, not life-sized, but their aim is the same as "Mein Herr's": to represent an entire territory—the whole world, in fact—in exhaustive one-to-one detail, without any of the selective simplification of paper maps. In many ways, these globes now contain *more* data than you could glean from the actual world with just a measuring stick or a camera. (Even the paradox-loving Lewis Carroll never proposed a map twice as exhaustive as the territory it depicted!)

Google Earth wasn't the first virtual globe, but it's certainly the industry leader now, with more than 700 million installations worldwide. It's so ubiquitous that it's hard to believe that the technology began life as a lowly video-game demo. In 1996, some Silicon Graphics engineers were looking for a way to show off the new texture-rendering abilities of their company's quarter-million-dollar workstations. Inspired by the famous 1968 short film *Powers of Ten*, which depicts the Earth at scales from the galactic to the microscopic, they produced "Space-to-Your-Face," a flyover demo in which the viewer zoomed down from a high Earth orbit to find a Nintendo 64 sitting on a pedestal atop the Matterhorn, with an SGI graphics chip inside. Three years later, Chris Tanner showed the video to Brian McClendon; both were part of a group of engineers who had left SGI to found their own game technology start-up, called Intrinsic Graphics. "The day I saw it," remembers McClendon, now vice president of engineering for Google Geo, "I said, 'We should start a separate company to do this.' The problem was, we weren't funded yet for the first company!"

As soon as Intrinsic had funding for its game library, the founders did spin off a new company, called Keyhole, to focus on geographic applications of their 3-D technology. The post-Internet-bubble period was a terrible time to found a start-up, so Keyhole told potential investors it was working on a tool for the real estate and travel industries, a way to let clients preview a property before renting. In reality, though, the Keyhole team knew what was compelling about its new product, and it wasn't beach condos. It was leaping through the stratosphere like a Mercury astronaut, like the boy with the seven-league boots from the fairy tale, and coming to rest, in one perfect fluid motion, in your own backyard. Their secret plan was to expand their little Realtor tool into an entire planet: Earth.com, in effect.

The watershed moment came in March 2003, when the United States invaded Iraq. McClendon, as it happens, had gone to junior high with CNN's vice president of engineering, and the news network bought rights to Keyhole's software in order to display 3-D views of the military campaign. Home viewers had never seen anything like these animated maps and fly-throughs and began buying copies for their home PCs, even though the software still sold for seventy dollars. The servers in Keyhole's tiny office could barely stand up to the demand, and employees were constantly running to Fry's, the local home electronics chain, to buy more hardware. A year later, the Keyhole team showed their software to Google founders Larry Page and Sergey Brin, and the demo was so compelling that an acquisition offer came the very next day, even though Google was in the middle of its hectic IPO. Keyhole's aerial imagery soon began appearing on Google's new map page, and for a while, Google Maps became a dreamy utopia, the vast majority of its users idly browsing the globe from space, not printing out driving directions from point A to point B. Two months later, when Google finally released Keyhole's application for free as Google Earth, demand exploded. "We nearly took down Google a couple times," laughs McClendon. "We actually had to turn off downloads of Google Earth because it was so popular. The first six days, it was nip and tuck."

When I met McClendon at the National Geographic Bee, he invited me to stop by his Mountain View, California, offices for "the nickel tour" if I was ever in the neighborhood. He was probably just being polite and had no way of knowing the level of my obsession with digital maps; I can spend days happily adrift over the pixelized Siberian taiga or gleefully rotating the 3-D buildings of the Manhattan skyline.

During the first couple of months of Google Earth's release, there were probably plenty of weekends when I spent more time on Google Earth than I did on our Earth. To a map obsessive like me, this casual invite was like a golden ticket to Willy Wonka's chocolate factory.

The Google Geo building isn't staffed by Oompa-Loompas, but it does have a few of the high-tech quirks I remember from past visits to the Google campus. When I step out of the elevator, the first thing I see is a foam-core map icon the size of a parking meter informing me that Al Gore's favorite spot in the Bay Area is the headquarters of Current TV, a cable network founded by, well, Al Gore. (The building is littered with these overgrown versions of the little pushpins that mark destinations on Google's online maps, remnants of a past celebrity promotion.) The oil paintings on the wall are by Bill Guffey, a rural Kentucky artist who paints cityscapes of places he's never been, based only on Google Street View photographs. This floor of the building has an ocean theme; surfboards line the walls, and in the common area outside the conference room where McClendon and I are chatting, a few programmers are working on their laptops while lounging on a giant plaster whale.

Brian McClendon is a tall, soft-spoken man in his midforties, with a deeply creased brow that always makes him look a little more concerned than he actually is. Maybe it's a sign of the unusual burden he carries as Google Earth's head engineer. After all, I've never met anyone in charge of his own planet before. You may scoff that Google Earth isn't a *real* planet, but consider: its architecture contains *hundreds of terabytes* of data. (A terabyte is equivalent to one thousand gigabytes; the entire text of every book in the Library of Congress could be stored in just twenty terabytes or so.) It's a mammoth responsibility, surely more complex than being the person in charge of, say, some uninhabitable iceball like Uranus or Neptune. But rank does have its privileges: the center of Google Earth (that is, the exact center of the map when the application opens) is an apparently random apartment building in Lawrence, Kansas—a secret salute to McClendon, who grew up in that very building.

Overseeing his digital dominion certainly isn't getting any easier. The library of aerial photographs that coats Google Earth—

taken from satellites, planes, hot-air balloons, even camera-equipped kites—is growing exponentially. "All the pictures that have ever been taken are less than what we're going to have next year," McClendon tells me.* The eventual goal is centimeter-per-pixel imagery for the entire globe: every square centimeter of the (real) Earth's surface would be its own pixel on Google Earth, not unlike Lewis Carroll's imaginary map. That goal is still more than twenty years away, McClendon guesses, since there are still places on Google Earth where the resolution is fifteen meters per pixel, more than a thousand times chunkier. And even once all three dimensions are sorted out, engineers must still grapple with the fourth dimension: time. Google Earth has assembled a library of historical photographs, so you can watch the years advance from orbit, but there's the future to worry about as well—the Sisyphean task of keeping the map up to date. Users can already watch real-time features like weather and traffic cross the surface of Google Earth, but, says McClendon, "The much harder truth is human truth. Does this business still exist? Is that a phone number? Is the location of the doorway here? These are the questions we have to get right if you're going to run the Google Maps navigation in your phone and get to the right business, which is effectively what pays the bills."

Google's mapping arm is a big moneymaker for the Internet giant; McClendon points out that 90 percent of all retail spending still happens offline, and that's powered by geographic technology like mapping and local search. But Google Maps and Earth have also become a lightning rod for geopolitical controversy. China might crack down

---

* Aerial photogrammetry is the technology that finally replaced large-scale trigonometric surveys as the state of the mapmaking art. It's much older than Google Earth, though—during the Peninsular Campaign of the Civil War, General George McClellan ordered some of his officers to ascend five hundred feet in a tethered silk balloon and make maps of the Confederate lines. The new West Point grad who spent the most time in the balloon, in fact, was none other than the young George Armstrong Custer. A century later, the very first U.S. military satellites were equipped with high-resolution cameras for taking aerial photos but had no way to develop the film or transmit its images back to Earth. As a result, the satellites were designed to drop film packets into the atmosphere with parachutes, where they could be retrieved in midair (most of the time, anyway) by a military transport plane.

because of Google "mistakes" like not labeling Taiwan as one of its provinces, or Nicaragua might use a misdrawn border in Google Maps as a rationale for a military incursion into Costa Rican territory. Sometimes Google will buy third-party images that have fabricated or blurred certain sensitive areas. Most famously, after 9/11, Vice President Dick Cheney's residence at the U.S. Naval Observatory stayed stubbornly fuzzy long after Google had found alternate sources that unblurred other sensitive spots, like the White House and the Capitol. Google finally secured uncensored photography of Chez Cheney and pushed it onto an Earth update as soon as they could—which happened to be Obama's inauguration day. ("I would have done it sooner had I found the pixels sooner!" McClendon still insists.) Scuffles like these have forced Google Earth to begin acting, in some ways, as an actual nation-state, negotiating with governments and even sending its own representative to meetings of the UN committee on place-names.

Should we be worried about the fact that a single company, however awesome its rotating holiday logos and employee snacks, has this much authoritative influence on the world's maps? At the dawn of the Internet mapping era, some geographers fretted about a coming "McDonaldization" of cartography, in which maps would become fast food: cheap and omnipresent but driven by distant, unaccountable corporations concerned more with ad revenue than quality. In reality, far from skimping on quality, Google has continued to add blow-your-mind features (3-D underwater terrain! Street View–level mapping of ski trails!* Interactive global warming models!) to its maps

---

* Yes, Google actually unveiled a Street View snowmobile when it published these photos during the 2010 Winter Olympics. During my visit to the Googleplex, I met Dan Ratner, who has helped design every vehicle in the Street View fleet. In addition to the cars and snowmobiles, there's also a "trike," which Ratner dreamed up during a visit to Barcelona when he noticed that many of the cobblestoned streets were too narrow for the regular Google cars. The trike has since been used to map national parks and theme parks, but whenever it rolls out, bystanders unaccountably mistake it for an ice cream vendor. Kids in Legoland asked the driver for ice cream, but so did a famous Nobel laureate once at a technology conference. Ratner also showed me the newest member of the Street View family: a trolley capable of capturing *indoor* imagery. Nobody would tell me where exactly the trolley will be filming. The Louvre? The Taj Mahal? The Playboy Mansion? It was top secret.

on a seemingly weekly basis. But Google Earth's unprecedented detail and popularity have led to more serious concerns about privacy and security. After all, any map of Mumbai that can help tourists find their hotel can also help terrorists attack that hotel.

There's not much that Google can do about how its maps are used, but at least their very popularity provides a safeguard against the mapmaker itself, whether it's Google or Microsoft or Yahoo!, trying to promote any sinister agenda with its maps. After all, every change they make to their data happens in front of millions of eyeballs. When mistakes are introduced (or even, if you prefer, when shady cartographic kowtowing takes place), locals notice and bloggers squawk and problems get fixed. In 2009, towns in the Indian border state of Arunachal Pradesh were briefly given Chinese names on Google Maps; when horrified Indians reacted, Google admitted its mistake the same day and reverted to the Hindi names.

Brian McClendon calls Google's Borgesian dream of a centimeter-per-pixel real-time world map "the end of resolution," and the phrase shocks me a little with its finality, because to me it implies the end of all mapmaking, the end of all discovery. It's one of the central paradoxes of maps: they make the world larger by showing us new vistas, but then they order and bean-count those new vistas into submission, and the world gets a little smaller as well. If Google Earth becomes the perfect map, the map of everything, why ever draw another one?

McClendon disagrees; he argues that virtual globes have actually led to a renaissance of discovery. After all, much of the aerial imagery that Google posts, old and new, has never been seen by human eyeballs before, and he's putting it in front of millions of curious armchair travelers. "There was so much of it that it was never visually inspected down to the bottom pixels. And sometimes there are things there at the bottom that were never known before."

In 1868, the element helium was discovered, revolutionizing children's birthday parties forever. Though Earth has large reserves of helium underground—some U.S. natural gas deposits are as much as 7 percent helium—the scientists who first discovered evidence of helium found it not under their feet but through spectroscopic analysis from one hundred million miles away. Helium was discovered on the Sun fifteen years before we found it here on Earth.* In much the same way, scientists and amateurs alike are nowadays discovering Earth's hidden secrets on Google Earth before they turn up on our real home planet. Meteor-impact craters in Western Australia, a Roman villa in Parma, the ruins of a lost Amazonian city that may have inspired the legends of El Dorado, a remote forest in Mozambique where hundreds of new species of plants and animals live—all these things were never on any map until they were spotted from space by Google Earth surfers.† In 2008, a team of German scientists studied Google images of more than eight thousand grazing cattle and three thousand wild deer in pastures all over the world. The vast majority, they were surprised to see, graze standing north to south, aligned to the Earth's poles. It was the first evidence that large mammals can sense and use the Earth's magnetic fields the way that migrating birds and turtles do, and it had been right under our noses all the time. People have watched livestock graze for millennia, but before Google Earth, nobody had ever noticed that they were all facing the same way. "I think you'll end up with both scientific and amateur studies solving problems that were intractable ten years ago," says McClendon. "I wouldn't be surprised if we discover *more* in the next twenty years than we ever did."

But the Google Earth team believes its software has changed maps in a more fundamental way than just adding detail. Because its globe looks like a real place, it blurs the distinction between map and territory in a way that would make Borges or Eco dizzy. When you see something on Google Earth, says McClendon, "You don't debate it.

---

* Which is why the element was named for the Greek sun god, Helios.

† One odd curio that isn't trotted out much in the Google press materials is the so-called forest swastika discovered in the 1990s in aerial photographs of northeastern Germany. During the 1930s heyday of the Third Reich, Nazi officials apparently planted a swastika of larch trees in a Brandenburg pine forest. The effect was invisible except during a few weeks each spring and autumn, when the paler larch leaves branded a bright yellow swastika across the treetops. The offending trees were cut down after German tabloids ran photos of the swastika in 2000.

You don't say, 'Is this somebody's representation? Did they draw this picture?' It's not somebody's version of reality. It *is* reality."

Map deconstructionists would have a field day with that claim! The trend in geography over the last thirty years has been to consider maps *not* as reality but as fallible narratives, each with its own quirks and agendas. This is a healthy kind of skepticism; maps work so well, generally, in getting us where we're going that we don't think to question the thousands of assumptions and biases that undergird them. Even a seemingly unimpeachable world map on a classroom wall isn't immune. Why should the top of the map be north, rather than south? Why is America arbitrarily at the center? Why is it easier to see political features than physical ones? Why include this city but not that one? Why label Taiwan as a country but not Palestine, or vice versa?

Mapmakers may make all these choices with the best of intentions, but the result is still, even if unconsciously, to reinforce some particular view of the world. I distinctly remember *not* believing, when my parents first told me, that Brazil was actually five times the size of Alaska. On the map of my bedroom wall, I could see *with my own eyes* that they were virtually twins! That's because my map was drawn according to the venerable Mercator Projection. In 1569, the Flemish cartographer Gerardus Mercator drew a world map using a cylindrical projection that would neatly render a rhumb line—a ship's course in a constant direction, like west or north-northeast—as a straight line.* The problem is that this kind of projection inflates the polar regions way out of proportion—in fact, on such a map, the poles can never even be drawn, because they're an *infinite* distance from the Equator.† Mercator maps were still used everywhere when I was growing up—classrooms, nightly newscasts, stamps, government briefing rooms—and so my generation grew up thinking that Greenland was bigger than Africa, since Greenland is oversized fourteenfold on Mercator maps.

---

* Rhumb lines are also called "loxodromes," which always sounds to me more like the name of some iffy pharmaceutical. "Ask your doctor if Loxodrome is right for you!"

† Even Mercator knew that his projection screwed up the poles. His very first map of the kind left off the Arctic entirely, displaying it as a special little polar inset, the way we do Alaska and Hawaii.

Of course, all map projections have to fudge somewhere, whether on area or on direction. Imagine trying to flatten an orange peel onto a flat surface, and as it tears and scrunches, you'll see the problem: something's got to give.* But the Mercator map stayed so popular in the West for so long, at least in part, because of how helpful its particular distortions were. Most obviously, it makes North America and Europe seem disproportionately important, while marginalizing much of the developing world. As a result, a 1996 study found that when students all over the world were asked to draw the contours of the continents, nearly all made Europe too big and Africa too small. Even when the test was given in Africa, the results were the same. And during the Cold War, we liked the sprawling, menacing Soviet Union that Mercator provided us, with the rest of Asia dangling halfheartedly beneath it.

As a high school junior, I walked into my Spanish class on the first day of school to see, replacing the familiar Mercator map on the teacher's wall, an equal-area Peters Projection map. This controversial map was unveiled with much fanfare in 1973 by the German historian Arno Peters, who told the media it was a revolutionary attack on the stodgy Mercator.† In fact, it was a simple retread of the 1855 Gall Orthographic Projection, and many cartographers disliked its north-south distortion of the equatorial regions, which stretched shape in order to properly represent area. The geographer Arthur Robinson compared Peters's continents to "wet, ragged long winter underwear hung out to dry on the Arctic Circle." But if Peters's goal was to shock, it worked on me. I stared at the map endlessly, marveling at the big,

---

* The only way to see all of a round globe from the same vantage point with no distortion is to visit the Mapparium, a wonderful Boston oddity built by the Christian Science Church in 1935. The Mapparium is a thirty-foot-tall globe of stained glass that visitors stand *inside* (passing through on an equatorial bridge), their eyes at the same distance from every point on Earth at once. Because of the difficulty of replacing the globe's 608 glass panels, the map is frozen in the year of its completion, still displaying long-gone places like Bechuanaland, Trucial Oman, and the Netherlands Indies to curious tourists.

† Peters's commitment to social justice started early; his father, Bruno, had been imprisoned by the Nazis in 1945 for labor union activism and would have been executed had the war not ended shortly thereafter.

muscular Africa dominating its center and the anemic Russia and Alaska hugging the North Pole. I'd been *told* that the maps I knew were lying to me about the globe, but it was quite another thing to see the evidence with my own eyes.

You can trace the decline of the Mercator Projection by looking at the set changes on *Saturday Night Live*'s "Weekend Update" faux newscast. The world outline map behind the newscasters was an acromegalic Mercator back in the Dan Aykroyd/Jane Curtin era, but under Dennis Miller it was replaced with a less absurd, modified Mercator called the Miller (no relation) cylindrical projection. Today the map behind Seth Meyers is an equirectangular projection called the *plate carrée,* useless for oceangoing but popular among computer map-

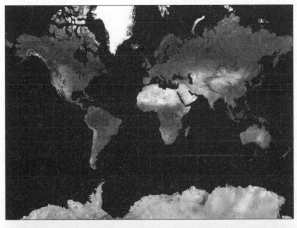

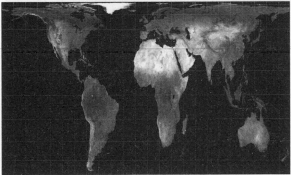

*The Mercator and Gall–Peters: Greenland's favorite
and least favorite map projections, respectively*

pers. But the Mercator map of our childhoods, though less visible today, is far from extinct. For example, use Google to bring up a map of your street or your city. Now zoom all the way out—yup, *all* the way, so the entire planet is on the map. See how Antarctica now looks bigger than every other continent put together? That's right: Google Maps still uses a Mercator Projection.*

So it's easy to quibble with McClendon's assertion that everything on Google's maps is unimpeachably *true* in some epistemological sense.† In some ways, it's as full of judgment calls and compromises as any other map. What he really means is that Google Earth is more convincing, more compelling, than a paper map and that this immersiveness gives it a unique ability to change the way we see the world.

"You trust that this picture is truly of this place. And when people see that, they get an emotional reaction. They feel like they're really visiting another place, and that's something no map has ever given before. You look at a traffic jam in Baghdad, and you realize, those guys are not much different than we are. How would it feel if *we* were getting bombed and we were losing buildings? That's what's happening to them right now. Same thing in Tehran. Here are these people that have a very Western city in many regards, but we see them as old-school Islamists that must be living in tents. But they're not. Tehran looks very European from the air, very densely populated."

"It sounds like you're almost saying that Google Earth is an ideological tool to bring peace to *real* Earth," I tell McClendon.

---

* For a very good reason: to preserve right angles in close-up. The earliest version of Google Maps used a better projection, but as a result, streets in high-latitude Scandinavian cities met at wonky angles.

† One counterexample is the West Lancashire town of Argleton, which appears on Google Maps and Google Earth but, sadly, not in real life. Google officially blamed the anomaly on "occasional errors" in its database and removed the label from the map, though you can still find it if you search for it. The discovery of Argleton made international headlines, making it the most famous nonexistent town since Goblu and Beatosu, Ohio, which appeared on the official state road map of Michigan in 1978. University of Michigan alum Peter Fletcher, who chaired the State Highway Commission at the time, inserted the fake towns to tease Ohio State fans. Their names mean "Go blue" and "Beat OSU," respectively.

He doesn't hesitate for a minute. "Yes. I say that, and I believe that. If it brings people that we're purportedly in conflict with close enough to us, then it's very hard to stay in conflict. If everybody had that—if North Koreans had that and could see what it's like in L.A. or small-town Middle America—they might not feel so isolated. But they have no access to any information."* It's a particularly Google approach to utopia: the notion that information *isn't* neutral, that on balance it's inherently good because of its power to help people understand one another.

At the dawn of the World Wide Web, much was made of the fact that this new "Internet" was a place without place—a geography-less void that was, like God, everywhere and nowhere. Cyberspace was *analogous* in some ways to space, but it would be navigated virtually, with no relation to our real three-dimensional world at all. There were two problems with this idea. First, it led to crappy "virtual reality" movies like *Virtuosity* and *The Lawnmower Man*. And second, in the long run, it turned out to be totally wrong. Fifteen years later, the hottest trend in information is "geotagging": ensuring that every bit of data on the Internet—every tweet, every YouTube video, every photo on Flickr—is coded with locational metadata tying it to a point on Earth.

Geotags may sound like a small change—just a latitude and a longitude on a Facebook status, big deal!—but they have the potential to revolutionize the Web. The dominant online search paradigm now is one of a librarian: we suggest subjects using keywords ("Tell me about dinosaur fossils" or "Tell me about 401(k) plans"), and resources come off the shelves. But on the "geoweb," data is indexed by place, not by theme, and so the search engine is a tour guide, not a librarian. You ask, "What's around here?" (and that query is probably automated,

---

* Avi Bar-Zeev, the Keyhole cofounder who wrote much of the early code for Google Earth, remembers a similar motivation for his decision to make point-to-point movement in the geobrowser a high-orbit "jump" rather than a "flight" at jetliner level: he wanted to use the software to emphasize the nearness and the interconnectedness of every place on the planet.

if you have a GPS-enabled phone), and the answers flood in: these friends, these businesses, these photos. In fact, the data is probably customized to the specific kinds of things you've decided you're likely to be looking for: these geocaches, these clients, these Ethiopian restaurants. The Internet overlays itself on the real world like—well, like a map, frankly.

In 2005, a DreamWorks animation tool developer named Paul Rademacher was looking for a new place to live in the Bay Area. This being the primitive pre-geoweb era, he was apartment hunting with stone knives and bearskins: a new sheaf of MapQuest printouts every time he left the house. The programmer part of his brain knew that this was wrong. It was inelegant. Google Maps had launched two months previously, and Rademacher admired its smoothly scrolling maps. Wait a minute, he thought. This map is just JavaScript running in my browser, so therefore I can change it. Why can't I just combine it with the list of for-rent apartments on Craigslist? Google Maps hadn't yet released an API—application programming interface, a guide for users to interact with the software—so Rademacher proceeded by trial and error, tweaking numbers at random in the unintelligible text representing map layout, just to see what would happen. A few weeks later, he ran his script and watched a scatter of apartments appear in his browser, neatly forming the shape of the San Francisco peninsula. It was the first Google Earth "mashup" ever created, but within a month there were dozens of copycats using Rademacher's code. Gas prices, movie showtimes, red-light cameras, package tracking, street crime—it seemed as if almost everything people wanted to look up on the Internet was a little more convenient displayed on a map.

"We all just hadn't realized that a map could be a platform," says Rademacher, who today works for Google Maps API team, managing the same interfaces he once hacked. Maps are millennia old, one of the earliest forms of representation ever devised by humankind, but new mobile technology has given them new versatility, and the result has been a map renaissance. Twenty years ago, most people probably consulted a map once every week or so, when they needed help navigating a highway or a shopping mall. Today it's not unusual for smart-phone owners to check a map many times an hour, for things that we wouldn't have associated with geography at all ten years ago—not just "Where's Romania?" but "Where's my pizza?" For geonerds, accustomed to the public perception of a map as something démodé and dull, it's like living in a golden age.

Wayne Coyne, the lead singer of the beloved indie-rock band the Flaming Lips, may have summed this up best. In 2009, Google Street View* users noticed that the map photos of Coyne's street in Oklahoma City included puzzling shots of the front man sitting, fully clothed, in a bathtub on his front lawn. He explained to an interviewer that he'd been trying out some props to scare neighborhood kids at a Halloween party and had no idea he was about to be immortalized by Google's amazingly comprehensive street photography. "A car that drives around on every street with a 360-degree camera?" he marveled. "We live in f——ing good times, don't we?"

But for every ebullient Wayne Coyne, it seems, there's some gloomy Cassandra warning against the new maps and the technologies they leverage. If you thought the worst part of location-based services was going to be advertisements that annoy you by name as you walk past them, like in *Minority Report,* think again. Jerome Dobson, a GIS pioneer and president of the American Geographical Society, has coined the word "geoslavery" to refer to the potential threat to our privacy and autonomy that GPS-powered maps might someday pose. If everything you do is geotagged, then everyone always knows where you are—which is awesome if you're hoping to meet some friends after work for a drink but maybe not so awesome if potential burglars are casing your neighborhood to find out who's not home, or if you're dealing with an abusive ex or a child predator or even some stranger who got mad about something you posted online. We're an Orwellian

---

* Google lore has it that the Street View project was born when company cofounder Larry Page filmed a driver's-eye view of his morning commute using a video camera and told the Geo team, "Do this." He may have lived to regret the idea, though. In 2008, in response to controversy over Street View "spying," a privacy watchdog group used Street View imagery to compile a report on Page's private life, using Google photos to reveal the name of his landscaping company and the license plate number of his Lexus SUV.

dystopia in the making, says Dobson, except that no shadowy government will be providing the surveillance. Instead, we're opting to do it to ourselves.

With Google's famous "Don't be evil" motto in mind, I ask Paul Rademacher if he worries about the new digital map technology—call it Maps 2.0—turning evil. He tells me that Michael Jones, Google Earth's chief technologist, often points out that *all* new technologies seem scary, but months later you find yourself wondering what you ever did without them. "He once gave the example of how cell phones now are cameras and how that seemed scary and invasive. You could just go in the bathroom and take pictures of everyone and put them on the Internet! But are we banning cell phones in bathrooms? I haven't seen that happen, because people just leave their cell phones in their pockets."

The example is telling. After all, no one actually *solved* the problem of camera-phone snooping; we've just decided to live with it because the advantages of camera phones outweigh, for now, the occasional abuses. If restroom spying ever turned into an epidemic, we'd look for legal or technological solutions—banning camera phones that can snap photos silently, for example. By the same token, abuse of location-based technologies could also be solved by smarter devices and better privacy settings. But those solutions work best in a free-market democracy. They'd be of little comfort if you were living in a North Korea–style dictatorship using this technology to keep tabs on every suspected dissident at every second or in a Taliban-style theocracy that wanted to keep college students in after dark or women out of movie theaters.

It goes without saying, of course, that Maps 2.0 has *saved* lives as well, from hikers stranded on mountainsides to Hurricane Katrina victims. In January 2010, a magnitude-seven earthquake flattened Port-au-Prince, the capital of Haiti. Rescue workers didn't know where to start; even the ones with GPS receivers quickly discovered that there were no good digital maps of Haiti. Google, to its credit, gave the United Nations full access to the usually proprietary data in its collaborative Map Maker tool, but the real hero of the hour was the OpenStreetMap project, an open-source alternative to

Map Maker. OpenStreetMap is essentially the Wikipedia of maps: anyone can use it, anyone can change it in real time, and its data is free and uncopyrighted in perpetuity. When the earthquake struck, late Tuesday afternoon, Haiti was a white void in OpenStreetMap. Within hours, thousands of amateur mappers were collaborating all over the world, adding roads and buildings from aerial imagery to the database, until every back alley and footpath in Port-au-Prince

Port-au-Prince, as it looked in OpenStreetMap when the earthquake hit and the way it looked a week later

had been charted. Relief workers updated the maps with traffic revisions, triage centers, and refugee centers, and just days later, the volunteer-drawn map was the United Nations' go-to source of transportation information. "Many thanks to all crisis mappers for great contributions," posted UNICEF emergency officer Jihad Abdalla. "You made my life much easier, since I'm a one-man show here . . . million thanks."

After reading about the lives saved in Haiti by OpenStreetMap, I used it to look at my own neighborhood and found that the cul-de-sac we live on was also missing from the map. After hesitating a moment—is it really okay to draw on a map?—I added and labeled my street by hand, Wikipedia-style. It was a surprising rush to add something new, however trivial, to the world's sum of geographical knowledge.* For a brief moment, I was Captain Cook charting the New Zealand coastline, a veritable Stanley of the suburbs.

Most of these new technologies are just reinventing how maps are made or the things they can be used for, but one particular innovation is changing the very definition of what a map *is*. "Augmented reality" is the practice of combining a real-world environment with computer-generated imagery, like those yellow "first down" lines that appear and disappear during televised football games. Until recently, augmented reality was a mostly theoretical idea, confined to laboratories where, no doubt, people used those big, clunky *Lawnmower Man* helmets to try it out. But augmented reality isn't virtual reality. The world it shows us isn't a new one: it's ours, only improved.

And in the age of GPS- and camera-enabled phones, you don't need the helmet anymore. Imagine this: you walk out of a Manhattan office building and wonder where the closest subway is. Instead of consulting a bird's-eye map, you just hold up your cell phone. The

---

* Google Map Maker has a complicated set of protocols in place to avoid Wiki-vandalism on its maps. "So if I draw imaginary highways to spell dirty words in the middle of Siberia, you'll catch me?" I asked Google's Jessica Pfund. "Oh, we've seen that," she said wearily.

screen shows your current point of view but augments it with a new layer of information: as you rotate the phone, symbols appear, hovering in the air in front of you as if fixed in place. There's one for the Lexington Avenue Line, just 325 feet to your right. Maybe a dotted pink trail appears on the sidewalk to guide you directly to the nearest entrance, and you have to look twice to be sure the trail's not there in real life. On the way, you notice that user reviews are fading into view when you point your phone at restaurants, and sightseeing links accompany tourist attractions. When you angle the camera upward, the windows of some of the apartments across the street have virtual FOR RENT signs with prices listed. This is all information you could glean from any number of digital maps, but there's a crucial difference: for thousands of years, we mentally projected ourselves into maps; now map information has the ability to project itself *outward,* onto us.

I'm so accustomed to the endless disappointments of futurism (in a year that begins with a 2, *why am I not living in a domed undersea city by now?*) that it comes as a shock when I read that augmented-reality phone apps already exist—not in labs and at trade shows but for reals: free in Apple's app store, even. I upgrade to a new iPhone just to try out some of these tools but wind up disappointed. One called Wikitude promises to embed my environment with information about nearby POIs, like a Web browser for the real world, but when I try it out in front of my house, all I see are logos for every Starbucks and Best Buy within five miles. Yelp's augmented-reality Monocle, the first AR app available for the iPhone, is a little better, bringing up an accurate text box about my favorite Thai place when I hold the phone up vertically and point it northwest, but neither program provides a very compelling experience. My version of the Apple operating system doesn't allow third parties to use incoming visual information, so these apps are trying to figure out what I'm looking at based solely on readings from the camera's GPS device and accelerometer. Even if I make slow, smooth phone movements, the AR data wiggles and jerks around unpredictably, destroying any illusion that it's painted over the real world. And a smart-phone screen is just too small and dim to be very immersive. You end up squinting and thinking for a minute and then saying, "Yeah, I guess that's kind of cool," sort of like when you were looking at those Magic Eye posters of dolphins back in the 1990s.

But these are temporary glitches; before long, no doubt, the imagery will be smoother and we'll all be wearing *Terminator* contact lenses with built-in heads-up displays for all the AR data. Not all the applications of augmented reality are map-related, of course. You could use it to interact with elaborate 3-D models that aren't really there, which would be a boon to architects visualizing buildings and surgeons trying to practice a tricky triple bypass without killing anyone. If you were so inclined, you could even use AR to turn the world into your own surreal wonderland, changing the color of the sky every thirty seconds or putting a werewolf mask or Groucho glasses on the face of every passerby, like a Merry Pranksters app for an audience of one. But most day-to-day uses of the technology will probably be locational, and that makes me wonder: can this kind of in-world navigation even be called a map? It *is* a pictorial way to represent geography, I suppose, but one without any significant abstraction: the map is nothing but the territory itself with very good footnotes, a 3-D version of the *Sylvie and Bruno* map.

I don't think that AR wayfinding will *replace* maps, because I can't use it for many things that I rely on maps for. It's good for telling me what's around me right now but not so good at showing me which counties of Florida voted for Barack Obama in 2008 or whether Peru is north or south of Ecuador. I do worry that augmented reality could continue the current trend of GPS-based mapping tools that are so convenient, so easy to use, that they stunt our built-in spatial senses. They are, in effect, maps so good that they make us bad at mapping.

GPS navigation is usually the whipping boy in this argument. Every driver who heads off a cliff or onto railroad tracks just because the GPS voice told him to—and there are thousands of these stories—is a symptom of a culture that is increasingly outsourcing its spatial thinking to technology, and once those jobs are gone, they may not come back. My favorite news story of GPS-crutch incompetence is that of an unnamed Swedish couple trying to drive from Venice to the sunny isle of Capri in 2009. Unfortunately, they accidentally misspelled the name of their destination when they entered it into their GPS, and arrived a few hours later at the industrial northern town of *Carpi,* where they wandered into the town hall and asked confused officials how to get to the Blue Grotto, Capri's famous sea cave. (The officials there assumed that "the Blue Grotto" must be some local restaurant they'd never heard of.) Ten seconds with a map, of course, would have told these tourists that

- you can't make the four-hundred-mile drive from Venice to Capri in just two hours;
- Capri is southeast of Venice, not west;
- and, crucially, that *it's a small island,* and the couple hadn't crossed a bridge or used a boat to get to Carpi, which is located on a landlocked inland plain!

But they didn't look at a map. They trusted GPS.

The decline of our wayfinding abilities didn't begin with GPS, of course. Nomadic cultures like the Bedouins still use all kinds of natural wayfinding cues in the stars and camel tracks that a modern American would never see because we've been able to rely on roads and signs and so forth in our cozy urban lives. Many human skills ceded to technology are no great loss—I'm not as good as my ancestors were at telling time based on the position of the sun in the sky, but that's okay because my wristwatch works just fine. But the end of navigation might be more serious. Reckoning with our environment isn't a single skill; it's a whole web of spatial senses and abilities, many so fundamental that we can't afford to lose them to machines. We know that thinking hard about navigation is what grows those neurons in our brains—what happens if we quit exercising those cells and they get flabby? "Society is geared toward shrinking the hippocampus," says Véronique Bohbot, a Montreal professor of psychiatry who specializes in spatial memory. "In the next twenty years, I think we're going to see dementia occurring earlier and earlier."

As a species, the loss of our spatial abilities might be a tragedy, but to a map nerd, an even sadder casualty of the digital map revolution might be paper maps themselves. As I wander into downtown

Seattle's biggest map store, I notice immediately that its new location, near the tourist-packed Pike Place Market, displays fewer travel maps than the previous store did. The cabinet of USGS topographical maps on the back wall is usually left alone; hikers get the trail maps they need on their cell phones. "The map business has slowed down a lot," the store's co-owner tells me. She gestures vaguely to a rack of folded pocket maps. "When a new map like that came out, we used to have to order twenty, twenty-five of them, or we'd sell out. Now we're lucky to sell one or two. We hope we can stay alive by diversifying." Indeed, this nominal "map store" now fills most of its space with travel items (backpacks and guidebooks) and vaguely geographical gifts (national flags, dodecahedral Earth globes, and novelty wall maps that use some design gimmick—$3,500 in rare hardwoods, for example, or cleverly placed notes on a series of musical staffs—to delineate the continents).

Allen Carroll, the chief cartographer at National Geographic, tells me that he's not worried about the market, because printed maps and Internet maps fulfill different functions. "So far, we haven't found that our atlas sales have been hurt by the Internet. Very different than is the case, obviously, with encyclopedias." Encyclopedia publishers like Britannica were caught unawares by the rise of CD-ROM encyclopedias in the 1990s, and their sales collapsed by 83 percent in just five years. Atlases may hold out longer, because no digital platform has yet managed to deliver browsable maps, in all their detail and versatility, as well as paper can. But what happens when that platform arrives, as it inevitably will? Could one killer iPad app doom atlases forever?

I may be part of the last generation to harbor a peculiar nostalgia for paper maps that stubbornly refuse to zoom or scroll or layer—in fact, that stubbornly refuse even to refold themselves into the neat rectangle you found in the glove compartment. That's what it is: nostalgia. Paper maps remind me of school libraries and the backseat of the family car on vacation. Pleasant times.

The name on nearly all those maps was "Rand McNally," America's best-known and best-selling map publisher for most of the last century. Founded in Chicago in 1868, the partnership between a Boston printer and a poor Irish immigrant soon branched out into the budding transportation industry, producing railroad tickets, guides, and timetables. The company was very nearly destroyed in the Chicago fire of 1871, but quick-thinking cofounder William Rand saved the day, rescuing two ticket-printing machines from the flames and burying them in the cool sand at a Lake Michigan beach three miles north of the city, where they'd be safe from the 3,000-degree inferno. Just three days later, before a survey had even been completed of the still-smoldering city, the buried machines were up and running in a rented building that had survived the flames. The very next year, Rand McNally printed its first map, a railway map of the United States and Canada, and the rest is history.

When I asked a Rand McNally publicist if I could stop by for a visit, I hoped its headquarters would retain some of the musty mid-century charm I associate with its maps—would cavernous brick vaults full of whirring printing presses be too much to ask? Instead my cab pulls up to an anonymous office park in suburban Skokie. I don't even see the iconic Rand McNally logo—a compass superimposed on an elliptical globe—until I'm in the lobby trying to figure out which floor reception is on.

"We finally moved out of the old place four months ago," explains Jane Szczepaniak, the assistant who arranged my visit. The company's two hundred employees don't seem to miss the windowless painted cinder-block walls and faded green filing cabinets of their longtime home. "It felt like an elementary school," Jane jokes. In the move, fifty years of old map film were tossed, and employees were invited to pillage a disorganized, dimly lit room full of thousands of past Rand McNally maps. Once everyone had a few souvenirs, the rest were thrown away.

Joel Minster, a former civil engineer, has been chief cartographer at Rand McNally for the past nine years. His office looks decidedly modern, with blue Earth hemispheres protruding from the walls as if they'd been beamed there by a *Star Trek* transporter, but he's adamant that old-fashioned paper maps are still Rand McNally's focus—for the moment. When I ask about the maps on the Rand McNally website, which still scroll and zoom chunkily in fixed increments, like MapQuest in 1999, he smiles wryly. "We're giving those away for free, so it's not really our goal to be number one." But even though road atlases sold to truckers and vacationers still pay the bills, he says that the company will keep a presence in GPS devices and e-reader atlases and smart-phone apps—not necessarily because it thinks those are the future but to have a toe in the water just in case. In fifteen or twenty years, he vows, "Rand McNally will still be in the business of travel planning. I have no idea what media we'll be using to deliver that information—a chip in your brain, sure—but we'll be there."

Despite my long history with paper maps, I wind up convinced by Minster's optimism: there will be nothing to lament when some new platform eventually replaces them, since that new technology, whatever it is, will by definition have to do all the things that paper maps do well. It will have to be portable and immediately intuitive. It will have to accommodate readers who need a specific piece of information *now,* as well as those just browsing for pleasure. And it will have to be a broader canvas than just a set of driving directions—not just how to get from A to B but a whole alphabet through Z of nearby suggestions and digressions. Maybe a few old-timers like me will always be annoying our grandkids with tales of how awesome maps used to be when they smelled like ink and crinkled like wood pulp, but, more likely than not, these will be stories of the walking-uphill-in-the-snow-to-school variety. "You kids today don't know how good you have it with your holographic globes that rotate by scanning your retinas! I had to do my homework with maps on paper—no, really, paper!—and they were unwieldy and hard to find stuff on and they were obsolete the moment they were printed. I'm telling you, it took *character* to be a map nerd back then!"

And—who knows?—maybe paper maps will be sticking around longer than we think. I rode in a cab twice during my visit to Chicago: once from the airport out to Rand McNally headquarters in Skokie and then from Skokie to my hotel. Both cabdrivers were enslaved to a dashboard GPS that told them exactly where to turn at every moment. Yet somehow we still managed to get lost along the way. Both times.

Chapter 12

RELIEF

[rē-'lēf] *n.*: differences in elevation on the Earth's surface,
as represented on a map by contours or shading

We shall not cease from exploration
And the end of all our exploring
Will be to arrive where we started
And know the place for the first time.

—T. S. ELIOT

My cell phone rings as I'm sitting with some friends, waiting for a concert to start. "Ken, this is Rodger. You left a message for me last week?"

"Right! Rodger! Thanks for calling me back. Your neighbor Kathy gave me your number. I hope that's okay." I take a deep breath, because what I'm about to say next is deeply weird. "Did you know that there's an integer degree confluence at the end of your driveway?"

A long pause. "There's a *what* in my driveway?"

The Degree Confluence Project was started in 1996 by a Massachusetts Web programmer named Alex Jarrett, a new GPS owner who noticed that his commute happened to take him across the nearby seventy-second meridian twice a day. The mathematical perfection of that line of longitude—seventy-two degrees west, no minutes, no seconds—sang to him like a row of zeroes on a rolling-over odometer. He and a friend biked ten miles to get to the point where the seventy-second meridian crossed their closest parallel, forty-three degrees north. The intersection turned out to be a nondescript spot of snowy woods next to a swamp. "We kept expecting there to be a monument at any location saying '43N/72W' but no such luck," Alex wrote on his website, where he posted pictures of the momentous expedition.

If you think about it, that very lack of a monument was what turned "confluence hunting" into a popular pastime, first for Jarrett and his friends and family and then for thousands of geography geeks who stumbled across his project on the Internet. There's no National Geodetic Survey benchmark in the ground to identify these integer confluences, and that means *nobody's ever found them before*. There are 16,340 "confluence points" worldwide,* and each one represents a chance to plant a flag like the explorers of old. Confluence hunters have dutifully braved army ants in the jungles of Ghana, leeches in Malaysian swamps, and armed nomads in the Algerian Sahara in pursuit of their quixotic goal, but there are still more than ten thousand primary confluences yet to be visited worldwide.

But not every confluence hunt need turn into an Indiana Jones adventure; in fact, no spot on Earth is more than forty-nine miles from one of these points of cartographic perfection. I was thrilled to find that Seattle's nearest confluence was less than a half hour from my front door—but my attempt to visit 48 degrees north, 122 degrees east came up short. There were no army ants or border guards, but there were no fewer than four NO TRESPASSING signs posted just a few tantalizing yards from my quarry. I found a few visits to the spot recorded on the confluence project's website, but most of the hunters had just bushwhacked halfway to the spot from a back road, and none had logged the spot in accordance with strict Degree Confluence Project guidelines—that is, with the permission of the landowner.

Which is why I tracked down Rodger. He seems unflustered by

---

* If you do the math, there are actually 64,422 latitude and longitude confluences, but most of them are located on water or on the polar icecaps. Jarrett and company have also disallowed many of the higher-latitude confluences because lines of longitude converge there. As you get further from the Equator, confluences crowd together until they're less than two miles apart at the poles.

his newfound claim to fame. "I knew the property was on the forty-eight-north line, but I had no idea about the—confluence, you called it?" But when I ask if I can visit the all-important square foot of land, I find out that it won't be possible for months. Rodger is a cook on a tugboat currently bound for Hawaii and then Wake Island—one of the Travelers' Century Club's most troublesome destinations, if you'll recall. "I'll call you when I get back," he promises.

I expect never to hear from him again, but two months later, Rodger's as good as his word. "When do you want to come up and see 48/122?" he asks. That very weekend, he and I are out trampling the ferns at the end of his driveway, swinging our respective GPS receivers around like blind men with white canes. Just like geocaching, only without anything tangible waiting to be found.

"Near as I can tell, it's right here," says Rodger finally. "Zero zero zero. All zeroes."

I wonder if I will feel some lightning crackle of Global Significance when I stand on the magic point, but nothing happens. I dutifully take a picture of the fateful ferns. Just as with the roadgeeks, attention must be paid.

"Do you feel like it's an honor to be the caretaker of 48° N 122° W?" I ask Rodger.

He shrugs. "I dunno. It's a two-edged sword. I might have to put up a sign at the end of the driveway now, so people can leave their phone numbers if they want to visit the spot."

"What about a plaque?" I joke.

"Yeah, I thought about that . . ." he says quite seriously, stroking his chin.

On the winding forest roads back to the freeway, the stentorian British tones of my GPS device inform me that I've missed my turnoff. "You turned the wrong way, dumb-ass," scolds Daniel. "Just do what I say." I must have been distracted by the thought of thousands of confluence hunters combing the Earth for perfectly arbitrary geometric points. At least members of the Highpointers Club are climbing to real geographical peaks, albeit minor ones in many cases. The earth's grid of latitude and longitude, on the other hand, is *entirely* arbitrary. The fact that we divide the circle into 360 degrees is an ancient artifact based on the Babylonians' (incorrect) estimate of the number of days in a year. Lines of longitude are even more arbitrary, since the Earth doesn't have any West Pole or East Pole. Our current zero-degree line of longitude, the Prime Meridian through Greenwich, was a convention chosen only after much political wrangling at the 1884 International Meridian Conference, called by mutton-chopped U.S. president Chester A. Arthur. France refused to vote for the London line and continued to use its own meridian, through Paris, for thirty years. If the French had been a little more persuasive or the ancient Babylonians a little less, Alex Jarrett and his fellow confluence hunters would have a totally different grid of intersections to contend with.

But that's the beauty of the Degree Confluence Project—its essential randomness. The photos on its website are just as homogeneous as the ones on any roadgeek site: the same unremarkable foliage and dry grass and mud seem to show up time and again, whether the magic spot was found in Botswana or Bakersfield. But the pictures remind us that it's never enough just to *be* at a place—anyone can do that. The trick is to know where you are. Columbus "discovered" America, in his own small Eurocentric way, but when the continent was named, he was snubbed in favor of Amerigo Vespucci. That wasn't just because Vespucci marketed the sexy natives better, I learned at the Library of Congress. It's also because he was the one who knew where he was, knew the context. Columbus thought he was in India; Vespucci realized that a new continent had been found. By the same token, Rodger had probably passed those ferns on the way to his garage many times, but it was the Degree Confluence Project that "discovered" what they meant. That's what maps are for: they provide the story of our locations and translocations. A $500 GPS device can tell you your position, but a $10 road atlas is still an infinitely more powerful tool for providing context.

The Degree Confluence Project isn't the *reductio ad absurdum* of our new constant awareness of latitude and longitude. That honor would belong to the "Earth sandwich" dreamed up in May 2006 by the Web humorist Ze Frank. In a short video, Frank instructed his fans to place two pieces of bread on the ground at diametrically opposite points, or antipodes,* on the Earth's surface, making the Earth, in effect, into a giant if inedible sandwich. He even broke out a tender "Imagine"-style ballad to commemorate his brainstorm. "As I lay this bread on the ground, I know my job ain't done," he crooned, "but if the Earth were a sandwich, we would all be one. (Sandwich.)" Frank's challenge was harder than you might think: looking at an antipodal map of the Earth's surface reveals that almost every bit of land on the planet sits directly opposite a large body of water—almost as if the God of your choice always intended the sandwich version of His creation to remain open-faced! One of the few possible sandwich sites is the Iberian Peninsula: if you were to dig a hole straight through the center of the Earth from Spain, you'd reemerge somewhere in the northern half of the island nation of New Zealand. Just weeks after Frank's challenge was posted, two Canadian brothers named Jonathan and Duncan Rawlinson, traveling from London to Portugal, made a side trip into the hills of southern Spain to lay a half baguette on the

---

* The singular form of "antipode" has three syllables, like "antipope," but the plural has four: "an-tip-uh-deez." This is because the word "antipode" shouldn't really exist at all. The correct Greek singular of *antipodes* is *antipous*; "antipode" is an iffy back-construction.

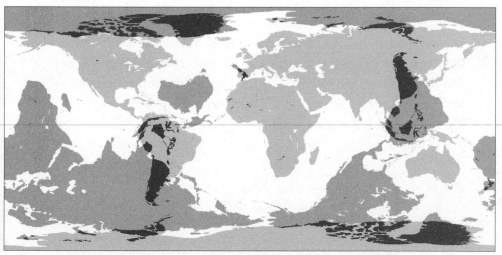

*The Earth, overlaid with its antipodal version. Very few
spots are sandwich-friendly in both hemispheres.*

dusty ground, while an Internet co-conspirator did the same thing near his home in Auckland, New Zealand. The first Earth sandwich in human history had been completed.

It's easy to dismiss the Earth sandwich as a silly (if ambitious) prank, the kind of conceptual art that the Liverpool cult band Echo & the Bunnymen practiced in the 1980s, when they would include odd locales like the Outer Hebrides of Scotland on their tour itineraries, so that the tour would form the shape of a rabbit's ears when seen on a map.* But as I reflect on the map freaks I've met on my journey, one of the things they all share is this same urge: to make the Earth—the entire Earth, its meridians and parallels and antipodes—into a giant plaything. Systematic travelers use jet planes and geocachers use GPS satellites and Google Earth fans use 3D-rendered aerial photography, but the impulse is the same one that's led people to pore over atlases for centuries: the need to place our little lives in the context of the Earth as a whole, to visualize them in the context of a grander scale. To this day, when we outline some ambitious plan, we still speak of how it will put us "on the map." We crave that wider glory and perspective.

We also crave exploration, and that's a thrill that's become scarcer as technology has advanced. When Alexander the Great saw the breadth of his domain, he wept, for there were no more worlds to conquer. Well, actually, I don't know if he did or not. That's a quote from Alan Rickman's German terrorist character in *Die Hard*. But the sentiment, at least, is true enough: human ambition requires new frontiers to cross, and for the last millennium, most of those frontiers were geographic in nature. In 1872, a surveyor named Almon Thompson explored the high desert plateaus of south-central Utah, mapping

---

* At the "Crystal Day" festival thrown by the Bunnymen to celebrate their hometown in 1984, the band led hundreds of Liverpudlian fans on a cycling tour of the city on a course designed to form the shape of a rabbit. The rabbit had been drawn on a city map by the band's eccentric manager, Bill Drummond, with the rabbit's navel placed at a manhole cover at the bottom of Mathew Street, in front of the city's famed Cavern Club. There were some last-minute adjustments to the course when it turned out that the hastily sketched route would require the peloton to cycle through the city's cathedral and then straight into the River Mersey.

a tributary of the Colorado called Potato Creek, which he renamed the Escalante River, and a thirty-mile mountain range now called the Henry Mountains. Thompson didn't know it, but his discoveries would be the last river and the last mountain range ever added to the map of the contiguous United States. Before Thompson's expedition, travelers had referred to the Henry range as "the Unknown Mountains," and Navajo in the area still call it Dzil Bizhi' Adini, "the mountain whose name is missing." But that's not true anymore: now all is named, all is neatly catalogued, just as the mapmakers thought they wanted. That frontier is gone.

Of course, the human yen for advancement didn't end when Conrad's "blank spaces" on the map were gone. We have turned our attention to "mapping" other things, like outer space and the human genome, but for those of us hardwired to organize the world spatially, cartographically, something is still missing. We're not content with discovering things that must be fuzzily visualized—quarks and quasars. We wish we could still discover real *places,* places we could visit, places that could surround us.

And so we reinvent exploration, albeit on a smaller and less perilous scale. We find ways to make even the most banal places new—by organizing them into made-up checklists, by planting geocaches in the parks there, by photographing the exit signs of the highways running through them, by studying their pixels in unprecedented detail on the Internet. Others forsake tidy modern maps altogether. Some recapture a sense of mystery with antique maps, with their wildly inaccurate coastlines and tentacled monstrosities at the margins. Others wander paths that are still unexplored because they exist only in the imagination. When I was a child, I could always add to a completed map of some fantasy kingdom simply by Scotch-taping a new piece of paper at one edge and continuing to draw. There will be no depressingly final "Potato Creek" on these inexhaustible maps.

It's been therapeutic for me to meet so many different kinds of geonuts. I can see that their rich diversity of obsessions all seem to be expressions of the very same gene, and it's the same instinct that made me an atlas collector at the same time that all my friends were more into He-Man and *Knight Rider*. But I've been most surprised by the response from friends who find out what I'm writing about. Since childhood, I've expected people to snort at the idea of maps being a bona fide hobby, so when I say, "It's a book about people who like maps," it comes out like an apology. Instead, those turn out to be the magic words that make me a secret confidant, a father confessor.

Laurie Borman, the editorial director at Rand McNally, said to me, "When I tell people where I work, you wouldn't believe how many people tell me, 'Really? I *love* maps!' It's more than you would think. But you can tell they think it's sort of an embarrassing confession to be a map geek." That's exactly what I find from my friends as well—even ones I've known for years, ones I'd never expect to be closet map fans.

"I can kill a whole afternoon just looking at rare maps on dealers' websites," says one friend. I knew he worked from home, but I had always naively assumed he was actually getting some work done sometimes. "Just drooling, not buying. It's like porn in our household."

"When my marriage was going south," says another friend, recently separated from his wife of five years, "I took my collection of *National Geographic*s from when I was a kid and threw them away, like my wife had been telling me to for years. But I couldn't bring myself to throw away the maps, so I took them out and hid them on top of the bookshelves."*

"As a kid, I'd beg my parents for the *Thomas Guide* every Christmas," yet another friend tells me, lowering her head and smirking guiltily at the sordid shame of it all.

The unlikeliest map booster of all turns out to be Mindy's obstetrician, whom I call the "monkey doctor," since, in addition to having delivered my daughter, Caitlin, she also delivers all the gorilla babies at Seattle's Woodland Park Zoo.† The monkey doctor keeps a world

---

* Take note, map lovers: your spouse may not believe you when you insist you just read *National Geographic* "for the articles."

† Yes, we are aware that this could explain a *lot* of things about our daughter. Particularly some of our potty-training difficulties.

map mounted on the wall of her exam room, because, she says, nothing distracts nervous patients better than a map does. I'm not sure this is the highest bar for map love to clear—"Maps: More Fun Than Thinking About an Imminent Pelvic Exam!" is unlikely to catch on as a geography slogan anytime soon—but the doctor has been surprised by how many patients ("more than you'd expect!") she finds completely engrossed in the map when she comes in.

Despite all the scare stories about American college students who can't find Africa on a world map, it seems there is a vast untapped reservoir of goodwill toward geography out there. It goes undercover; it keeps its head down until it knows it's in friendly company. But those alarmist newspaper articles about map-dumb kids wouldn't be written *at all* if, on some level at least, our society didn't still feel like maps were an important marker of knowledge and culture and interest.

I'm convinced—and relieved—that, as a maphead, I'm not the lonely oddity I always thought I was. But this is even better news for the world at large: people still like maps! Despite the media fearmongering, our kids still like maps. If they're failing geography tests en masse, it's only because *we're* letting them down. We're not teaching geography or spatial literacy the right way or giving them a long enough leash to explore their environments on their own. We're inadvertently convincing them in a million little ways that maps are old-fashioned and dull and that there's something a little weird about looking at them for fun.

But no matter what we do, I think maps are destined to win the battle. For five hundred years, maps changed barely at all, so it's no surprise that our enthusiasm for them has faded a bit. But today we are poised at the brink of a potentially Gutenberg-like sea change for maps. There's nothing dull about a flight through a three-dimensional Grand Canyon on Google Earth, or a map that shows where all your friends are in real time, or a comprehensive world atlas—down to street-level detail!—that you can carry with you on a cell phone. These technologies are so compelling that they could convert even the most spatially confused map skeptic, the way video games turned thousands of not-otherwise-destined-for-geekdom kids into computer science majors. For the first time in decades, there is reason to think that we might be entering a geographic renaissance. *Viva la revolución.*

If the geographers and psychologists I've talked to are right and map love is just a symptom of a gift for spatial thinking, it makes sense that maps could be passed through families genetically, like curly hair or color blindness. That's certainly true in my case; my parents liked looking at maps. So did my grandparents, my mom's parents. The second atlas I ever owned as a kid, after the Hammond atlas I saved up all year for, was a Rand McNally *Cosmopolitan World Atlas* that my grandma mailed to me in Korea. I can still picture the ballpoint-pen inscription on the title page, in her neat, round handwriting: "Merry Christmas 1983! Atlases are some of our favorite things too! Love, Grandma and Grandpa." That meant a lot to me at that age, the idea that someone besides me *understood*—that atlases were, in fact, an acceptable thing for adults to say they liked.

Grandma died of a lung ailment almost ten years ago, shortly after Mindy and I were married. She never got to meet her great-grandkids, and, I realize now, I never got to talk maps with her as a grown-up. My grandpa is still doing as well as one could hope to at eighty-two, and since he lives nearby, we have him over for dinner every Wednesday night. It's not hard to get him to talk about his late wife, whom he clearly still misses very much.

"Why did Grandma always love maps and atlases?" I ask him one night as we clear the table after dinner.

"Well, her mother married a man called Elcock." (From many past conversations with my grandpa, I'm not surprised that this story seems to (a) begin decades before I thought it did and (b) involve people I've never met.) "He was a bounder. A drunk. Betty remembers getting sent out to the bars to try to get him to come home." He still refers to his wife in the present tense; he also sometimes slips and calls her "your mother," a habit he must have fallen into while raising his three daughters.

"Betty's mother divorced this man Elcock, then remarried him, then divorced him. After the divorce, her mother had to start working full-time. They moved a lot. One time when we were in Salt Lake City, we drove around all afternoon looking at all the places where she'd lived. I remember four, five, six of them. During the summer, she and Teddy"—that's Grandma's younger sister, my great-aunt—"were sent to live with relatives because her mother was working such long hours. They'd sit in the public library all day, and your mother would look at atlases." That was where it all started, then: a turbulent home life and a welcoming library with pages and pages of beautiful maps. Werner Muensterberger, who wrote about antique maps in his book *Collecting: An Unruly Passion*, has noticed that map lovers often seem to come from broken homes (like Grandma's) or families that moved around a lot (like mine). Maps give us a sense of place and stability and origin that we otherwise lack.

"She was smart as a whip," he says ruefully. "That was her great disappointment, never finishing school."

"Did she still like to look at maps when you were married?"

"Well, she believed in history. In the 1960s she started attending genealogy seminars, and you couldn't do genealogy without telling the history of a town or an area. Hanging over my bed—her bed—is a *National Geographic* map of New England. She traced her family all the way back to colonial days and then back to England. I still have the map. I haven't moved a lot of her stuff." He pauses to think. "Maybe I should, but I haven't done it."

I like the notion that I come from a long heritage of maps, that I belong in a long line of keepers of the flame, like a cartographic version of the Knights Templar. I know from my grandma's years of genealogy work that her family was descended from the Mormon pioneers who settled Utah beginning in 1847. This means, I suppose, that I wouldn't even *exist* without those great nineteenth-century maps of the West that I glimpsed in the Library of Congress. Without the maps of one Charles Preuss, the German-born cartographer for John C. Frémont's expeditions, Brigham Young would never have made it to the Great Salt Lake.

But I've been worried of late that I might not have passed along my map genes in robust enough fashion. My own kids, despite adopting a new all-consuming obsession every week or so, have never seemed too interested in maps. We bought them a wall-sized cloth U.S. map from FAO Schwarz a few Christmases ago and hung it in the playroom, but I've never seen them spend much time with it. At the moment, all the little Velcro pieces (landmarks and crops and whatnot) are randomly stuck onto the waters of the Gulf of Mexico—the only part of the map that my three-year-old can reach. They both love the GPS navigator in our car, but "Daniel" gives driving directions so well that you never *have* to look at a map—he's the antimap, in many ways. Obviously my love for my children doesn't depend on whether or not they know that Santa Fe, New Mexico, is the highest-altitude state capital or that Thimphu, the capital of Bhutan, has no traffic lights. But I remember how important maps were to me at their age, and I'd like to be able to share that joy again with them, now that I'm a cranky old geonerd instead of a starry-eyed young one.

I poke my head into Dylan's room one night to tuck him into bed. "Nine o'clock, guy. Lights out."

"Are you almost done with your map book?" he asks sleepily.

He asks this a lot, but out of pure self-interest, not cartophilia. "The map book" is always the reason I give when I can't play with him every waking hour. You want me to wear a ninja mask while you shoot suction-cup-tipped Nerf bullets at my forehead? Sorry, map book.

"Actually, I'm almost done," I say. "Today I was trying to figure out which parts of the book should actually have maps to illustrate them."

"You can put my map in your book if you want. I drew it today."

"Really? You drew a map? Let me see."

The map—the first map—is sitting in a pile of books at the head of his bed, just where I used to keep my *Medallion World Atlas*. "This is the Sea of Sharks," he says. "You have to follow this dotted line through the sharks and the octopuses and jellyfish to get to the X-marks-the-spot."

"What's at the X?"

This is apparently the silliest question anyone has ever asked.

"That's the treasure!" He yawns. "Tomorrow I'm going to make a map of my submarine. Will you put it in your book?"

"We'll see. Good night, kiddo."

"Good night, Dad."

Maybe the map gene lives after all. I walk downstairs smiling, and Dylan, I can only assume, drifts off to explore the Sea of Sharks.

NOTES

CHAPTER 1: ECCENTRICITY

1 "My wound is geography": Pat Conroy, *The Prince of Tides* (New York: Dial, 1986), p. 1.

2 "Weirton, West Virginia": Located at the narrowest part of West Virginia's pointy little panhandle part, Weirton extends from the Ohio border in the west all the way to Pennsylvania on the east—even though the town is only five miles wide.

3 "Now when I was a little chap": Joseph Conrad, *Heart of Darkness* (New York: Norton, 1902/2005), p. 7.

4 Karen Keller: Cindy Rodriguez, "Population: 1," *The Boston Globe*, Apr. 19, 2001.

6 folding his *keffiyeh:* Said K. Aburish, *Arafat: From Defender to Dictator* (New York: Bloomsbury, 1998), p. 82.

7 a stretched leopard skin: Stephanie Meece, "A Bird's Eye View—of a Leopard's Spots," *Anatolian Studies* 56 (2006), pp. 1–16.

8 evolved gradually over millennia: Angus Stocking, "The World's Oldest Map," *The American Surveyor*, June 2006.

9 ancestors of all modern jigsaw puzzles: Margaret Drabble, *The Pattern in the Carpet: A Personal History with Jigsaws* (New York: Houghton Mifflin Harcourt, 2009), p. 111.

9 "very pretty . . . pale blue": Samuel Beckett, *Waiting for Godot* (New York: Grove, 1954), p. 5.

9 "map of the world": Letter to Charles Darwin, Feb. 1, 1846. *The Correspondence of Charles Darwin: 1844–1846* (Cambridge, England: Cambridge University Press, 1987), p. 283.

CHAPTER 2: BEARING

13   "An individual is not": Quoted in Edward Relph, *Place and Placelessness* (London: Pion, 1976), p. 43.

13   Stephen Dedalus: James Joyce, *A Portrait of the Artist as a Young Man* (New York: Norton, 1916/2007), p. 13.

14   asked in a 1985 address: Peirce Lewis, "Beyond Description," *Annals of the Association of American Geographers* 75, no. 4 (December 1985), pp. 465–477.

14   geographer Yi-Fu Tuan: *Topophilia: A Study of Environmental Perception, Attitudes and Values* (New York: Prentice Hall, 1974).

14   no less than W. H. Auden: Introduction to John Betjeman, *Slick but Not Streamlined* (New York: Doubleday, 1947), p. 11.

16   "That map set": Quoted in Gianni Granzotto, *Christopher Columbus* (New York: Doubleday, 1985), p. 57.

16   "He did not doubt": Quoted in Henry Vignaud, *Toscanelli and Columbus* (London: Sands, 1902), p. 220.

17   A famous 2000 study: Eleanor A. Maguire et al., "Navigation-related Structural Change in the Hippocampi of Taxi Drivers," *Proceedings of the National Academy of Sciences* 97, no. 8 (April 11, 2000), pp. 4398–4403.

18   grokking diagonals: Barbara Tversky, "Distortions in Memory for Maps," *Cognitive Psychology* 13 (1981), pp. 407–433.

18   Harm de Blij has claimed: Harm de Blij, *Why Geography Matters* (New York: Oxford University Press, 2005), p. 27.

19   one researcher noted: Most of these findings about children and maps come from Lynn S. Liben's work at Penn State. A good summary is her "The Road to Understanding Maps," *Current Directions in Psychological Science* 18, no. 6 (December 2009), pp. 310–315.

20   something innate: This no-longer-fashionable notion was most famously advanced in the "natural mapping" theory of James Blaut.

20   hundreds of other: David Woodward and G. Malcolm Lewis, *The History of Cartography*, vol. 2, book 3 (Chicago: University of Chicago Press, 1998), p. 4.

21   "cognitive map" was first coined: By the Berkeley behavioral psychologist Edward Tolman.

21   animals can perform: Many of these wayfinding examples are drawn from Colin Ellard, *You Are Here: Why We Can Find Our Way to the Moon but Get Lost in the Mall* (New York: Doubleday, 2009). The shearwater anecdote is the subject of Rosario Mazzeo, "Homing of the Manx Shearwater," *The Auk* 70, no. 2 (April 1953), pp. 200–201.

22   The frillfin goby: Stéphan Reebs, *Fish Behavior in the Aquarium and in the Wild* (Ithaca, N.Y.: Cornell University Press, 2001), p. 84.

24 both dogs and chimpanzees: This experiment was first performed by Emil Menzel at SUNY–Stony Brook. See "Chimpanzee spatial memory organization," *Science* 182, no. 4115 (November 30, 1973), pp. 943–945.

26 "laid out like a map": "Log of Glenn's Historic Day Circling Globe," *Chicago Daily Tribune,* Feb. 21, 1962.

26 allegorical maps: Many of these beautiful maps are reproduced in Katharine Harmon, *You Are Here: Personal Geographies and Other Maps of the Imagination* (Princeton, N.J.: Princeton Architectural Press, 2003). Matt Groening's homage is found in the largest book I own: *Kramer's Ergot 7* (Oakland, Calif.: Buenaventura Press, 2008).

30 "Third Culture Kids": "Third Culture Kids: Focus of Major Study," *Newslinks* 12, no. 3 (January 1993), p. 1. Now that the president of the United States is himself a TCK, the term seems a little less exotic.

31 "To be rooted": Simone Weil, *The Need for Roots: Prelude to a Declaration of Duties Toward Mankind* (Boston: Beacon Press, 1955), p. 42.

CHAPTER 3: FAULT

32 "To the people of Bolivia!": Steve Neal, "A Casual Approach Amid Controversy," *Chicago Tribune,* Jan. 9, 1983.

32 David Helgren sprang: The best account of Helgren's fateful brush with fame is the article he himself wrote on the subject: "Place Name Ignorance Is National News," *Journal of Geography* 82 (July–August 1983), pp. 176–178.

35 kidnapped a young woman: This was the notorious Gary Steven Krist case. His victim, Barbara Jane Mackle, lived to retell the story in her book *83 Hours till Dawn* (New York: Doubleday, 1971).

36 *Nouvelle Géographie:* Quoted in "Old Maps and New," *Blackwood's Edinburgh Magazine* 94, no. 577 (November 1863), pp. 540–553.

37 Henry Kissinger told: In *Years of Renewal* (New York: Touchstone, 1999), p. 72, quoted in de Blij, *Why Geography Matters,* p. 13.

37 "Over the last": www.snopes.com/politics/obama/57states.asp.

37 "the importance of": Lourdes Heredia, "Spain Puzzled by McCain Comments," BBC News, Sept. 18, 2008.

37 Africa was a country: Frank Rich, "The Moose Stops Here," *The New York Times,* Nov. 16, 2008.

38 Al Franken's favorite: A YouTube search for "al franken map" will return at least three such clips, spanning over twenty years.

38 "I personally believe": Rebecca Traister, "Miss Dumb Blond USA?," Salon.com, Aug. 29, 2007. Upton later spun her geographical ignorance

into a contestant spot on CBS's globetrotting reality show *The Amazing Race*; she and her boyfriend, Brent, finished third.

39 "in the great majority": Andrew Dickson White, *Autobiography*, vol. 1 (New York: Century, 1905), p. 258.

39 "Geographic illiterates": Howard Wilson, "Americans Held Lax on Geography," *The New York Times*, Jan. 2, 1942.

39 1950 study: Kenneth J. Williams, "A Survey of the Knowledge of Incoming Students in College Geography," *Journal of Geography* 51, no. 4 (April 1952), pp. 157–162.

41 fifteenth-anniversary follow-up: "Fifteen Year Follow-up Geography Skills Test Administered in Indiana, 1987 and 2002," *Journal of Geography* 108, no. 1 (January 2009), pp. 30–36.

41 recent National Geographic polls: The National Geographic Society and Roper conduct these polls and wag their fingers at America every four years or so; the most recent findings can be perused at www.national geographic.com/roper2006/findings.html.

42 in nine different countries: National Geographic–Roper 2002 Global Geographic Literary Survey, www.nationalgeographic.com/geosurvey2002.

42 "Just a conspiracy": Tom Stoppard, *Rosencrantz and Guildenstern Are Dead* (New York: Grove, 1967), p. 108.

43 made geopolitics seem: de Blij, *Why Geography Matters*, pp. 15, 45.

43 Arthur Jay Klinghoffer: Arthur Jay Klinghoffer, *The Power of Projections: How Maps Reflect Global Politics and History* (Westport, Conn.: Praeger, 2006), p. 126.

43 children have it worst: These statistics are drawn from the books that have been written on today's hypercushioned, outdoors-hating children, especially Lenore Skenazy, *Free Range Kids: Giving Children the Freedom We Had Without Going Nuts with Worry* (San Francisco: Jossey-Bass, 2009) and Richard Louv, *Last Child in the Woods: Saving Our Children from Nature-Deficit Disorder* (Chapel Hill, N.C.: Algonquin, 2005), and their associated websites.

44 A mom in Columbus: "The Walk Felt 'Round the World," *The Commercial Dispatch*, Mar. 23, 2009.

45 adult recruits' parents: Nancy Gibbs, "The Growing Backlash Against Overparenting," *Time*, Nov. 20, 2009.

45 measures of outdoor activity: Oliver Pergams and Patricia A. Zaradic, "Evidence for a Fundamental and Pervasive Shift Away from Nature-Based Recreation," *Proceedings of the National Academy of Sciences* 105, no. 7 (February 19, 2008), pp. 2295–2300.

45 panicked: Craig Lambert, "Nonstop," *Harvard Magazine*, March–April 2010.

45 British moms now refuse: Julie Henry, "Countryside Ban for Children Because Mums Cannot Read Maps and Hate Mud," *The Daily Telegraph*, Feb. 20, 2010.

45 "Geography is an earthly subject": James Prior, *Memoir of the Life and Character of the Right Hon. Edmund Burke*, vol. 1 (London: Baldwin, Cradock, and Joy, 1826), p. 512.

46 "Geography is not a university subject!": David N. Livingstone, *The Geographical Tradition: Episodes in the History of a Contested Enterprise* (Oxford, England: Blackwell, 1992), p. 311.

47 "All maps distort reality": Mark Monmonier, *How to Lie with Maps* (Chicago: University of Chicago Press, 1996), p. xi.

49 "You think": Jean-Jacques Rousseau, *Émile* (London: J. M. Dent and Sons, 1762/1911), p. 74.

49 "I know of no other": Peirce Lewis, "Beyond Description," *Annals of the Association of American Geographers* 75, no. 4 (December 1985), pp. 465–477.

50 "until every hamlet": "Old Maps and New," p. 540.

51 In 2008, a survey: "Cool Survey Results from Nokia Maps Guys," Nokia "Conversations" blog, http://conversations.nokia.com/2008/11/26/cool-survey-results-from-nokia-maps-guys/.

51 Jessica Lynch: Richard Serrano and Mark Fineman, "Army Describes What Went Wrong for Jessica Lynch's Unit," *Los Angeles Times*, Jul. 10, 2003.

51 "graphicacy": "Graphicacy Should Be the Fourth Ace in the Pack," *The Cartographer* 3, no. 1 (June 1966), pp. 23–28.

52 Jerome Bruner complained: *In Search of Pedagogy*, vol. 1 (New York: Routledge, 2006), p. 36.

53 "Its meanings have shifted": Robert Harbison, *Eccentric Spaces* (Cambridge, Mass.: MIT Press, 1977/2000), p. 124.

55 more than $100 million: "Geography Catches Up," National Geographic press release, July 14, 2005.

CHAPTER 4: BENCHMARKS

56 "This information": Barry Lopez, "The Mappist," in *Light Action in the Caribbean* (New York: Knopf, 2000), p. 159.

58 "River of Doubt": This ill-fated expedition—the only time, as far as I know, that a U.S. president has defeated flesh-eating bacteria—is fascinatingly detailed in Candice Millard, *The River of Doubt: Theodore Roosevelt's Darkest Journey* (New York: Anchor, 2006).

59 *Zelig*-like role: The Snow and Normandy maps, among many others,

can be seen in Jeremy Harwood, *To the Ends of the Earth: 100 Maps That Changed the World* (Newton Abbot, Devon: Davis & Charles, 2006).

59 The *Apollo 11* crew pored: John Noble Wilford, *The Mapmakers* (New York: Vintage, 2000), p. 427.

59 the library's very first shipment: Ralph E. Ehrenberg, *Library of Congress Geography and Maps: An Illustrated Guide* (Washington, D.C.: Library of Congress, 1996).

60 "cover for small detachments": Mark Monmonier, *How to Lie with Maps* (Chicago: University of Chicago Press, 1996), p. 127.

60 783 feet by 383 feet: James R. Akerman and Robert W. Karrow, Jr., eds., *Maps: Finding Our Place in the World* (Chicago: University of Chicago Press, 2007), p. 156. The only completely blank USGS map in the Great Salt Lake is, I believe, 41112C6, known as "Rozel Point SW," but there are several others that show only a single train trestle or boundary line.

63 the ghosts of dead mapmakers: Ibid., p. 137.

64 the "pink bits": This was the "British Empire Map of the World," the brainchild of the Canadian schoolteacher George Parkin. Klinghoffer, *The Power of Projections*, p. 79.

64 localized versions: You can view a comparison at "Disputed Territory? Google Maps Localizes Borders Based on Local Laws," Search Engine Roundtable, Dec. 1, 2009, www.seroundtable.com/archives/021249 .html.

64 God would strike her down: Nadav Shragai et al., "Olmert Backs Tamir's Proposal to Include Green Line in Textbook Maps," *Ha'aretz*, June 12, 2006.

65 1,807 feet east: Elizabeth White, "Four Corners Marker Is Off Target," *Denver Post*, Apr. 23, 2009.

65 Mike Parker has noted: In his very entertaining *Map Addict* (London: Collins, 2009), p. 131. *Map Addict* was released while I was writing *Maphead* and is a very British version of this book's own map-nerd-memoir mission statement.

67 the Mount McKinley controversy: James W. Loewen, *Lies Across America: What Our Historic Sites Get Wrong* (New York: Touchstone, 2007), p. 39.

67 "Whorehouse Meadow": Mark Monmonier, *From Squaw Tit to Whorehouse Meadow: How Maps Name, Claim, and Inflame* (Chicago: University of Chicago Press, 2006), p. 64. Monmonier's book is a particularly good exploration of politically incorrect toponyms and the issues they raise.

68 tantalizing place-names: Wilford, *The Mapmakers*, p. 165.

68 Ortelius's 1596 note: James Romm, "A New Forerunner of Continental Drift," *Nature* 367 (February 3, 1994), pp. 407–408.

69 the eccentric town toponyms: I took most of these examples from David Jouris's clever *All over the Map: An Extraordinary Atlas of the United States* (Berkeley: Ten Speed Press, 1994). If you're looking for U.S. maps depicting 75 Christmas-themed town names or 250 towns with the same names as famous writers, this is the book for you.

69 an enterprising local tailor: Meic Stephens, *The Oxford Companion to the Literature of Wales* (Oxford: Oxford University Press, 1986), p. 354.

69 back to being Halfway, Oregon: William Drenttel, "What Ever Happened to Half.com, Oregon?," Design Observer, Aug. 29, 2006, www .designobserver.com/observatory/entry.html?entry=4707.

70 Sharer, Kentucky, turned down: "Gambling Site Offers to Buy Town's Name," Associated Press, Sept. 26, 2005.

70 Butt Hole Road: "Residents of 'Butt Hole Road' Club Together to Change Street's Unfortunate Name," *Daily Mail*, May 26, 2009.

70 "I feel sure": David Usborne, "The Town That Refuses to Be Ashamed of Its Name," *The Independent*, Mar. 22, 1995.

71 every place got a cozy: Harwood, *To the Ends of the Earth*, p. 80.

71 suspiciously un-Japanese names: Vincent Virga, *Cartographia: Mapping Civilizations* (New York: Little, Brown, 2007), p. 76.

72 "Under the influence": Michael Theodoulou, "Ideological Gulf Enflames Iran," *The Times*, Dec. 3, 2004.

73 tensions in the Gulf are still running high: Tom Hundley, "A Gulf by Any Other Name," GlobalPost, Mar. 15, 2010, www.globalpost.com /dispatch/middle-east/100312/persian-gulf-arabian.

73 "Even on a stormy day": Marcel Proust, *Swann's Way* (New York: Modern Library, 1913/2003), pp. 550–551.

75 "No lost maps": This quote, and other historical details about the map's creation and discovery, were drawn from Toby Lester, *The Fourth Part of the World: The Race to the Ends of the Earth, and the Epic Story of the Map That Gave America Its Name* (New York: Free Press, 2009).

77 "They . . . are excessively": Jack Hitt, "Original Spin: How Lurid Sex Fantasies Gave Us 'America,'" *Washington Monthly*, Mar. 1993, p. 25.

78 "The science of geography": *Biography for Beginners* (London, T. W. Laurie, 1905), p. 5.

CHAPTER 5: ELEVATION

82 a record price: "Million-Dollar Map Tops Julia's Winter Auction," Antiques and the Arts Online, Feb. 9, 2010, http://antiquesandthearts .com/Antiques/AuctionWatch/2010–02–09__11–49–11.html.

84 making its final appearance: Raymond H. Ramsey, *No Longer on the*

Map: Discovering Places That Never Were (New York: Viking, 1972), p. 215.

84 The Mountains of Kong: James R. Akerman and Robert W. Karrow, Jr., eds., *Maps: Finding Our Place in the World* (Chicago: University of Chicago Press, 2007), p. 145.

87 Columbus relied: Vincent Virga, *Cartographia: Mapping Civilizations* (New York: Little, Brown, 2007), p. 24.

87 the vast "Billington Sea": I first saw this wonderful anecdote in John Noble Wilford, *The Mapmakers* (New York: Vintage, 2000, p. 167) and learned about Francis's checkered past in William Bradford's own journals, *The Mayflower Papers* (London: Penguin, 2007), p. 120.

87 "The Great American Desert": Virga, *Cartographia*, p. 206.

88 "Your work has cost me": Harwood, *To the Ends of the Earth: 100 Maps That Changed the World* (Newton Abbott, Devon: Davis & Charles, 2006), p. 108.

88 new sanitation systems: Akerman and Karrow, *Maps*, p. 155.

89 fell to their deaths: Harwood, *To the Ends of the Earth*, p. 125.

89 James Rennell: Clements R. Markham, *Major James Rennell and the Rise of Modern English Geography* (London: Cassell, 1895), p. 48.

89 Nain Singh: Singh's remarkable story has been told many times; I've relied here on the chapter on pundits in John Noble Wilford, *The Mapmakers*.

90 "God had endowed": Charles Kendall Adams, *Christopher Columbus: His Life and His Work* (New York: Dodd, Mead, and Co., 1892), p. 20.

90 Vespucci was a map collector: C. Edwards Lester, *The Life and Voyages of Americus Vespucius* (New Haven, Conn.: Horace Mansfield, 1858), p. 70.

91 a "Palin effect": Gemma Bowes, "Eastern Europe Braced for Palin Effect," *The Observer*, Sept. 16, 2007. In U.S. electoral politics, the "Palin effect" is something different, don'tcha know.

92 In 1504, King Manuel I: As a result of a deft bit of map theft by an Italian spy named Alberto Cantino. Harwood, *To the Ends of the Earth*, p. 64.

92 "Almost everything was changed": Bill Keller, "Soviet Aide Admits Maps Were Faked for 50 Years," *The New York Times*, Sept. 3, 1988.

93 E. Forbes Smiley III: The best reporting on the Smiley case was done by Kim Martineau in the *Hartford Courant* and by William Finnegan in "A Theft in the Library: The Case of the Missing Maps," *The New Yorker*, Oct. 17, 2005, pp. 64–78.

95 "If you take": Lillian Thomas, "Valuable Maps Too Easily Stolen from Books, Libraries," *Pittsburgh Post-Gazette*, Aug. 16, 2005.

96 Farhad Hakimzadeh: Sandra Laville, "British Library Seeks £300,000 Damages from Book Vandal," *The Guardian*, Jan. 17, 2009.

98 Handel enraged him: Philipp Blom, *To Have and To Hold: An Intimate History of Collectors and Collecting* (New York: Overlook, 2003), p. 82.

98 an amazing hodgepodge: From inventories I found in Blom's book as well as in Umberto Eco, *The Infinity of Lists* (New York: Rizzoli, 2009).

99 "some to beautify their halls": In his preface to *The English Euclid.*

99 "took great delight": John Aubrey, *Brief Lives* (Oxford, England: Clarendon, 1898), p. 329.

99 Samuel Pepys had: Jonathan Potter, *Collecting Antique Maps: An Introduction to the History of Cartography* (London: Jonathan Potter, 2002), p. 10.

99 by 1560, a quarter: Catherine Delano Smith, "Map Ownership in Sixteenth-Century Cambridge," *Imago Mundi* 17, no. 1 (1995), pp. 67–93.

99 Vermeer was a particular map fan: James A. Welu, "Vermeer: His Cartographic Sources," *Art Bulletin* 57 (December 1975), pp. 529–547.

101 Christian mapmakers were constrained: Daniel Boorstin, *The Discoverers* (New York: Vintage, 1985), p. 148.

CHAPTER 6: LEGEND

105 "Most of us": C. S. Lewis, *The Voyage of the Dawn Treader* (New York: HarperCollins, 1952), p. 5.

106 "This view looks like Islandia": The Wrights' recollections of their father can be found in Sylvia Wright's introduction to the second edition of *Islandia* (New York: Rinehart, 1958).

107 "trompe-l'oeil, on a vast scale": "Daydream," *Time*, May 18, 1942, p. 86. *Time* was so taken by the geography of Islandia that its editors commissioned a new map of the island to run alongside its review.

107 even contemplating suicide: Jo Piazza, "Audiences Experience *Avatar* Blues," CNN, January 11, 2010.

108 *Treasure Island:* Lloyd Osbourne, *An Intimate Portrait of R.L.S.* (New York: Scribner's, 1924), p. 41.

108 "I am told": Robert Louis Stevenson, "My First Book," *McClure's* no. 3 (September 1894), p. 283.

108 "I don't know": *Peter and Wendy* (Oxford: Oxford University Press, 1911/1991), p. 73.

110 Delvoye is also the artist: Katharine Harmon, *You Are Here; Personal Geographies and Other Maps of the Imagination* (Princeton, N.J.: Princeton Architectural Press, 2003), p. 186.

112 gay map buffs: Mike Parker, *Map Addict* (London: Collins, 2009), p. 258.

114 Tolkien never read *Islandia:* According to a letter he wrote to a reader in 1957. Douglas A. Anderson, *Tales Before Tolkien* (New York: Del Rey, 2003), p. 372.

115 Narnia was itself named: Walter Hooper and Roger Lancelyn Green, *C. S. Lewis: A Biography* (New York: HarperCollins, 2002), p. 306.

115 she had some cartographic training: "Pauline Baynes," obituary, *The Daily Telegraph,* Aug. 8, 2008.

115 he doodled the map first: David and Lee Eddings, *The Rivan Codex* (New York: Del Rey, 1998), p. 10.

117 Baldwin Street in Dunedin: Simon Warren, *100 Greatest Cycling Climbs* (London: Frances Lincoln, 2010), p. 10.

117 "The achievement of": *The Romance of the Commonplace* (San Francisco: Paul Elder and Morgan Shepherd, 1902), p. 91.

120 "Nothing seems crasser": Robert Harbison, *Eccentric Spaces* (Cambridge, Mass.: MIT Press, 1977/2000), p. 125.

CHAPTER 7: RECKONING

133 "Rote memorization must be emphasized": "National Geography Bee?," *FOCUS on Geography* 38, no. 2 (Summer 1988), pp. 33–36.

135 the old record had been shattered: David Brooks, "Mount Washington Gust Record Gone with the Wind," *Nashua Telegraph,* Jan. 27, 2010.

136 the second best design: "The Great British Design Quest," *The Culture Show,* BBC Two, Mar. 2, 2006.

136 "removing the smile": Mark Easton, "Map of the Week: London without the Thames," BBC News, Sept. 16, 2009.

136 "Can't believe that the Thames disappeared": @MayorOfLondon, Twitter status, Sept. 17, 2009.

136 The Swedish crown jewels: Peter Barber and Christopher Board, *Tales from the Map Room: Fact and Fiction About Maps and Their Makers* (London: BBC Books, 1993), p. 74.

138 an elaborate farm system: Ben Paynter, "Why Are Indian Kids So Good at Spelling?," Slate, June 2, 2010, www.slate.com/id/2255622.

139 Deborah Tannen says: Missy Globerman, "Linguist and Author Lectures on Differences in Men's and Women's Conversational Styles," *Cornell Chronicle,* Jul. 10, 1997.

140 John and Ashley Sims: Mike Parker, *Map Addict* (London: Collins, 2009), p. 254.

CHAPTER 8: MEANDER

148 without ever leaving their monasteries: James R. Akerman and Robert W. Karrow, Jr., eds., *Maps: Finding Our Place in the World* (Chicago: University of Chicago Press, 2007), p. 35.

149 international cleanup efforts: Gopal Sharma, "Everest 'Death Zone' Set for a Spring Clean Up," Reuters, Apr. 19, 2010.

151 hovered around 20 percent: Lornet Turnbull, "Many in U.S. to Need Passport," *The Seattle Times,* Apr. 6, 2005.

152 "I've worked all my life": Katie Couric, "Exclusive: Palin on Foreign Policy," *CBS Evening News,* Sept. 25, 2008.

155 "My God!" he remembered marveling: Jack Longacre, "The Birth of the Highpointers Club," *Apex to Zenith* (newsletter) 14 (3rd quarter 1991), p. 9.

156 least accessible U.S. high point: Helen O'Neill, "Why Molehill Is Nation's Most Challenging Mountain," *Los Angeles Times,* July 2, 2000.

156 "I would lose": Julie Jargon, "A Fan Hits a Roadblock on a Drive to See Every Starbucks," *The Wall Street Journal,* May 23, 2009.

157 forty-five Detroit-area McDonald's: Susan Sheehan and Howard Means, *The Banana Sculptor, the Purple Lady, and the All-Night Swimmer* (New York: Simon & Schuster, 2002), p. 104.

157 A documentary: *Starbucking,* directed by Bill Tangeman, Heretic Films, 2005.

159 He's been mugged: These calamities are drawn from a list Veley compiled of his worst travel experiences. John Flinn, "I've Been Everywhere, Man," *San Francisco Chronicle,* Sept. 25, 2005.

161 the island of Ferdinandea: Richard Owen, "Italy Stakes Early Claim to Submerged Island," *The Times,* Nov. 27, 2002.

162 a man comfortable with the amenities: A phrase I've stolen from the great Scottish cartoonist Eddie Campbell.

164 "It was like finishing": Rolf Potts, "Mister Universe," *The New York Times,* Nov. 16, 2008.

165 "I want to be": Roger Rowlett, "An Interview with Club Founder Jack Longacre," *Apex to Zenith* (newsletter) 57 (2nd quarter 2002), p. 10.

CHAPTER 9: TRANSIT

166 "There are map people": John Steinbeck, *Travels with Charley: In Search of America* (London: Penguin 1962/1997), p. 55.

168 a cross-country convoy: Numerical data about this grueling expedition was drawn from William Greany, "Principal Facts Concerning the First Transcontinental Army Motor Transport Expedition, Washington to San Francisco, July 7 to September 6, 1919," Dwight D. Eisenhower Presidential Library and Museum, www.eisenhower.archives.gov/research /digital_documents/1919Convoy/New%20PDFs/Principal%20facts.pdf.

169 the size of the state of Delaware: U.S. Bureau of Public Roads, 1961, www.fhwa.dot.gov/infrastructure/50size.cfm.

170   the traffic light in Syracuse's: "Irish in Syracuse Keep Green on Top, Even on Stop Light," *The New York Times,* Apr. 7, 1976.

170   the nation's highest-numbered road: This is a much-contested distinction, confused by the fact that some areas (like my former home state of Utah) add two zeroes to their numbered streets, calling a road something like "800 South" when it's effectively 8th South. 1010th Street in rural Wisconsin is the highest number so far discovered by the obsessives on the misc.transport.road newsgroup.

170   US-321 through Elizabethton: According to the misc.transport.road FAQ, this is the only U.S. highway that switches from north–south to south–north signposting, though nearly thirty others switch from north–south to east–west at some point.

170   The numbering was out of order: Shuster insisted that the name I-99 would be more "catchy." Sean D. Hamill, "Road Stirs Up Debate, Even on Its Name," *The New York Times,* Dec. 27, 2008.

171   "Guerrilla Public Service": Craig Stephens, "Richard Ankrom's Freeway Art," *L.A. Weekly,* Dec. 30, 2009.

173   fabled wonders of roadgeek America: Both superlatives drawn, again, from the FAQ periodically posted to misc.transport.road.

174   the Daleks from *Doctor Who*: "Daleks Get Stamp of Approval," BBC News, Feb. 5, 1999.

174   millions every year: "From One Revolution to Another," Ordnance Survey, www.ordnancesurvey.co.uk/oswebsite/about-us/our-history/index.html.

174   "Coming from a country": *Notes from a Small Island* (New York: William Morrow, 1995), p. 94.

175   Weimar-era maps: Arthur Jay Klinghoffer, *The Power of Projections: How Maps Reflect Global Politics and History* (Westport, Conn.: Praeger, 2006), p. 90.

175   as he and his new bride: Douglas A. Yorke and John Margolies, *Hitting the Road: The Art of the American Road Map* (San Francisco: Chronicle, 1996), p. 17.

176   a jaw-droppingly bold: Ibid., p. 40.

176   Eight billion: Ibid., p. 6.

184   "There is a game": "The Purloined Letter," *Edgar Allan Poe: Poetry and Tales* (New York: Library of America, 1984), p. 694.

CHAPTER 10: OVEREDGE

187   Neal Lane announced: "On the President's Announcement on the Global Positioning System," White House Office of Science and Technology Policy press release, May 1, 2000.

188 "Now that SA": "The Great American GPS Stash Hunt!," sci.geo
.satellite-nav Usenet newsgroup, May 3, 2000. The lightning-quick
spread of geocaching in its first few weeks can be read firsthand in the
archives of this now mostly defunct newsgroup.

191 "the biggest hobby in the world": Nicole Tsong, "Geocachers to Descend
on Seattle This Weekend in Search of the 'Triad,'" *The Seattle Times,* July
1, 2010.

193 "Look at this list": Mia Farrow enthused about geocaching to *Time Out
New York* in November 2006, while Ryan Phillippe brought it up on
George Lopez's talk show in May 2010. Wil Wheaton and Rikki Rock-
ett used to geocache as GroundskeeperWillie (awesome handle!) and
PoisonDrummer (not-so-awesome handle), respectively, though neither
has logged a find in years.

197 1,157 caches in a single day: Steve O'Gara, "New World Record—1157
Geocache Finds in 24 Hours," Groundspeak forums, Oct. 2, 2010,
http://forums.groundspeak.com/GC/index.php?showtopic=261055.

201 "OK, OK": "Giving Up . . ." GPSStash list, Yahoo! Groups, message
2040, Jun. 17, 2001.

202 "Viajero Perdido": "Primero de Nicaragua," cache GCH30B, www.geo
caching.com. His geohandle means, quite appropriately, "lost traveler."

202 "Hukilaulau," from Long Island: "Geocaching Level of Addiction,
What's Yours?," Geocaching Topics forum, June 23, 2008, forums
.groundspeak.com/GC/index.php?showtoic=196941. In the same thread,
he confesses that when he spends too much time online looking at geocaches, he appeases his wife by telling her he's looking at porn.

205 "the worst has happened": Apsley Cherry-Garrard, *The Worst Journey in
the World* (New York: Carroll & Graf, 1922/1965), p. 525.

207 "I can imagine no more": Niall Ferguson, *Empire: The Rise and Demise
of British World Order and the Lessons for Global Power* (New York: Basic
Books, 2003), p. 200.

207 Serbian geographer Jovan Cvijić: Vincent Virga, *Cartographia: Mapping
Civilizations* (New York: Little, Brown, 2007), p. 153.

208 "I don't do anything": Charles Hoskinson, "GPS Receivers Add Twist to
Hide and Seek," *The Washington Times,* Nov. 7, 2004.

208 "I started to miss": *Geocache,* directed by David Liban, 2007, www
.geofilm.net.

208 "Was out enjoying": "Sugar's Compost Pile," cache GC229E8, www
.geocaching.com.

CHAPTER 11: FRONTIER

212 "Our age today": Quoted in John Noble Wilford, *The Mapmakers* (New York: Vintage, 2000), p. 112.

212 "Mein Herr": Lewis Carroll, *Sylvie and Bruno Concluded* (London: Macmillan, 1893), p. 169.

212 1982 essay: Umberto Eco, "On the Impossibility of Drawing a Map of the Empire on a Scale of 1 to 1," in *How to Travel with a Salmon and Other Essays* (Orlando, Fla.: Harcourt, 1994), p. 95.

216 twenty terabytes or so: Stewart Brand, *The Clock of the Long Now: Time and Responsibility* (New York: Basic Books, 1999), p. 87.

217 George Armstrong Custer: Jeffry D. Wert, *Custer* (New York: Touchstone, 1996), p. 50.

217 drop film packets: Nicholas M. Short, *The Remote Sensing Tutorial* (Washington, D.C.: Federation of American Scientists, 2001), http://rst.gsfc.nasa.gov/Intro/Part2_26e.html.

218 a military incursion: Daniel Hernandez, "Tensions High Between Nicaragua, Costa Rica in Border Dispute," *Los Angeles Times,* Nov. 19, 2010.

218 "McDonaldization" of cartography: Martin Dodge and Chris Perkins, "Reclaiming the Map: British Geography and Ambivalent Cartographic Practice," *Environment and Planning A* 40, no. 6 (June 2008), pp. 1271–1276.

219 briefly given Chinese names: "Google Admits 'Mistake' of Wrong Depiction of Arunachal," *The Times of India,* Aug. 8, 2009.

220 Meteor-impact craters: Richard Macey, "Opal Miner Stumbles on Mega Meteorite Crater," *The Sydney Morning Herald,* Nov. 23, 2008.

220 a Roman villa in Parma: "Internet Maps Reveal Roman Villa," BBC News, Sept. 21, 2005.

220 a lost Amazonian city: Ed Caesar, "Google Earth Helps Find El Dorado," *The Sunday Times,* Jan. 10, 2010.

220 a remote forest in Mozambique: Louise Gray, "Scientists Discover New Forest with Undiscovered Species on Google Earth," *The Daily Telegraph,* Dec. 21, 2008.

220 the so-called forest swastika: "German Forest Loses Swastika," BBC News, Dec. 4, 2000.

220 eight thousand grazing cattle: Thomas H. Maugh II, "Tip Them Over and They Still Point North," *Los Angeles Times,* Aug. 26, 2008.

221 Greenland is oversized fourteenfold: Ralph E. Ehrenberg, *Mapping the World: An Illustrated History of Cartography* (Washington, D.C.: National Geographic, 2006), p. 111.

222 nearly all made Europe too big: Thomas F. Saarinen, Michael Parton, and Roy Billberg, "Relative Size of Continents on World Sketch Maps,"

Cartographica 33, no. 2 (Summer 1996), pp. 37–48.

222 "wet, ragged long winter underwear": "Arno Peters and His New Geography," *American Cartographer* 12 (1985), pp. 103–111.

223 West Lancashire town of Argleton: Rebecca Lefort, "Mystery of Argleton, the 'Google' Town That Only Exists Online," *The Daily Telegraph,* Oct. 31, 2009.

224 Goblu and Beatosu, Ohio: Mark Monmonier, *How to Lie with Maps,* (Chicago: University of Chicago Press, 1996), p. 50.

227 a report on Page's private life: "Google Executive," National Legal and Policy Center, Jun. 30, 2008, www.nlpc.org/pdfs/googleexecutive.pdf.

227 "we live in": John Sellers, "Wayne Coyne Confirms Google Street View Sighting," True/Slant, Feb. 5, 2010, http://trueslant.com/john sellers/2010/02/05/wayne-coyne-flaming-lips-confirms-google-street-view-sighting/.

227 "geoslavery": Jerome Dobson and Peter Fisher, "Geoslavery," *IEEE Technology and Society Magazine* 22, no. 1 (Spring 2003), pp. 47–52.

229 thousands of amateur mappers: Amy Davidson, "A Map of Thousands," *The New Yorker,* "Close Read" blog, Feb. 24, 2010, www.newyorker.com /online/blogs/closeread/2010/02/a-map-of-thousands.html.

229 "Many thanks": Google Groups, "CrisisMappers," Feb. 4, 2010, http:// groups.google.com/group/crisismappers/msg/54a9be63091dbab9.

232 an unnamed Swedish couple: "Swedish Tourists Miss Island Due to GPS Typo," *Seattle Times,* July 28, 2009.

233 "Society is geared": Alex Hutchinson, "Global Impositioning Systems," *The Walrus,* Nov. 2009, pp. 67–71.

234 sales collapsed by 83 percent: Richard Melcher, "Dusting Off the *Britannica," BusinessWeek,* Oct. 20, 1997, pp. 143–146.

235 William Rand saved the day: Richard Cahan, *Chicago: Rising from the Prairie* (Carlsbad, Calif.: Heritage Media, 2000), p. 323.

235 zoom chunkily in fixed increments: In 2010, about a year after I spoke with Minster (and just months after he left the company), Rand McNally did finally upgrade the map interface on its site.

CHAPTER 12: RELIEF

237 "We shall not cease": T. S. Eliot, "Little Gidding," *Collected Poems, 1909– 1962* (New York: Harcourt Brace Jovanovich, 1991), p. 208.

238 "We kept expecting": "43°N 72°W (visit #1)," Degree Confluence Project, Feb. 20, 1996, http://confluence.org/confluence.php?visitid=1.

238 16,340 "confluence points" worldwide: "Frequently Asked Questions," Degree Confluence Project, http://confluence.org/faq.php.

238 Confluence hunters have dutifully braved: Joseph Kerski, "To the Nth Degree . . . and Minute, and Second: Confluence Hunting on Planet Earth," Earthzine, Dec. 8, 2009, www.earthzine.org/2009/12/08/to-the-nth-degree%E2%80%A6and-minute-and-second-confluence-hunting-on-planet-earth/.

240 the "Earth sandwich": "If the Earth Were a Sandwich," www.zefrank .com/sandwich/.

242 the shape of a rabbit's ears: Robert Sandall, "Bill Drummond: Pop's Prankster Heads for Destruction," *The Daily Telegraph*, Aug. 19, 2008.

242 the "Crystal Day" festival: Chris Adams, *Turquoise Days: The Weird World of Echo & the Bunnymen* (New York: Soft Skull Press, 2002), p. 153.

243 the last river and the last mountain range: Bradford J. Frye, *From Barrier to Crossroads: An Administrative History of Capitol Reef National Park, Utah*, National Park Service, www.nps.gov/history/history/online _books/care/adhi/adhi3.htm.

INDEX

Page numbers in italics indicate illustrations.